Stanley Greenberg

Olmsted Trees

Stanley Greenberg

Olmsted Trees

HIRMER

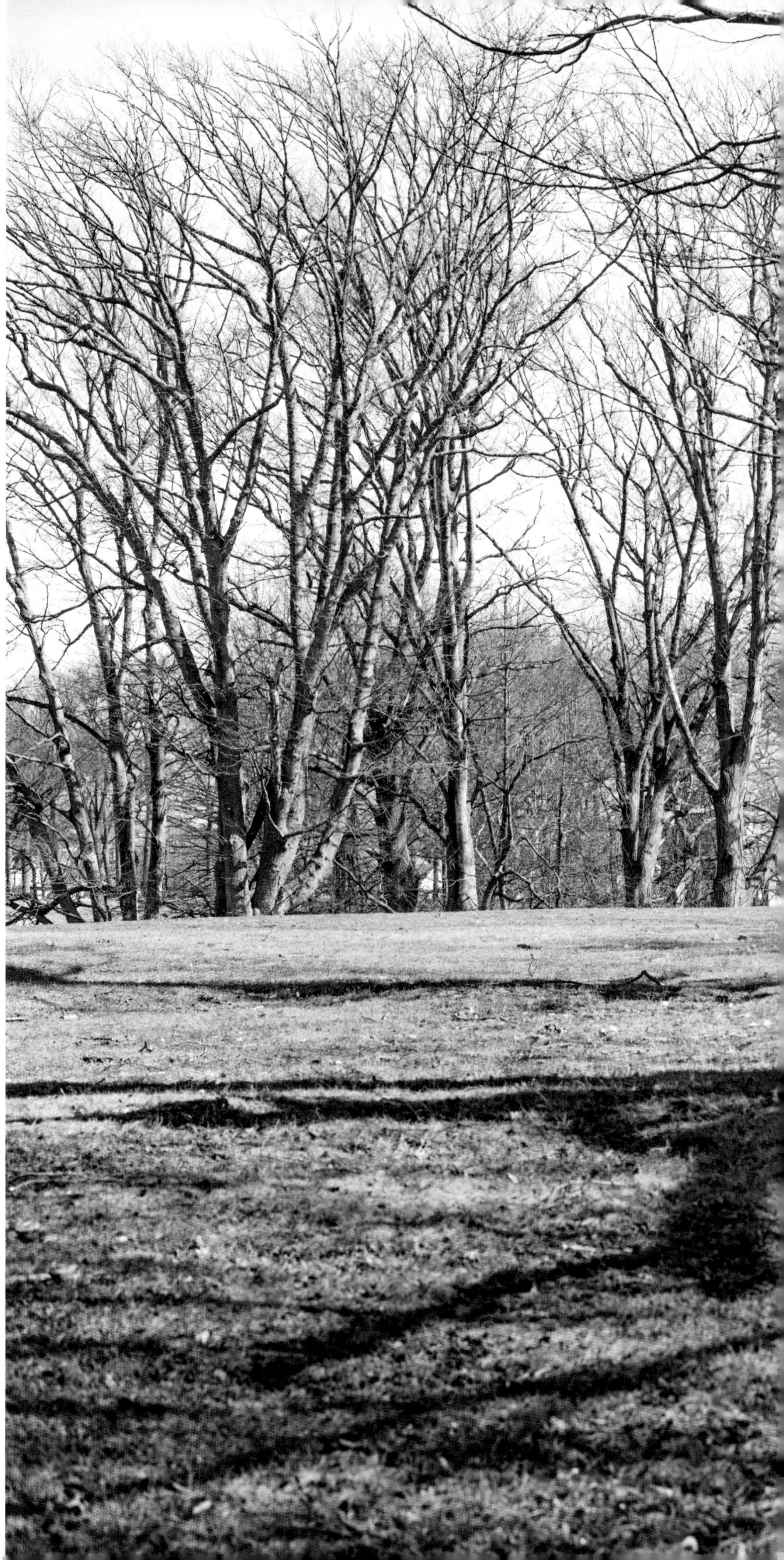

Fagus sylvatica,
European Beech, Rot-Buche
– Franklin Park, Boston,
Massachusetts, 2020

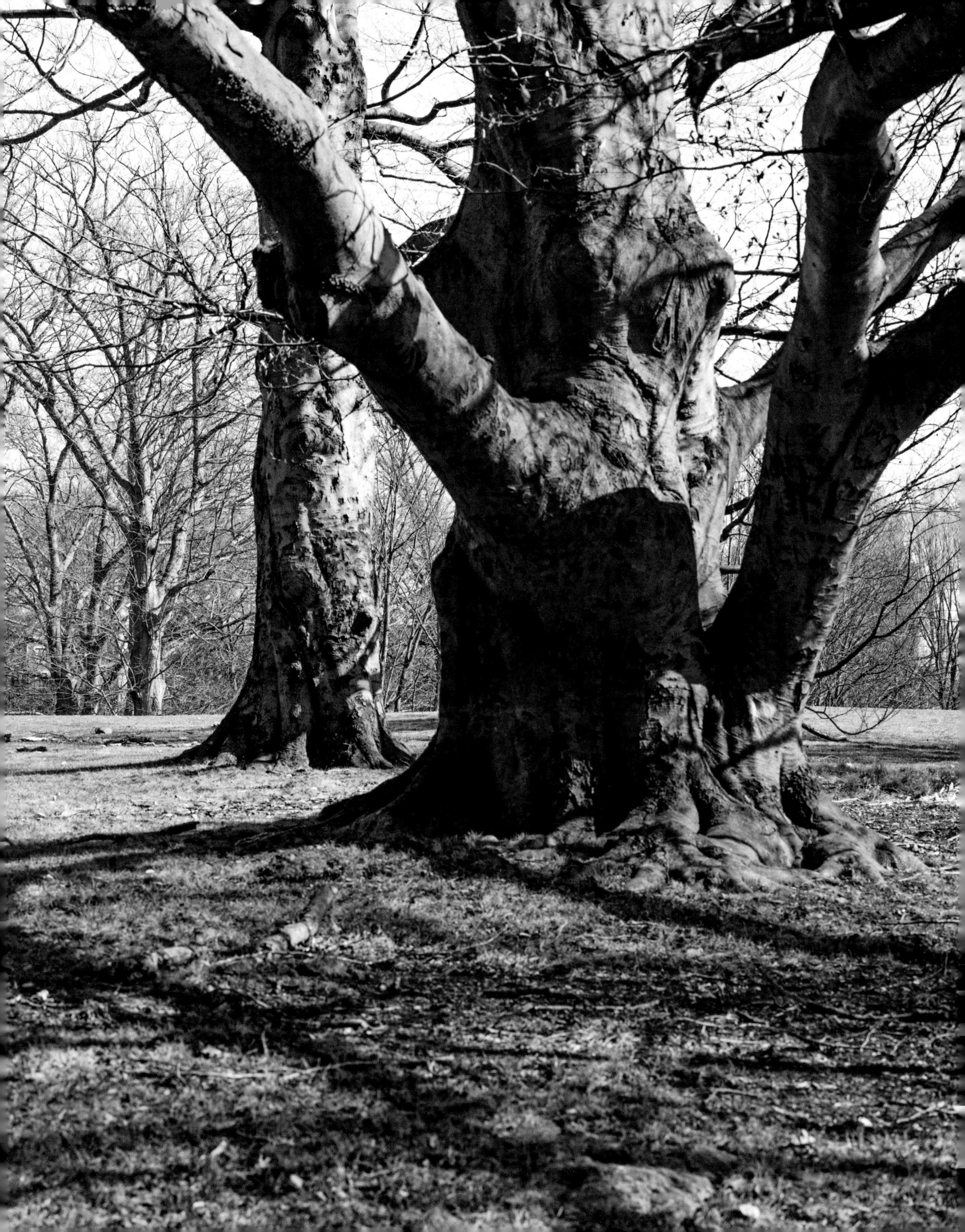

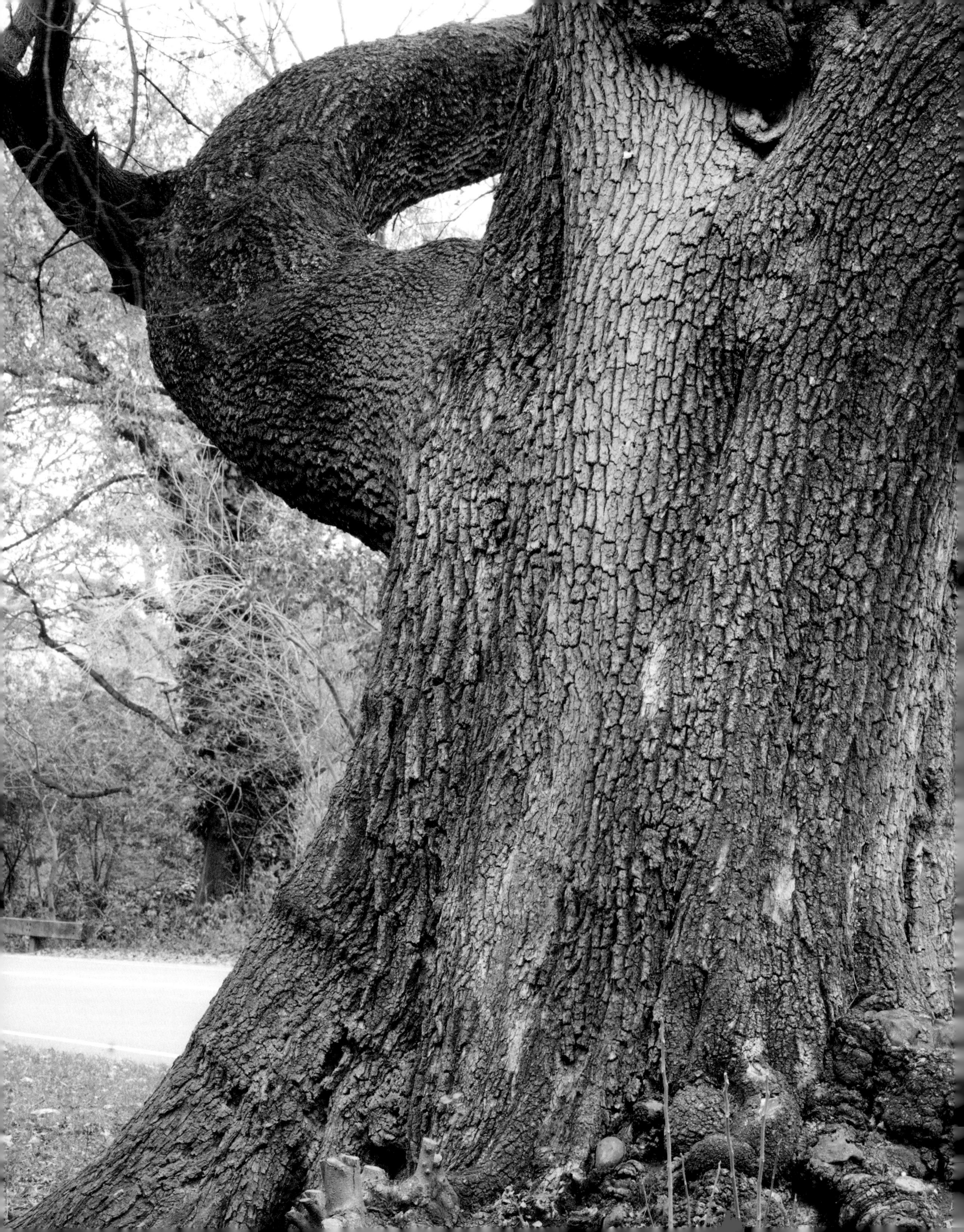

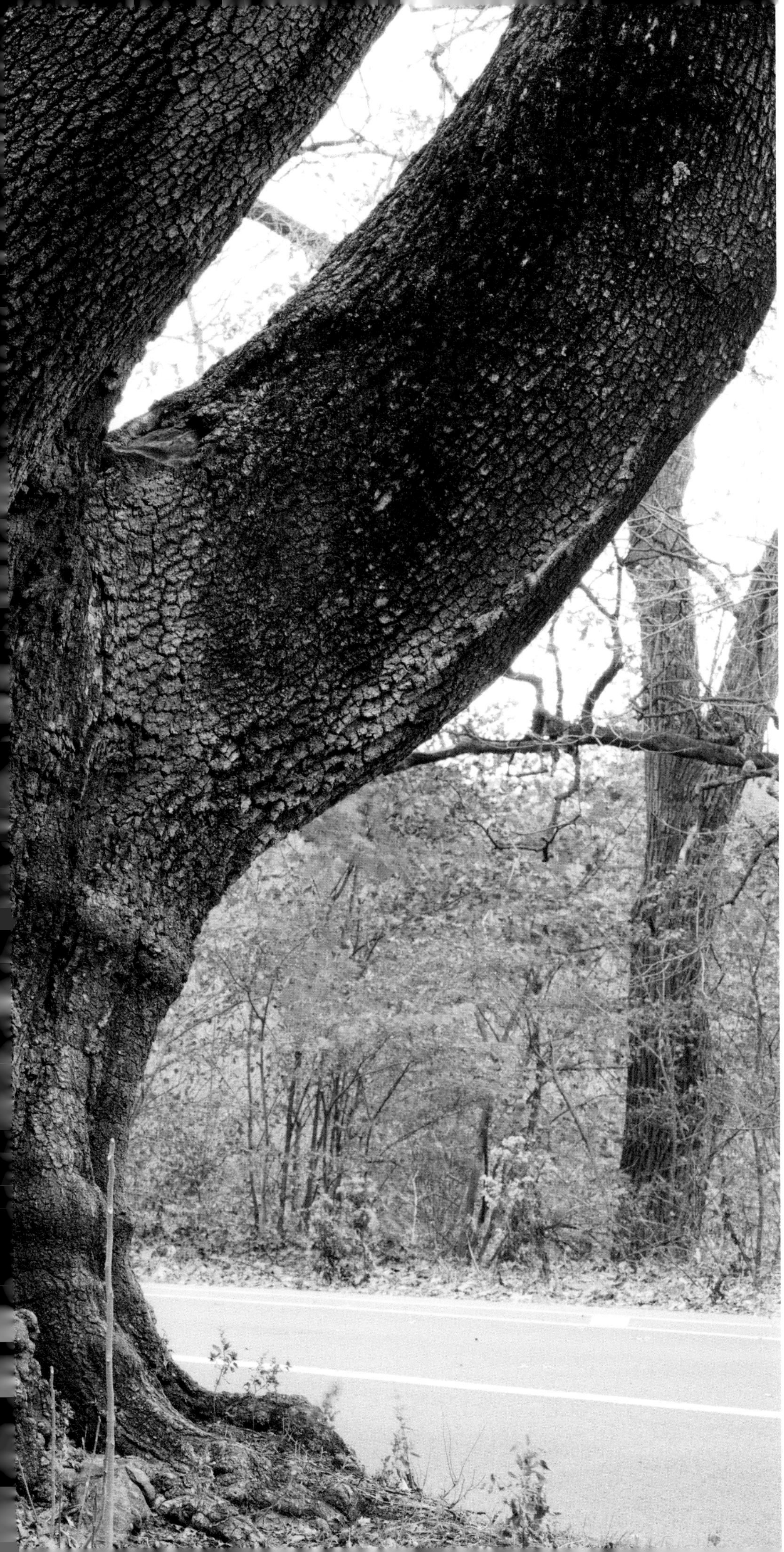

Ulmus rubra,
Slippery Elm, Rot-Ulme –
Prospect Park, Brooklyn,
New York, 2019

Fest verwurzelt

Kevin Baker

»Wenn der Mensch nicht vom Brot allein lebt,
was könnte er dann Besseres tun, als Bäume zu pflanzen.«
— Frederick Law Olmsted[1]

Frederick Law Olmsted war ein Mensch, der beinahe sein gesamtes Leben in Bewegung verbrachte. Deshalb entbehrt es nicht einer gewissen Ironie, dass Bäume einen so prominenten Platz in den von ihm geschaffenen Landschaften einnehmen. Zu jener Zeit, als er die Anlage des Central Park in New York übernahm, sein erstes Projekt als Landschaftsarchitekt 1857, hatte er bereits ausgedehnte Reisen durch England sowie den Nordosten und Süden der USA unternommen und war von New York nach China und wieder zurück gesegelt. Zu seinen späteren Reisen gehört die Durchquerung des Isthmus von Panama – zur damaligen Zeit ein lebensbedrohliches Unternehmen.

Sein rastloses Wesen drückte sich nicht nur durch häufigen Ortswechsel aus. Im Alter von 35 Jahren hatte sich Olmsted auch bereits als Landvermesser, Verkäufer, Seemann, Landarbeiter, Gutsbesitzer, Journalist, Autor und Verleger versucht. Des Weiteren leitete er eine Goldmine in Kalifornien, war Generalsekretär der US Sanitary Commission, die die umfangreichen Hilfsaktionen für kranke und verwundete Soldaten der Union während des Bürgerkriegs koordinierte, und wirkte bei der Rekrutierung und Ausrüstung der ersten drei Regimenter von Afroamerikanern mit, die in diesem Krieg aufgestellt wurden. Außerdem zählt er zu den Vorkämpfern der amerikanischen Umweltbewegung.

Zwar hatte Olmsted bei Ausübung all dieser Berufe auch das Geld seines Vaters im Rücken, doch war er beileibe kein Dilettant. Er arbeitete stets hart bis zur Erschöpfung und schonte seine Gesundheit nicht. Allein auf seiner Fahrt nach China zog er sich Typhus und Skorbut zu und konnte infolge eines Sturzes einen Monat lang nur eingeschränkt seinen rechten Arm benutzen. Obwohl er nie eine Universität besuchte, erwarb er sich durch eigene Arbeit, Lektüre und seine Beobachtungsgabe das, was Lewis Mumford die »amerikanische Erziehung in ihrer besten Form«[2] nannte.

1 Charles E. Beveridge u. a. (Hg.), The Papers of Frederick Law Olmsted (Bd. VIII): The Early Boston Years, 1882–1890, Baltimore 2013, S. 61.
2 Witold Rybczynski, A Clearing in the Distance: Frederick Law Olmsted and America in the Nineteenth Century, New York 2000, S. 91.

Rooted in Place

Kevin Baker

> "If man is not to live by bread alone,
> what is better worth doing well than the planting of trees."
> — Frederick Law Olmsted[1]

Frederick Law Olmsted was a man who lived almost his entire life in motion, which makes it ironic that he should have made trees such an essential part of his landscapes. By the time he began construction of New York's Central Park, his first landscaping project, in 1857, he had already traveled extensively throughout England, the American Northeast and South, and sailed from New York to China and back. Later travels would include a passage through the Isthmus of Panama, at the time a life-threatening expedition.

Nor was his restlessness confined to physical movement. By the age of thirty-five, Olmsted had tried his hand at being a surveyor, a dry goods clerk, a sailor, a farmhand, a gentleman farmer, a journalist, an author, and a publisher. He would go on to manage a gold-mining project in California, direct the work of the US Sanitary Commission—the vast effort to provide succor for sick and wounded Union soldiers during the Civil War—help recruit and outfit three of the first African-American regiments during the war, and serve as an early leader of the American conservation movement.

Olmsted was able to try many of these professions thanks to his father's money, but he was not a dilettante. He worked hard, often to the point of exhausting himself and endangering his health. On his voyage to China alone, he contracted typhoid and scurvy, and suffered a fall so bad that he was unable to fully use his right arm for a month. While he never attended college, his work, his reading, and his gift for observation combined to give him what Lewis Mumford called "American education at its best."[2]

Olmsted finally found his life's calling as a landscape architect, but here, too, his interests were wide and varied. He and his collaborators designed parks and park systems and parkways, including Boston's Emerald Necklace, Milwaukee's Grand Necklace of Parks, Detroit's Belle Isle, Mount Royal in Montreal, and Prospect Park and Ocean Parkway in

1 Charles E. Beveridge et al., eds., *The Papers of Frederick Law Olmsted (Vol. VIII): The Early Boston Years, 1882–1890* (Baltimore: Johns Hopkins University Press, 2013), 61.

2 Witold Rybczynski, *A Clearing in the Distance: Frederick Law Olmsted and America in the Nineteenth Century* (New York: Scribner, 2000), 91.

Seine Berufung fand Olmsted schließlich in der Landschaftsarchitektur, und auch hier waren seine Interessen breit gefächert und vielseitig. Er und seine Mitarbeiter entwarfen Parks, Parksysteme sowie Boulevards und Panoramastraßen, Parkways genannt. Dazu zählen das Emerald Necklace (»Smaragdkollier«) in Boston, eine Reihe miteinander verbundener Parkanlagen, das Grand Necklace of Parks von Milwaukee, die Belle Isle, eine Parkinsel im Detroit River, der Parc du Mont Royal, eine der wichtigsten Parkanlagen von Montreal, sowie der Prospect Park und der Ocean Parkway in Brooklyn. Sie gestalteten Gelände für Privatschulen wie Groton und Lawrenceville, für Colleges wie Smith und Bryn Mawr, Ausstellungsgelände, Krankenhausanlagen, Wohnsiedlungen und gelegentlich auch ein privates Anwesen. Mit seinen wichtigsten Werken schuf er urbane Landschaften in bedeutenden Städten wie New York, Chicago und Washington und dachte sie neu. Daneben arbeitete er auch an Projekten in kleinerem Maßstab wie dem Walnut Hill Park in New Britain und vollendete den Friedhof Willowbrook in Westport, beide in Connecticut gelegen. Viele weitere Entwürfe für Parks, Universitäten und Schulen wurden, nicht selten aus Unverständnis, abgelehnt oder erst nach seinem Tod vollendet.

Olmsted war unermüdlich in seiner Arbeit, aber er war auch eigensinnig, hartnäckig und entschlossen. Nicht selten überwarf er sich mit Kunden und Auftraggebern – nicht ungewöhnlich zur damaligen Zeit. Bemerkenswert ist allerdings, wie oft es ihm gelang, auch strittige Projekte abzuschließen. Es war für ihn am Ende ebenso oft zu- wie abträglich, dass er so häufig einfach recht behielt.

Sein Leben war turbulent. Doch obwohl selbst ständig in Bewegung, war die erste Landschaft, die Olmsted zunächst auf dem Papier entwarf und dann im Gelände realisierte, von Bäumen definiert. Die Gestaltung des Central Park begann er mit der »Promenade« oder »Mall«, ein schnurgerader, etwa 400 Meter langer Boulevard für Spaziergänger, beidseitig gesäumt von Doppelreihen Amerikanischer Ulmen. Die Mall war ein Zugeständnis von Olmsted und seinem engsten Mitarbeiter, Calvert Vaux, an die Vorstellungen der Parkverwaltung, deren Mitglieder streng formal angelegte Stadtparks mit orthogonalem Wegenetz und klar gegliederten Blumenrabatten bevorzugten. Damit machten Olmsted und Vaux eine seltene Ausnahme von ihrer ansonsten favorisierten Idee der »natürlichen Landschaft«, wie sie in Amerika ursprünglich von ihrem Mentor, dem Landschaftsarchitekten und Gartenbaukünstler Andrew Jackson Downing, vertreten worden war.

Wovon Downing – ein Romantiker und eine etwas geheimnisvolle Persönlichkeit, der höchstwahrscheinlich mit der Anlage des Central Park betraut worden wäre, hätte er nicht einige Jahre zuvor auf tragische Weise beim Brand eines Dampfschiffs sein Leben verloren – jedoch wirklich überzeugt war, das war die englische Idee der verbesserten, »idealisierten Natur«. Gemeint ist damit eine geschickt so arrangierte Landschaft, dass sich aus jedem Blickwinkel eine besonders pittoreske Aussicht ergibt.

Uns Heutigen erscheint die Vorstellung befremdlich, wir könnten die Natur verbessern, doch Vaux und Olmsted taten dies auf eine Weise, die ihresgleichen sucht. Ich erinnere

Brooklyn. They designed school campuses for Groton and Lawrenceville, college campuses at Smith and Bryn Mawr, fairgrounds, hospital grounds, planned communities, and the occasional private estate. His major works would reshape and reimagine vast spaces in cities as great as New York, Chicago, and Washington, DC. Yet he also worked on a scale small enough to design Walnut Hill Park in New Britain and finish Willowbrook Cemetery in Westport, both in Connecticut. Still more designs, for parks and universities and schools, were rejected (often foolishly) or only completed after his death.

Olmsted was, as always, industrious in this work—and also stubborn, persistent, and determined. He had frequent fallings-out with clients and bosses, which was not that unusual for the time, but what is remarkable is how often he would manage to finish the project in question. He was, in the end, both hindered and served by how often he was right.

It was a whirlwind of a life. But for all the time he spent on the move, the first piece of landscape that Olmsted designed, on paper and on the ground, was one defined by trees. The very first feature of Central Park was the “Promenade,” or “Mall,” a straight pedestrian boulevard a quarter of a mile long, bounded by double rows of American elm trees on each side. The Mall was a concession by Olmsted and his greatest collaborator, Calvert Vaux, to most of the park’s commissioners, who held with the idea of formal urban parks full of Cartesian paths cut through beds of well-regimented flowers. His concession was a rare departure from the idea of “natural landscape” that Olmsted and Vaux favored, and that had originally been championed in America by their mentor, the landscape architect and horticulturalist Andrew Jackson Downing.

Yet what Downing—a romantic, somewhat mysterious figure who would have been hired to build Central Park himself had he not died in a terrible steamboat accident a few years earlier—really believed in was the English idea of “improved nature.” That is, nature adroitly rearranged to produce the most inspiring, rustic views possible for any vista.

Today we would be loath to presume we could ever improve upon nature, but Vaux and Olmsted did it without peer. I can still remember how awed I was when, many years ago, a professor took our geology class on a survey of Central Park, and casually remarked on how this and that great boulder was not native to the area but had been brought there to shape it. I have lived my whole adult life in a place bounded by three great Olmsted-Vaux parks—Manhattan’s Central, Riverside, and Morningside parks—and I still cannot get over what intricate creations they are, at once concealing and revealing, full of mechanisms and sleights-of-hand so subtle that one rarely notices them.

In Central Park, the transverse roads were sunk below the park level and hidden from view. The swampy wetlands were turned into bright ponds, navigated by rowboats and even gondolas, and were spanned by ornate little bridges that also kept the pathways at the same grade level. The existing rocky jumble of the land became outcroppings from a Gothic novel.

mich noch daran, wie beeindruckt ich war, als uns vor vielen Jahren unser Geologieprofessor auf einen Ausflug in den Central Park mitnahm und beiläufig bemerkte, dieser und jener große Fels habe ursprünglich gar nicht dort gelegen, sondern sei eigens des Gesamteindrucks wegen herbeigeschafft worden. Praktisch mein gesamtes Leben als Erwachsener spielte sich an einem Ort ab, der von drei großen Parkanlagen von Olmsted und Vaux begrenzt wird – Manhattans Central Park, dem Riverside Park und dem Morningside Park – und es fasziniert mich bis heute, um welch komplexe, zugleich verbergende und enthüllende Schöpfungen es sich dabei handelt, wie sie voller Kniffe und Kunststückchen stecken, die so feinsinnig sind, dass man sie oft gar nicht bemerkt.

Die den Central Park querenden Straßen wurden unter das Landschaftsniveau abgesenkt und sind so dem Blick entzogen. Die sumpfigen Bereiche wurden in klare Seen verwandelt, befahren von Ruderbooten und sogar Gondeln, und mit schmucken kleinen Brücken überspannt, die eine ebene Wegführung ermöglichten. Bestehende zerklüftete Felslandschaften wurden so gestaltet, als seien sie einem Schauerroman entsprungen.

Unvorstellbar, dass heutzutage jemand etwas so Wohlüberlegtes, so minutiös Geplantes, so Umfassendes schafft wie die Parks von Olmsted und Vaux. Im Grunde verstehen wir ihre Anlage nicht mehr, weshalb wir sie auch oft so schlecht erhalten, die Kieswege und das Kopfsteinpflaster asphaltieren, die Pflanzungen vernachlässigen, unsensibel neue Polizei- und Wartungsgebäude hineinsetzen, und wo immer es uns dienlich scheint, auch Parkplätze anlegen.

Allerdings hatte Olmsted stets befürwortet, dass seine Parks benutzt und dabei auch verändert werden.

»[W]ir waren uns einig, dass man vor Ablauf von vier Jahrzehnten keinerlei Ergebnisse erzielen kann«, schrieb er später an seinen Sohn und Schützling Frederick Jr. »Mein Leben lang habe ich die zukünftige Wirkung mitbedacht und den unmittelbaren Erfolg und Beifall dem der Zukunft geopfert.«[3]

Ein wesentlicher Bestandteil dieser »zukünftigen Wirkung« waren Olmsteds Bäume, die er so sehr liebte. Nichts anderes »verbessere« sich über die Zeit mit solcher Dramatik und Anmut. Im Fall der Central Park Mall sind die Bäume vierzehn Jahre nach ihrer Pflanzung zu »einem grünen Tunnel« herangewachsen, einem »Baldachin aus neuen Blättern«, die »ein gesprenkeltes Muster aus Licht und Schatten auf den Kies des Weges werfen«, so Olmsteds Biograf Witold Rybczynski.[4] Das tun sie noch heute, 160 Jahre später, und führen so Spaziergängerinnen und Spaziergänger zur Bethesda Terrace und einem Wasserbecken, in dessen Mitte sich Emma Stebbins ergreifende, den heilenden Kräften gewidmete Statue *The Angel of the Waters* erhebt.

Zugleich sind diese Bäume jedoch auch eine Art Tür. Wenn man aus der Allee heraustritt, blickt man über die Sheep Meadow, die Baseball- und Softballfelder und weiten Wiesen des Parks, die sich meilenweit zu erstrecken scheinen. Immer wieder dienen in Olmsteds Parks Bäume zur Orientierung, sie trennen Aktivitäts- und Stimmungsbereiche, sie gewähren Schutz und Obdach – und sie erfreuen. Olmsted füllte seine Parks mit Bäumen –

3 Ebd., S. 385f.
4 Ebd., S. 317.

It is impossible to conceive of us building today something so coordinated, so minutely planned, so all-encompassing as the Olmsted-Vaux parks. We do not really understand them, which is why we are often so bad at maintaining them, dumping asphalt over their dirt and cobblestoned paths, neglecting their gardens, throwing up crude new police and maintenance buildings, and installing parking lots, wherever it suits us.

Yet Olmsted always embraced the idea that his parks were to be used, and to change as they were used.

"[W]e determined to think of no results to be realized in less than forty years," he later wrote to his son and protégé, Frederick Jr. "I have all my life been considering distant effects and always sacrificing immediate success and applause to that of the future."[3]

Vital to these "distant effects" were Olmsted's trees, which he loved. Nothing else would "improve" so dramatically or so gracefully over time. In the case of the Central Park Promenade, fourteen years after its trees were planted they would, in the words of Olmsted biographer Witold Rybczynski, "create a green tunnel," a "canopy of new leaves" that "throws dappled patterns of light and shade on the gravel walk."[4] They still do today, 160 years later, guiding walkers to the Bethesda Terrace and a pond surrounding Emma Stebbins's moving statue dedicated to healing, *The Angel of the Waters.*

Yet the trees are, as well, a sort of door. Step outside them and you are gazing upon the Sheep Meadow and the park ballfields, rolling meadows that seem to stretch out for miles. Again and again, in Olmsted's parks, trees serve to guide, to separate different sorts of activities and even moods, to protect, to shelter—and to delight. He filled his parks with them—300,000 trees and shrubs in Central Park alone—and he used species from all over America, as well as from other continents.

All of which is why it is so important for us to see Stanley Greenberg's extraordinary photographs of Olmsted's trees when they have become "distant effects," many years after they were planted. By focusing so closely upon their trunks in most of these pictures, he shows us how individual, how splendid and enduring they are.

Greenberg has included a wide variety of trees—as Olmsted did. Elms and oaks, beeches and sycamores, ashes and pecans, maples and planes, lindens and Osage oranges, a cottonwood and a katsura tree. They are, all of them, old trees, and through Greenberg's lens we react to them almost as though they were human, or animals. We worry about the fate of the northern red oak in Newburgh, marked with its ominous "X"; admire the pluck of its cousin in the Back Bay Fens, flourishing despite a sawed-off branch that here feels like a missing limb. The beeches in Washington and Trenton and Central Park, with names and hearts so thoughtlessly cut into them, also seem anthropomorphic, their carvings looking like nothing so much as tattoos on aged, sagging skin. The bark on the slippery elm in Prospect Park, the European beeches in Franklin and Central Park, the pin oak in Morningside, and more: they look like the hides of great,

3 Rybczynski, *Clearing in the Distance*, 386, 385.
4 Rybczynski, *Clearing in the Distance*, 317.

allein im Central Park wurden 300 000 Bäume und Büsche gepflanzt – und er nutzte dazu Arten aus ganz Amerika sowie von anderen Kontinenten.

All dies sind Gründe genug, Stanley Greenbergs wunderbare Fotos von Olmsteds Bäumen zu betrachten, die nun, viele Jahre nach ihrer Pflanzung, ihre »zukünftige Wirkung« entfaltet haben. Durch die Konzentration auf die Stämme in den meisten seiner Bilder zeigt er uns, wie individuell, wie prächtig und beständig sie sind.

Greenberg hat sich – ebenso wie Olmsted – einer breiten Palette von Bäumen zugewandt: Ulmen und Eichen, Buchen und Platanen, Eschen und Pekannussbäumen, Ahornbäumen, Linden und Milchorangenbäumen, einer Schwarz-Pappel und einem Katsurabaum. Es sind sämtlich alte Bäume, die durch Greenbergs Objektiv gesehen beinahe menschlich auf uns wirken, oder wie Tiere. Wir machen uns Gedanken über das Schicksal der Rot-Eiche in Newburgh, die mit einem ominösen »X« gekennzeichnet ist, bewundern den Schneid ihres Bruders in den Back Bay Fens, der trotz eines abgesägten Astes, der wie ein amputierter Arm wirkt, zu gedeihen scheint. Auch den Birken in Washington, Trenton und im Central Park, in die so rücksichtslos Namen und Herzen geschnitten wurden, haftet etwas Menschliches an, die eingekerbten Inschriften wirken wie Tätowierungen auf gealterter, schlaffer Haut. Die Rinde der Rot-Ulme im Prospect Park, der Rot-Buchen im Franklin und im Central Park, der Sumpf-Eiche in Morningside und anderer Bäume, sie wirkt jeweils wie die Haut großer, wettergegerbter Tiere, Elefanten oder Nashörner. Die Rot-Buche am Jamaica Pond ähnelt einem in sich zusammengesunkenen Tintenfisch. Aus dem Stamm der Winterlinde im Prospect Park holt Greenberg gar ein menschliches Antlitz heraus.

In jedem Bild steckt eine Hommage an die Herrlichkeit des Alters. Greenberg verwandelt jeden Knoten und Sprössling, jede alte Kerbe und knorrige Wurzel in ein Ehrenzeichen – und eine Herausforderung. Wir lieben die eleganten, gleichmäßigen Furchen der Holländischen Ulme auf dem Gelände des Kapitols in Washington, und die mächtige Rot-Eiche, die in einsamer Würde im Olmsted Park in Boston steht, allein und gewaltig. Die Rot-Ulme im Prospect Park erscheint uns lebendig wie ein Geschöpf in höchster Qual, ein Wesen, das um sein Überleben inmitten der Elemente kämpft – nichts anderes ist ein Baum in Wahrheit auch.

Mit seinen Bäumen hinterließ uns Olmsted gigantische Wächter und Beschützer, die zusammen mit uns alt werden und uns beständig zugleich an die Zerbrechlichkeit der Natur wie ihr Durchhaltevermögen in der städtischsten aller Umgebungen erinnern. Greenbergs Porträts, persönlich und liebevoll, erwecken sie für uns zum Leben, selbst wenn wir ihnen nur in einem Buch begegnen. Die Parks von Olmsted und Vaux beabsichtigten die Menschen und die Natur gleichermaßen zu einem Besseren zu führen, und auch wenn wir heute womöglich nicht genau mit ihnen darüber übereinstimmen, was das im Einzelnen bedeutet, erleben wir doch in der Tat eine Veredelung, und das jedes Mal, wenn wir uns unter diese treuen Gefährten begeben.

rugged beasts, elephants or rhinoceroses. The European beech at Jamaica Pond resembles a slumping squid. Greenberg even seems to draw a human face out of the trunk of the littleleaf linden in Prospect Park.

Everywhere, in every picture, is an essay on the magnificence of age. Greenberg turns each knot and second growth, every ancient groove and gnarled root into a badge of honor—and defiance. We love the elegant, matching furrows of the Dutch elm on the US Capitol Grounds, and the solitary dignity of the northern red oak, alone and immense, in Boston's Olmsted Park. The slippery elm in Prospect Park seems most vividly like a creature in active torment, a live thing actively struggling to survive amidst the elements. Which of course it is.

In the form of these trees, Olmsted provided us with gigantic guides and protectors that would grow old along with us, and serve as constant reminders of both the fragility of natural life and its persistence in the most urban of environments. Greenberg's portraits, intimate and loving, bring them alive to us even at the remove of a book. Olmsted-Vaux parks were intended to improve people as well as nature, and while today we might not share the exact same view of what that means, we are indeed improved, every time we intermingle with these faithful companions.

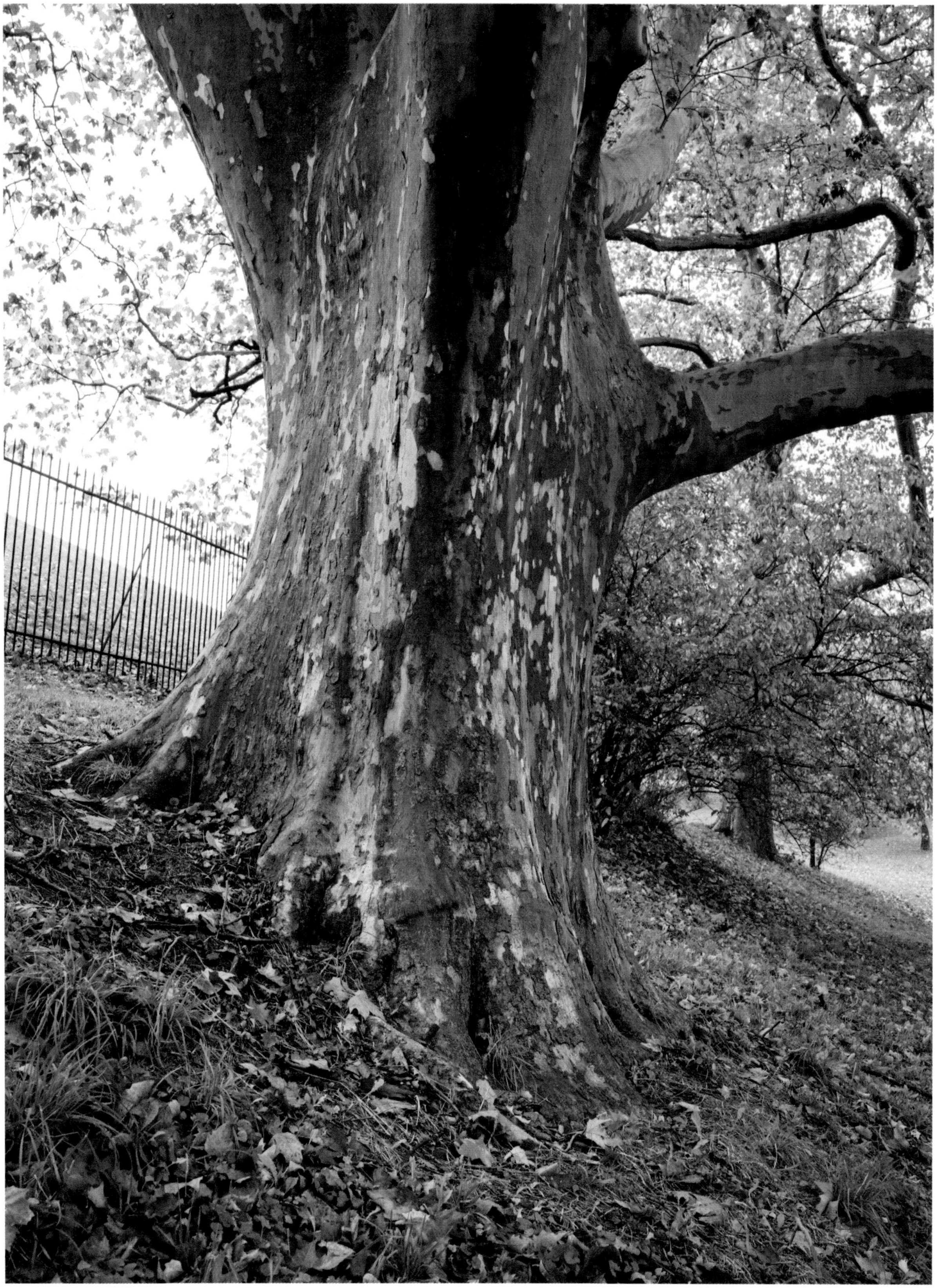

Platanus × acerifolia, London Plane, Ahornblättrige Platane – Highland Park, Rochester, New York, 2020

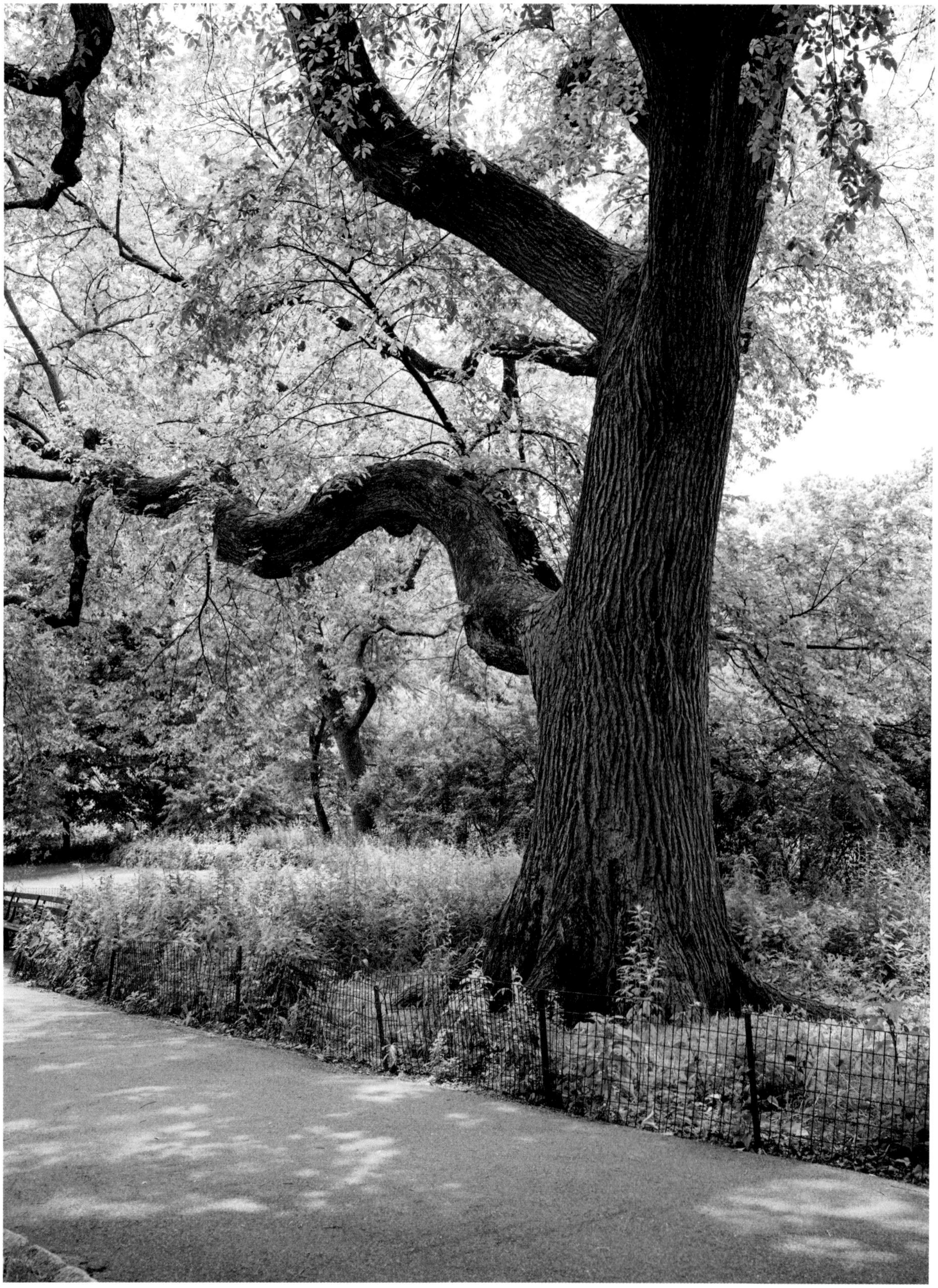

Ulmus americana, American Elm, Amerikanische Ulme – Central Park, New York, New York, 2021

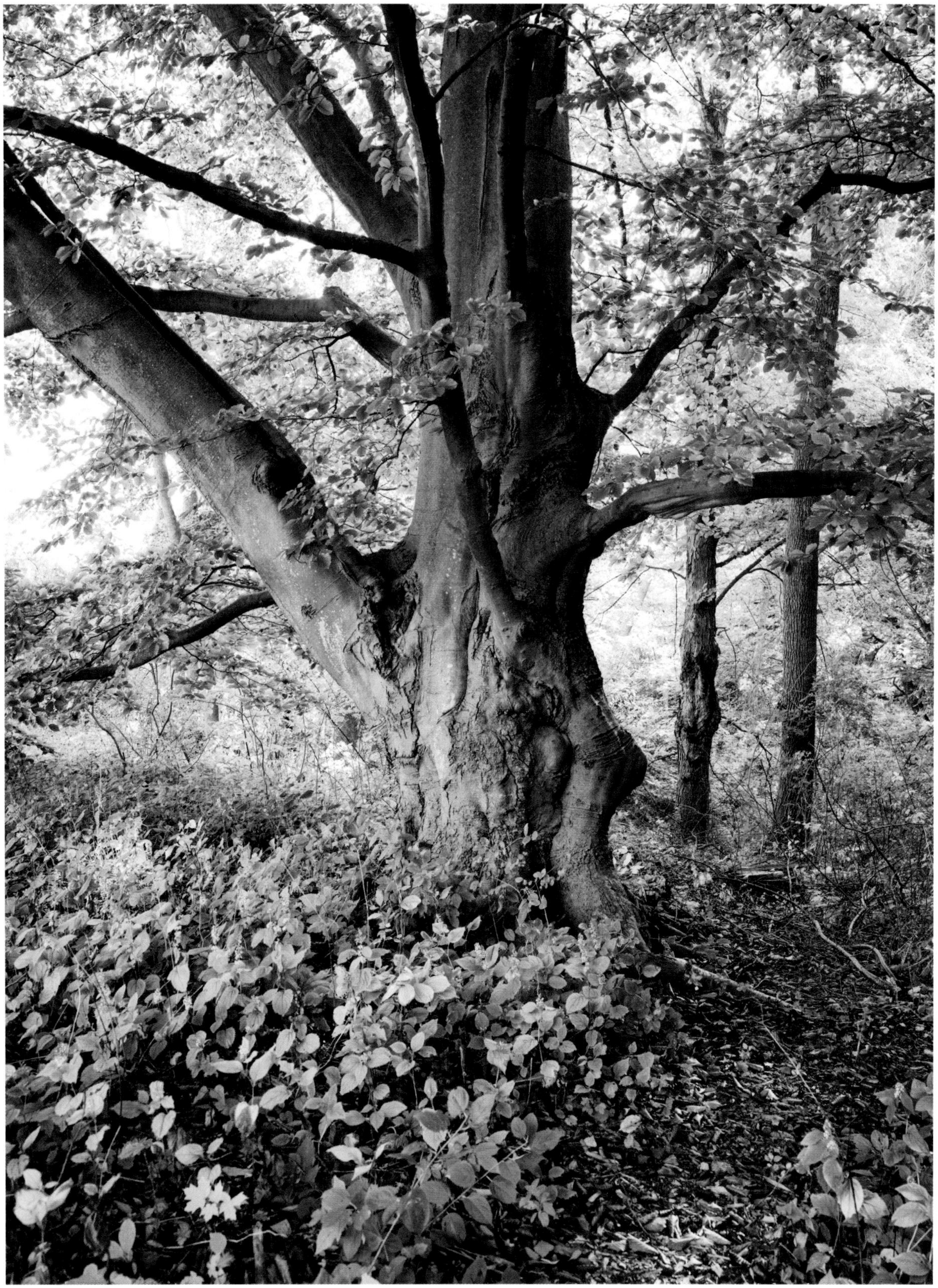

Fagus sylvatica, European Beech, Rot-Buche – Lake Park, Milwaukee, Wisconsin, 2021

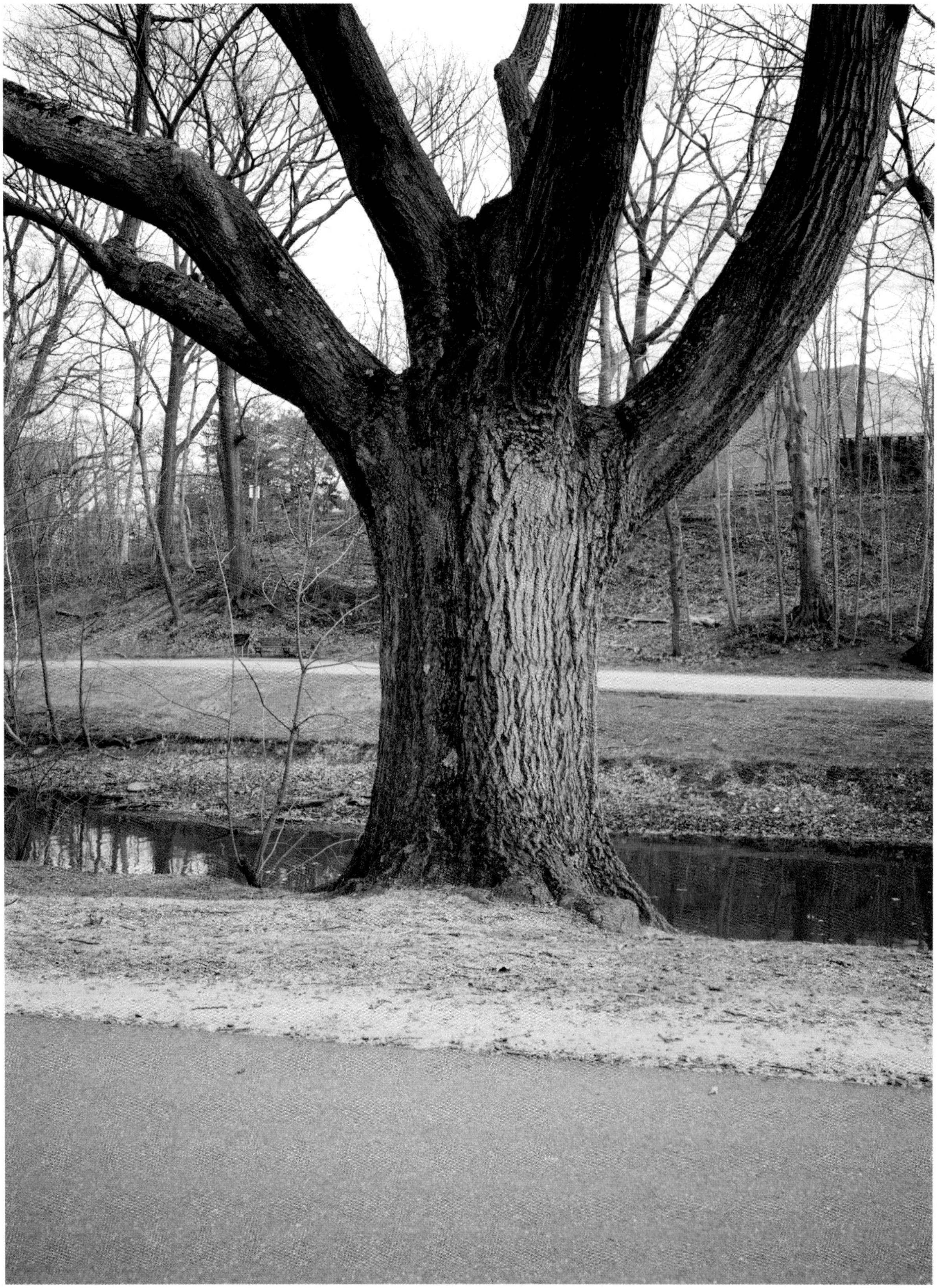

Quercus rubra, Northern Red Oak, Rot-Eiche – Riverway, Boston, Massachusetts, 2020

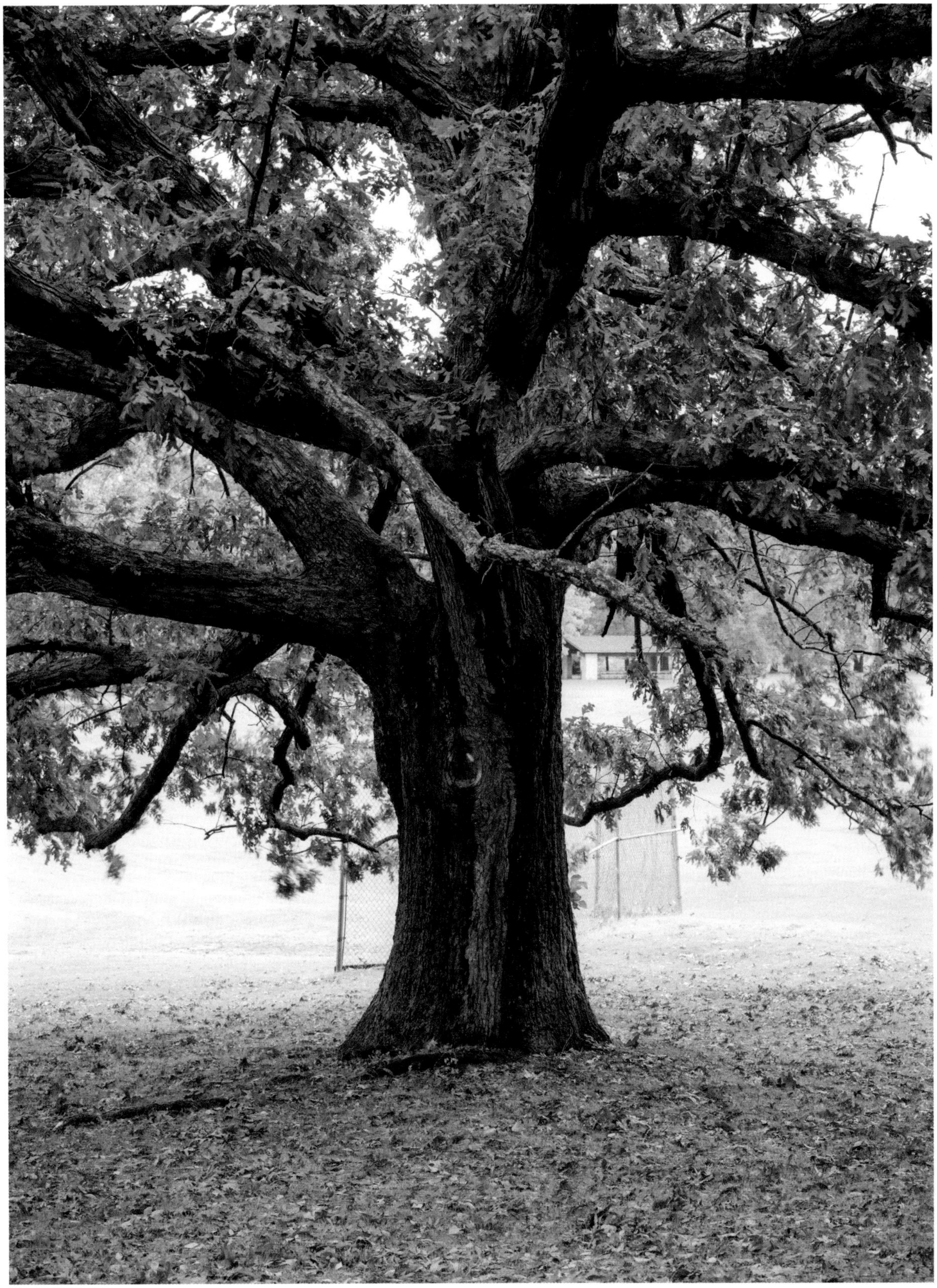

Quercus alba, White Oak, Amerikanische Weiß-Eiche – Genesee Valley Park, Rochester, New York, 2020

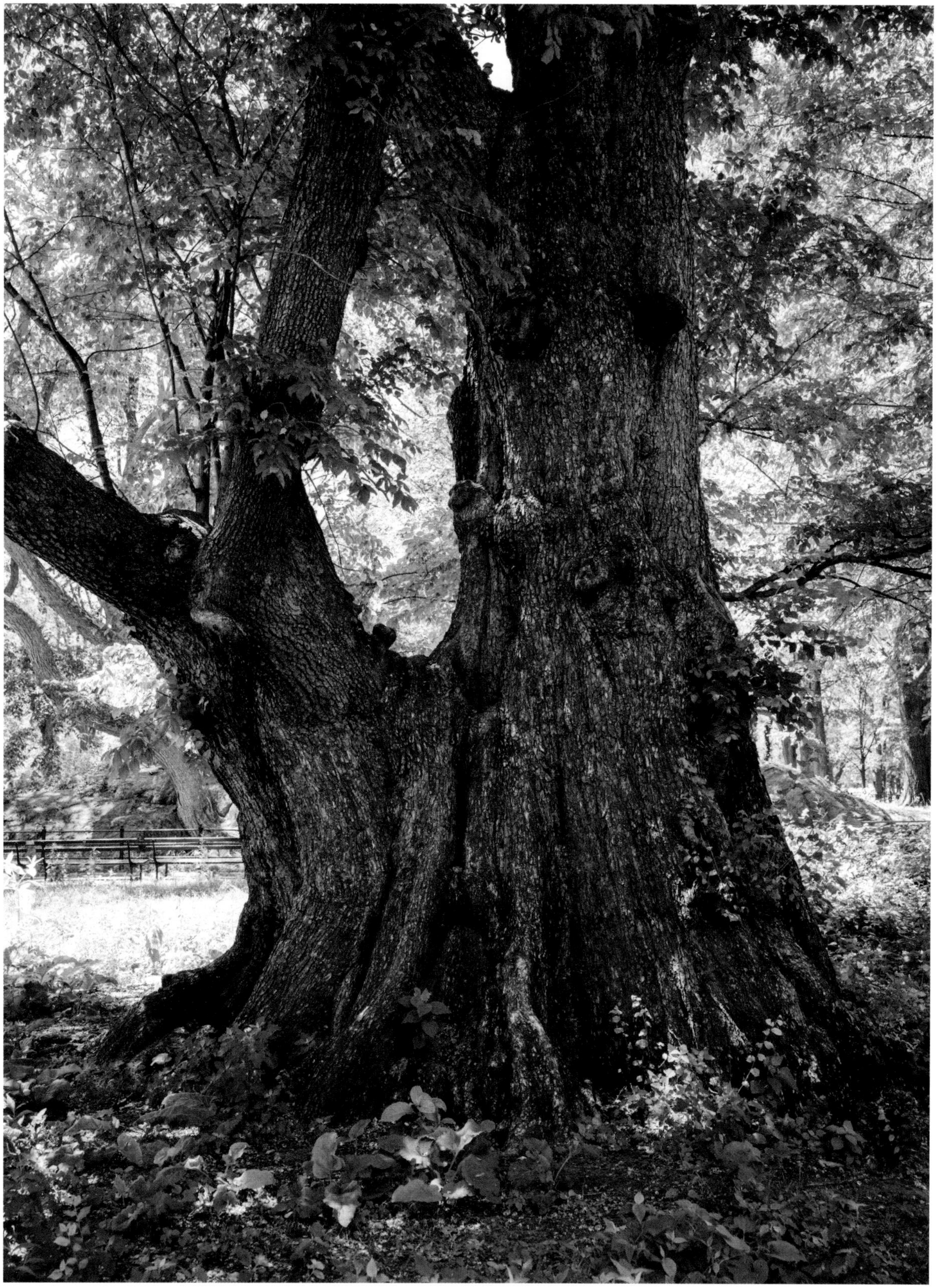

Ulmus minor, English Elm, Feld-Ulme – Central Park, New York, New York, 2021

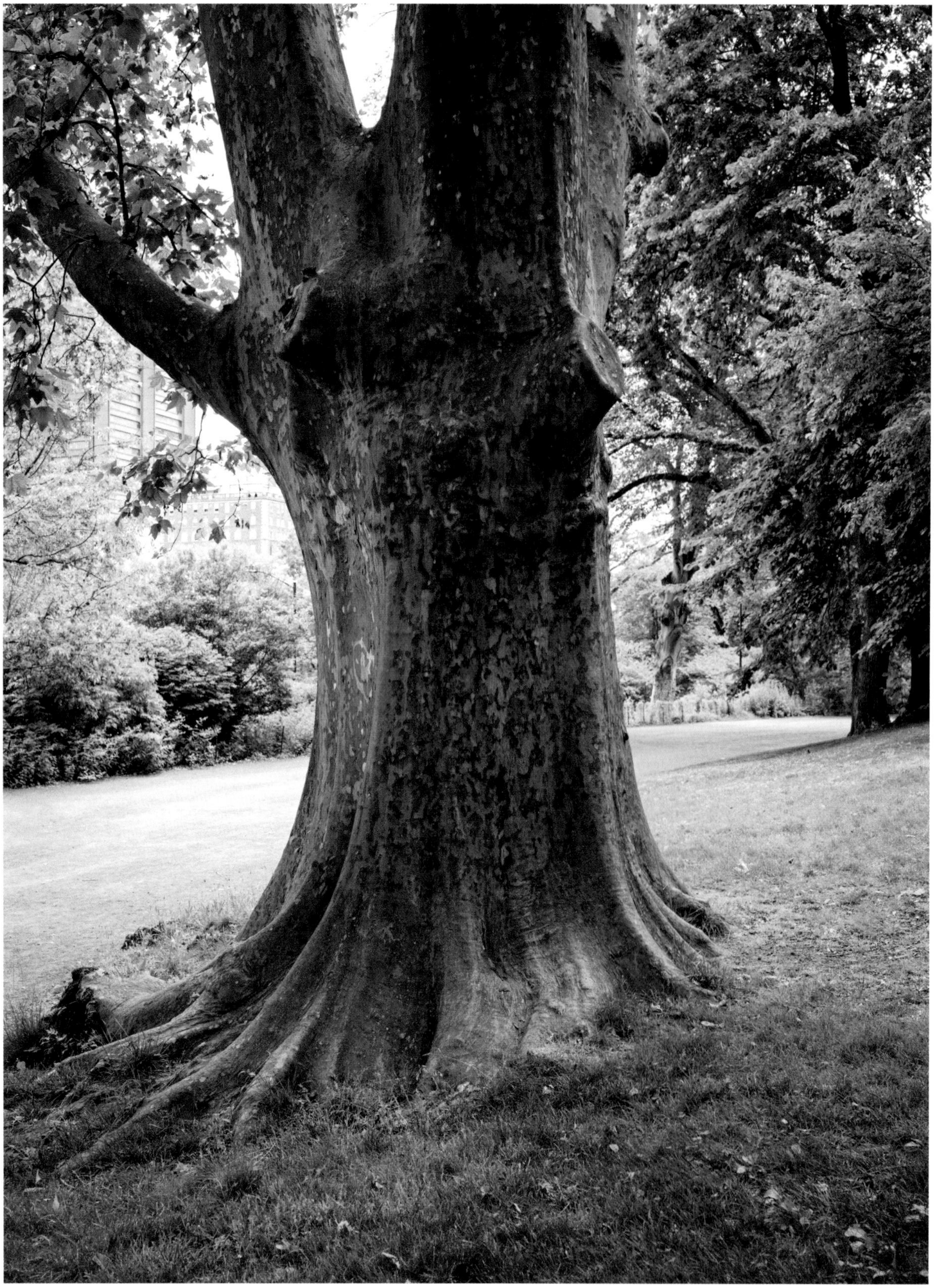

Platanus × acerifolia, London Plane, Ahornblättrige Platane – Central Park, New York, New York, 2021

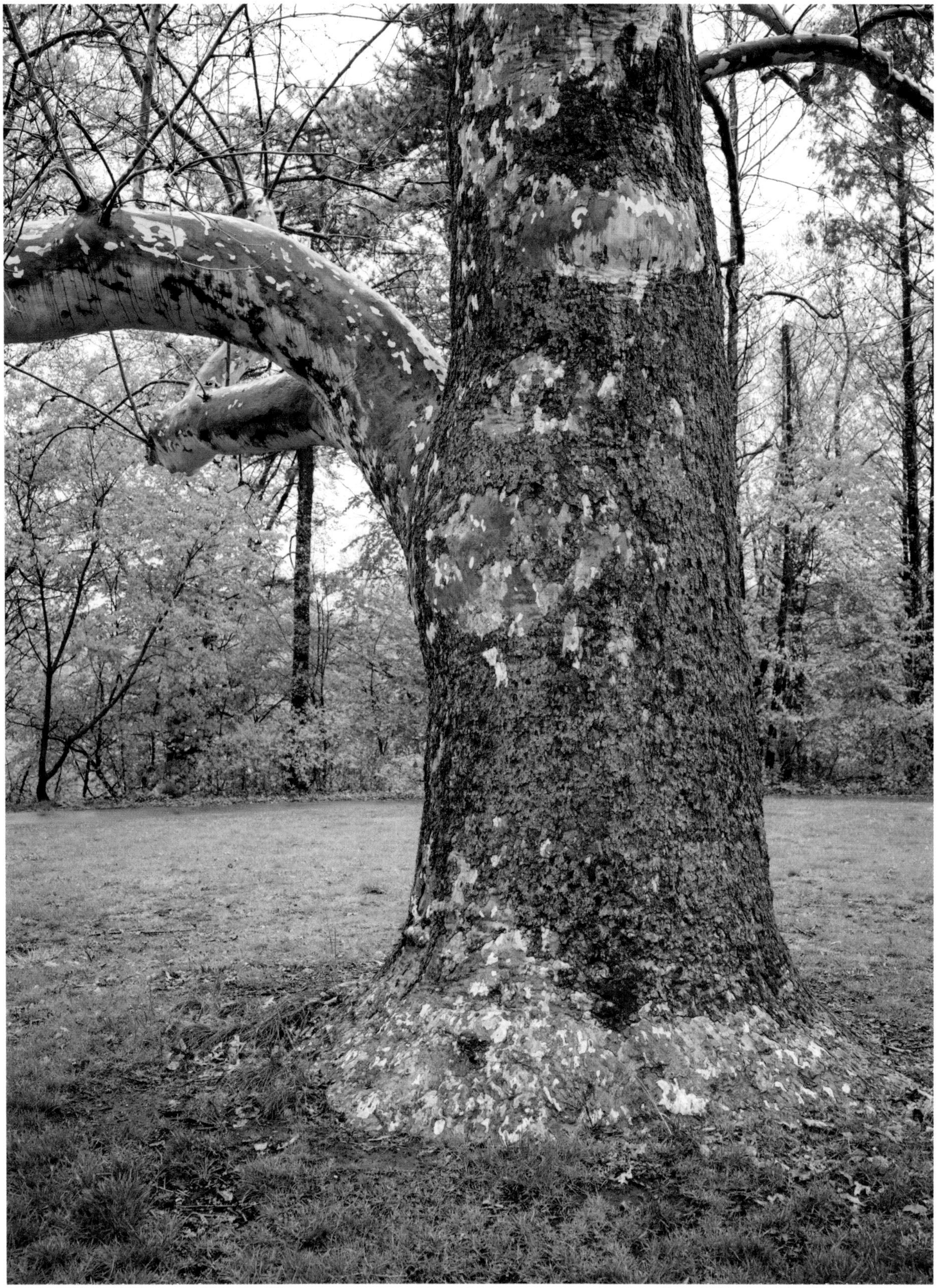

Platanus occidentalis, American Sycamore, Amerikanische Platane – Jamaica Pond, Boston, Massachusetts, 2020

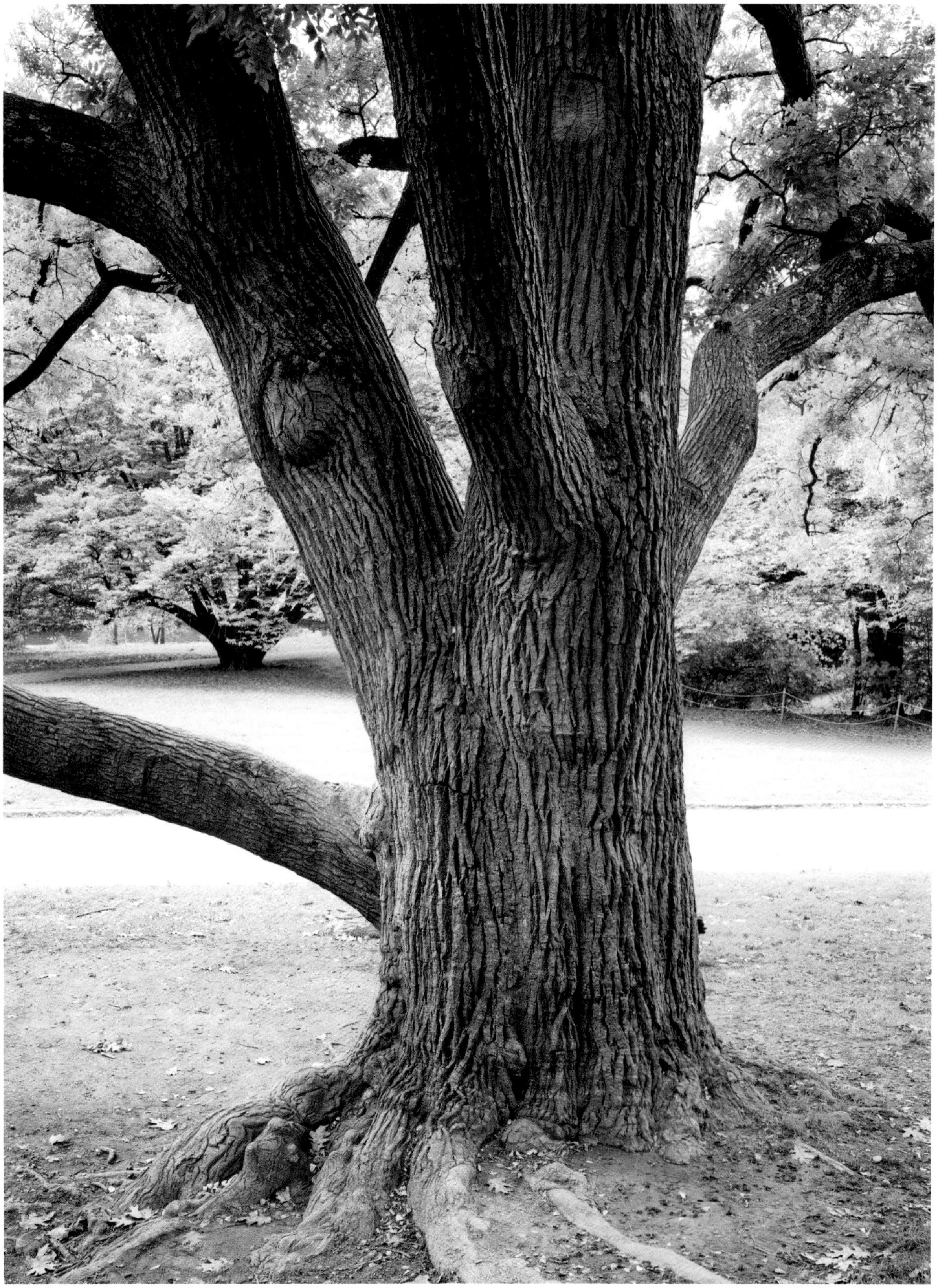

Styphnolobium japonicum, Pagoda Tree, Japanischer Schnurbaum – Prospect Park, Brooklyn, New York, 2021

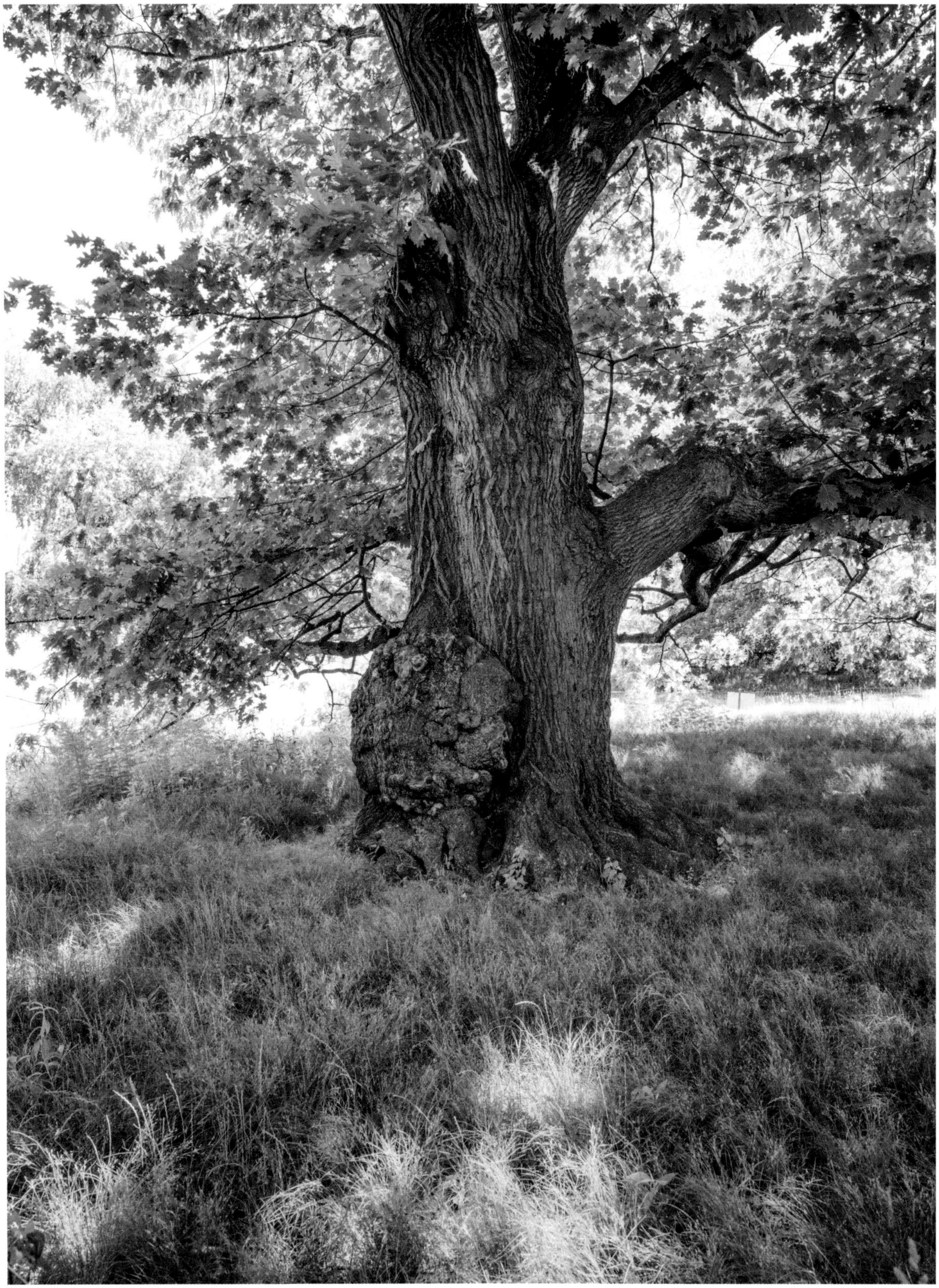

Quercus rubra, Northern Red Oak, Rot-Eiche – Central Park, New York, New York, 2021

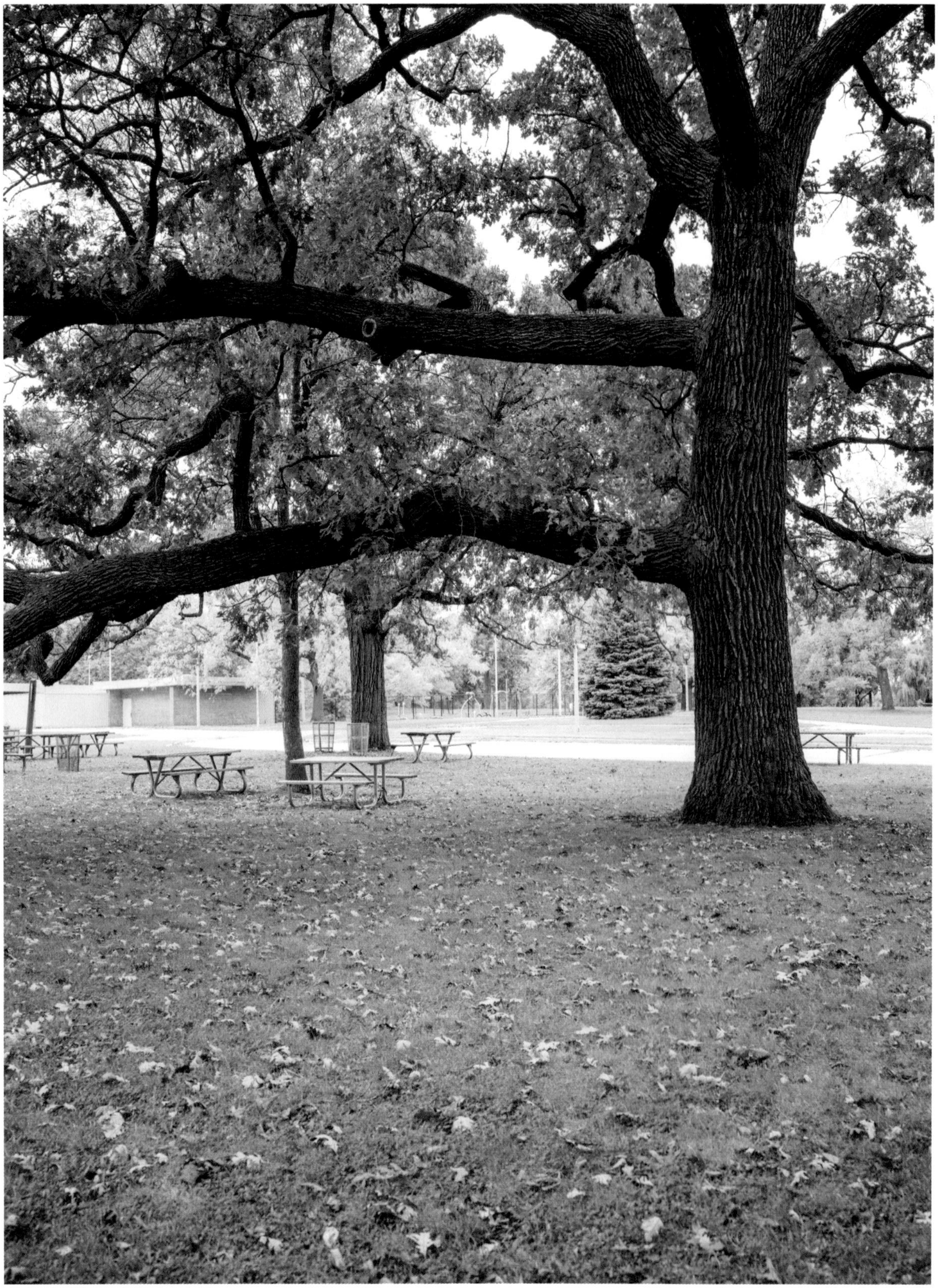

Quercus macrocarpa, Burr Oak, Bur-Eiche – Washington Park, Milwaukee, Wisconsin, 2021

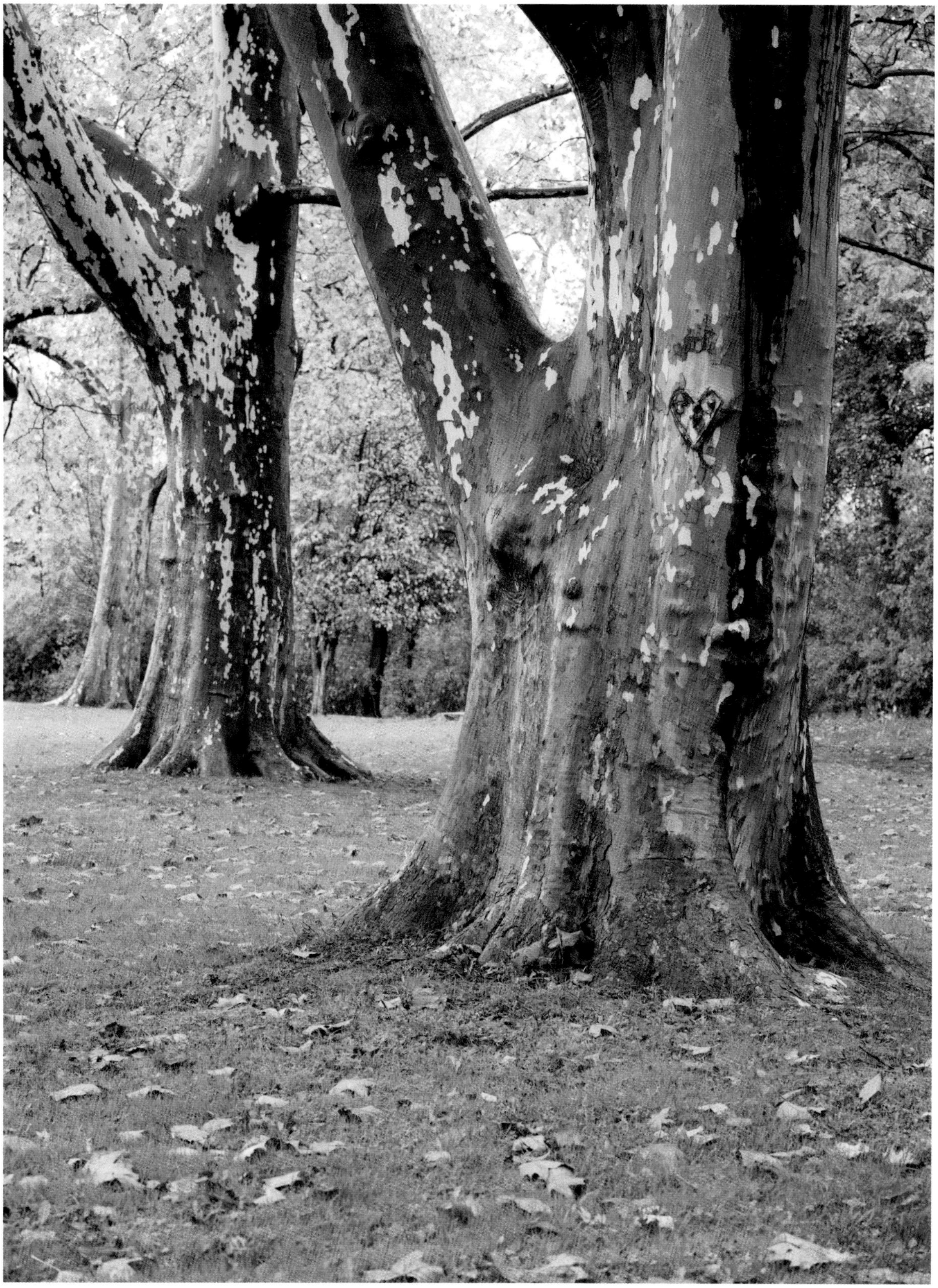

Platanus × acerifolia, London Plane, Ahornblättrige Platane – Delaware Park, Buffalo, New York, 2020

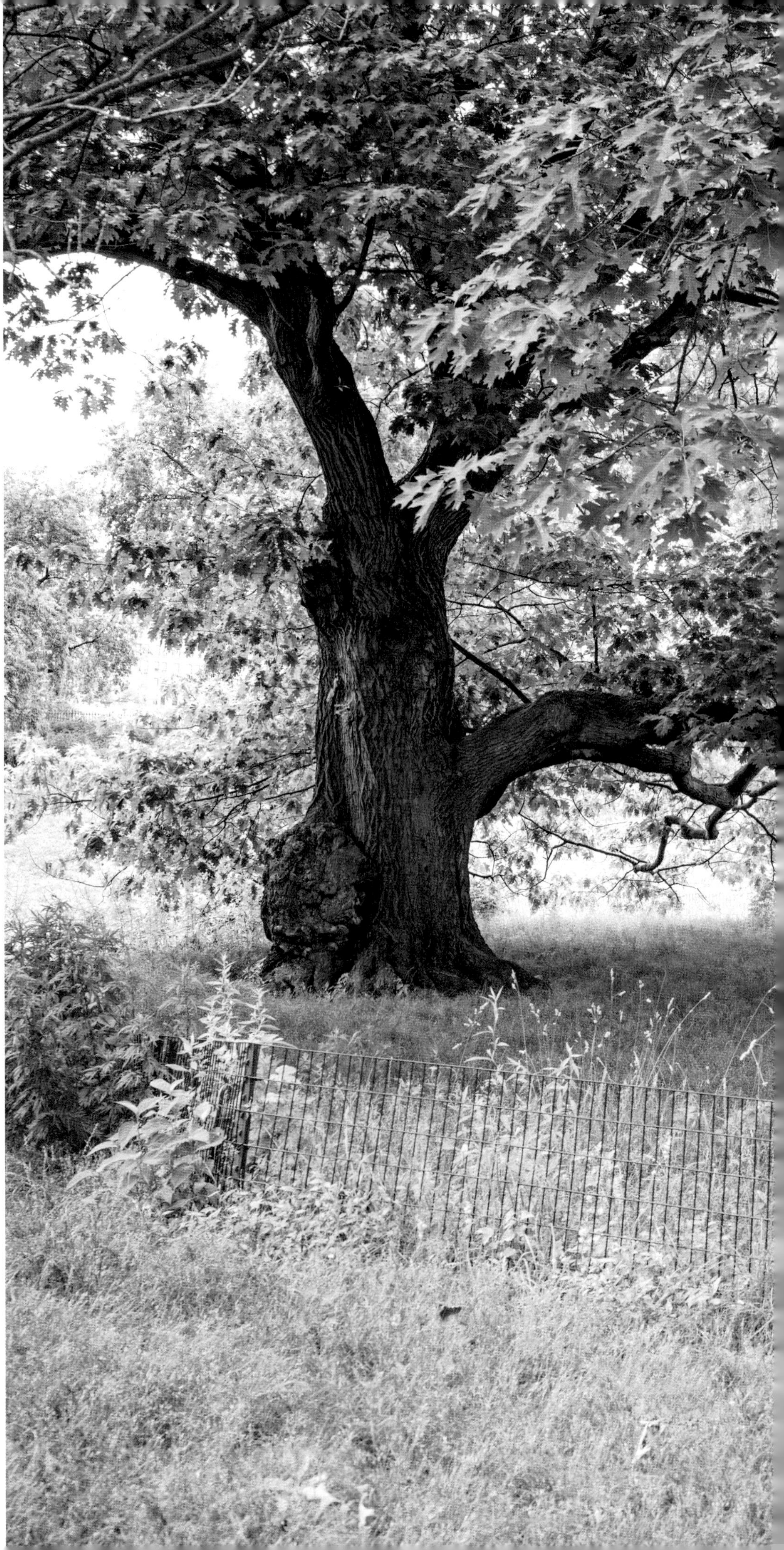

Quercus rubra,
Northern Red Oak, Rot-Eiche
– Central Park, New York,
New York, 2021

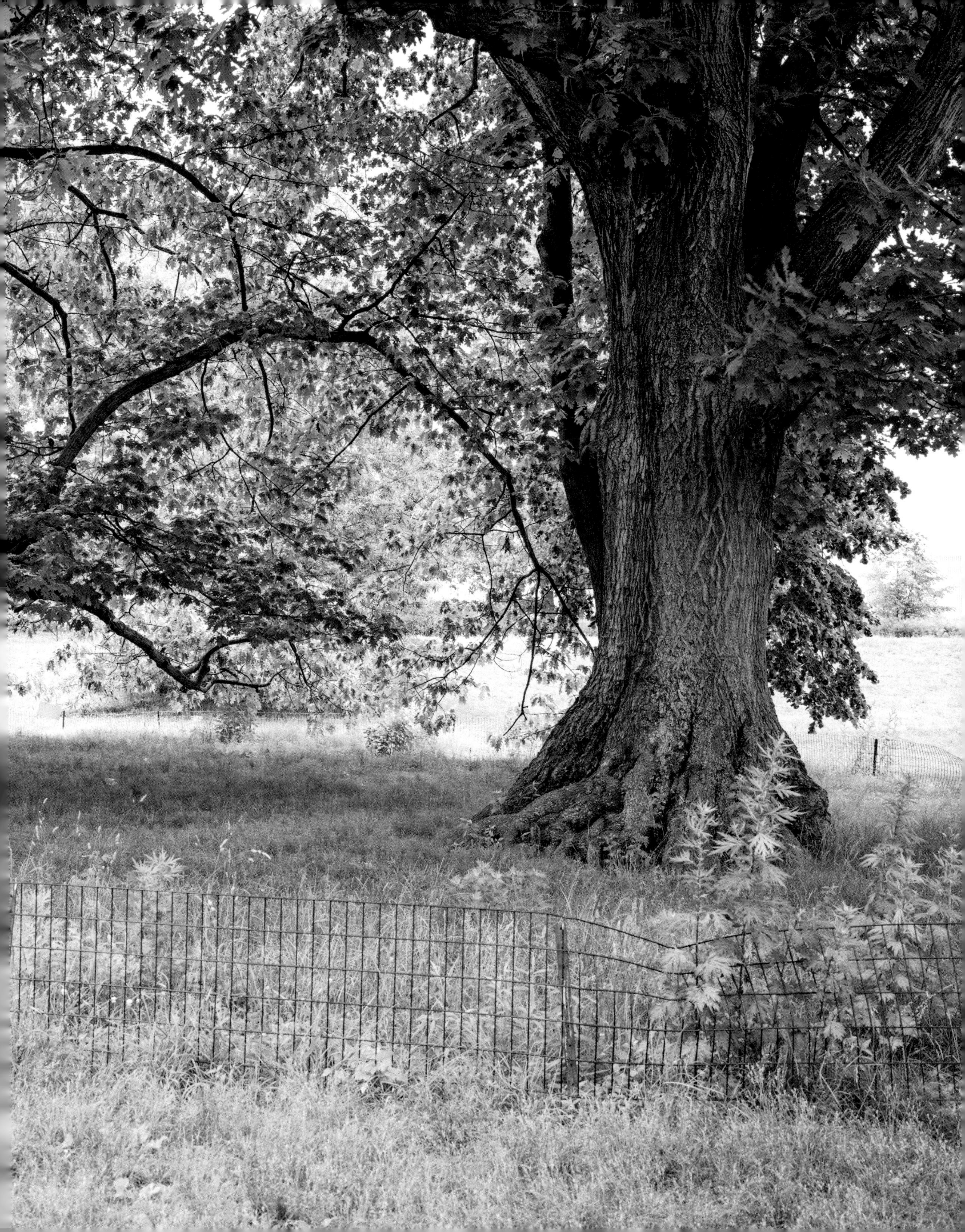

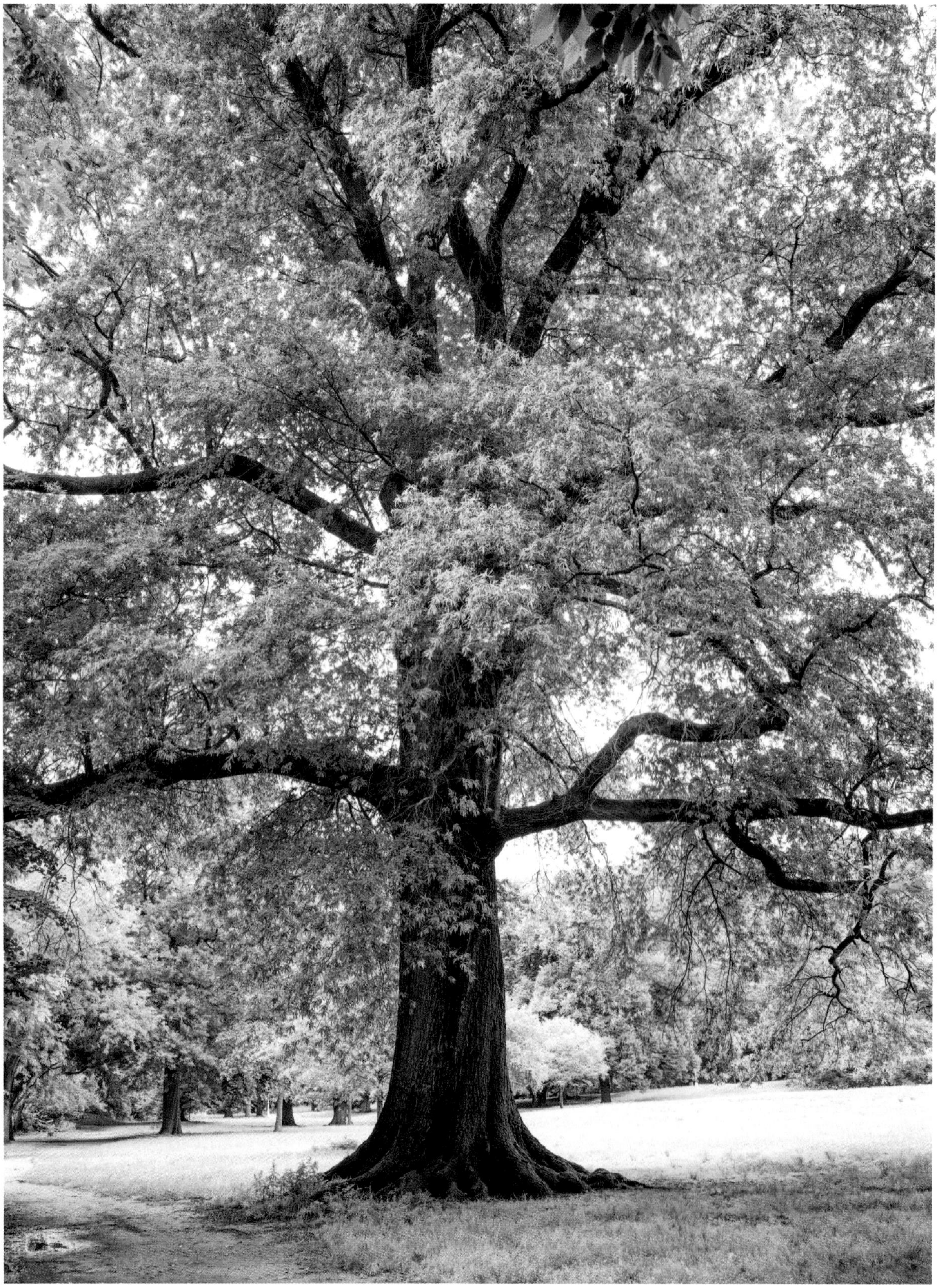

Quercus phellos, Willow Oak, Weiden-Eiche – Prospect Park, Brooklyn, New York, 2021

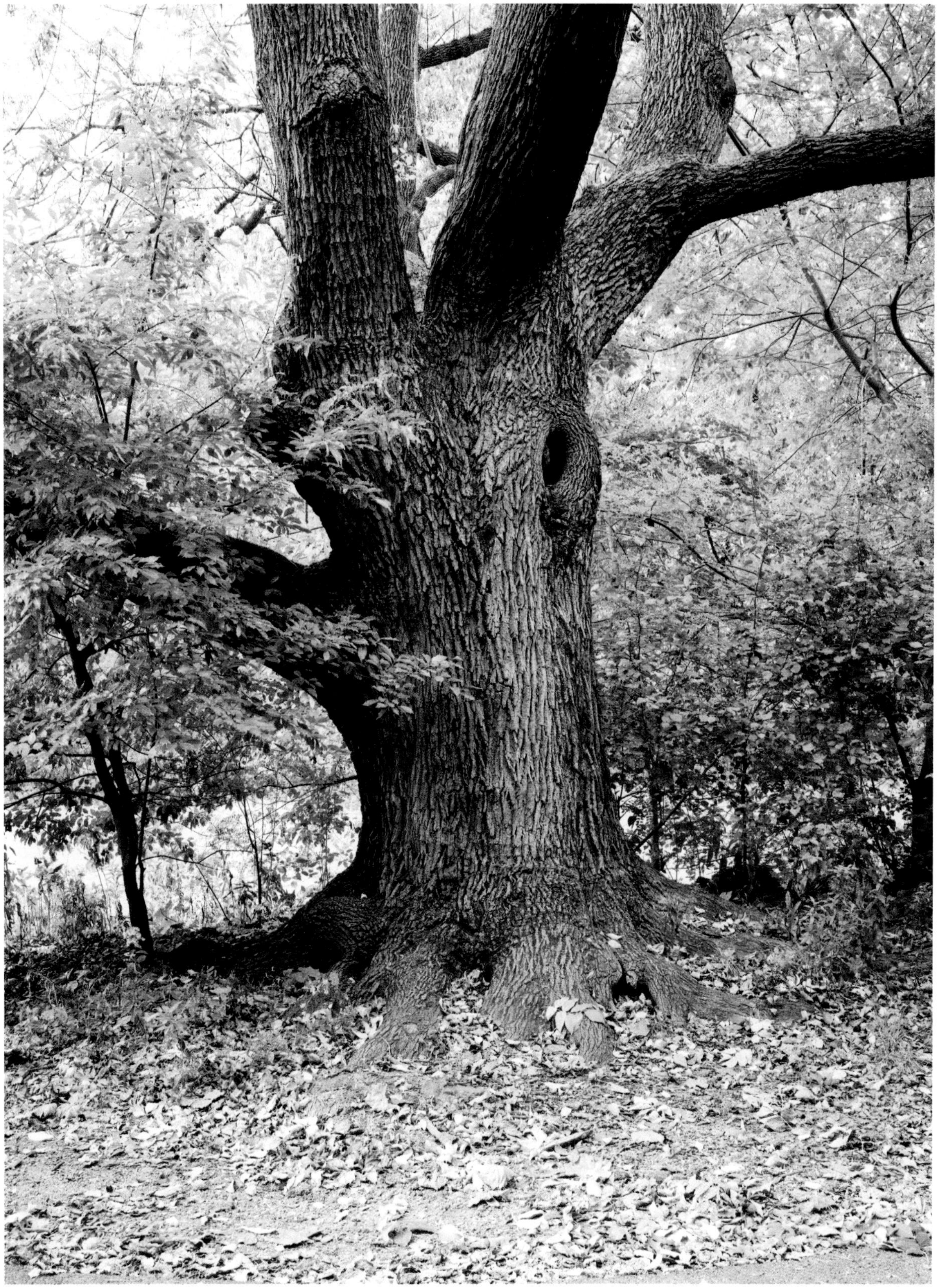

Fraxinus americana, White Ash, Weiß-Esche – Prospect Park, Brooklyn, New York, 2021

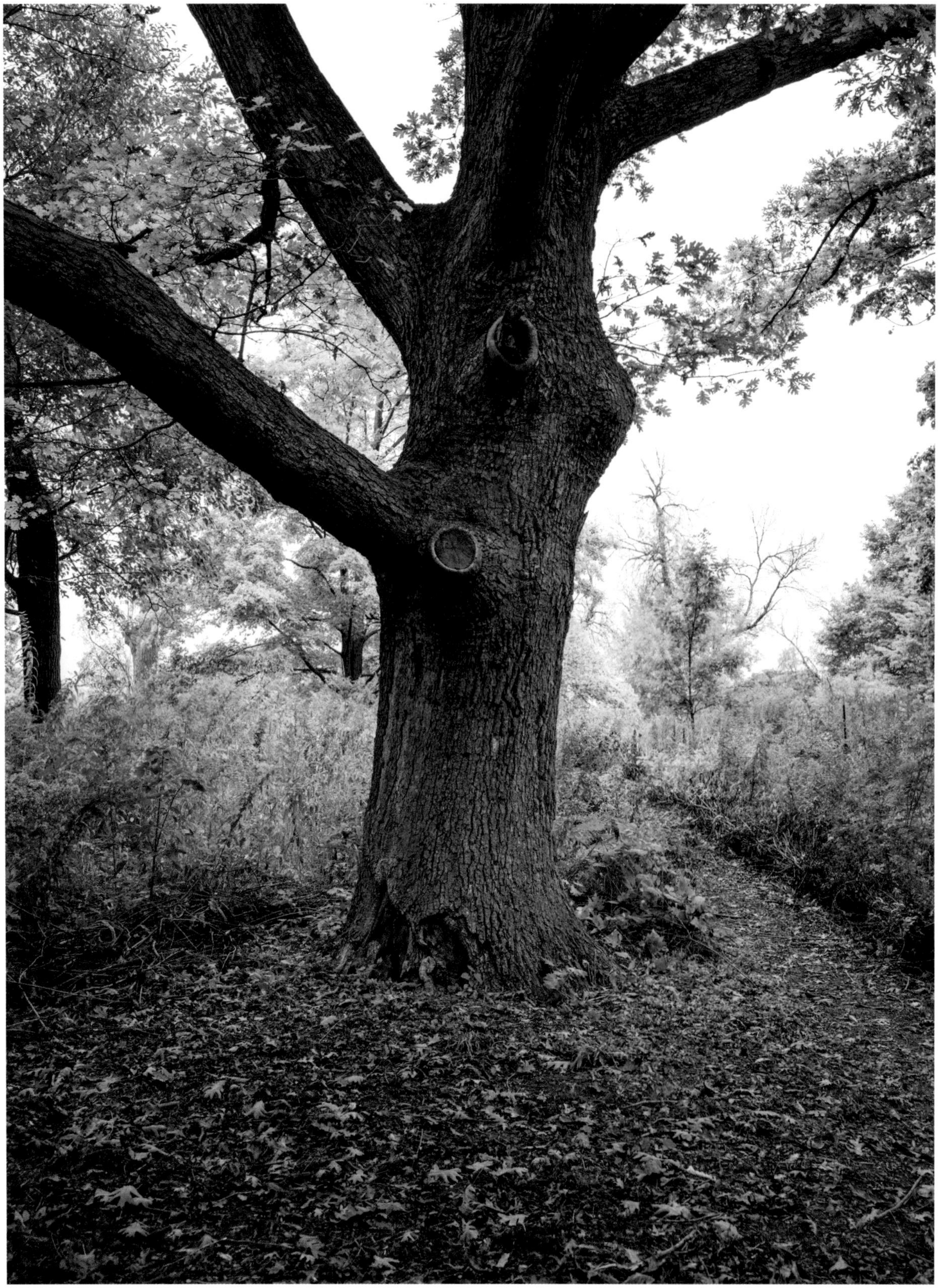

Quercus alba, White Oak, Amerikanische Weiß-Eiche – Washington Park, Milwaukee, Wisconsin, 2021

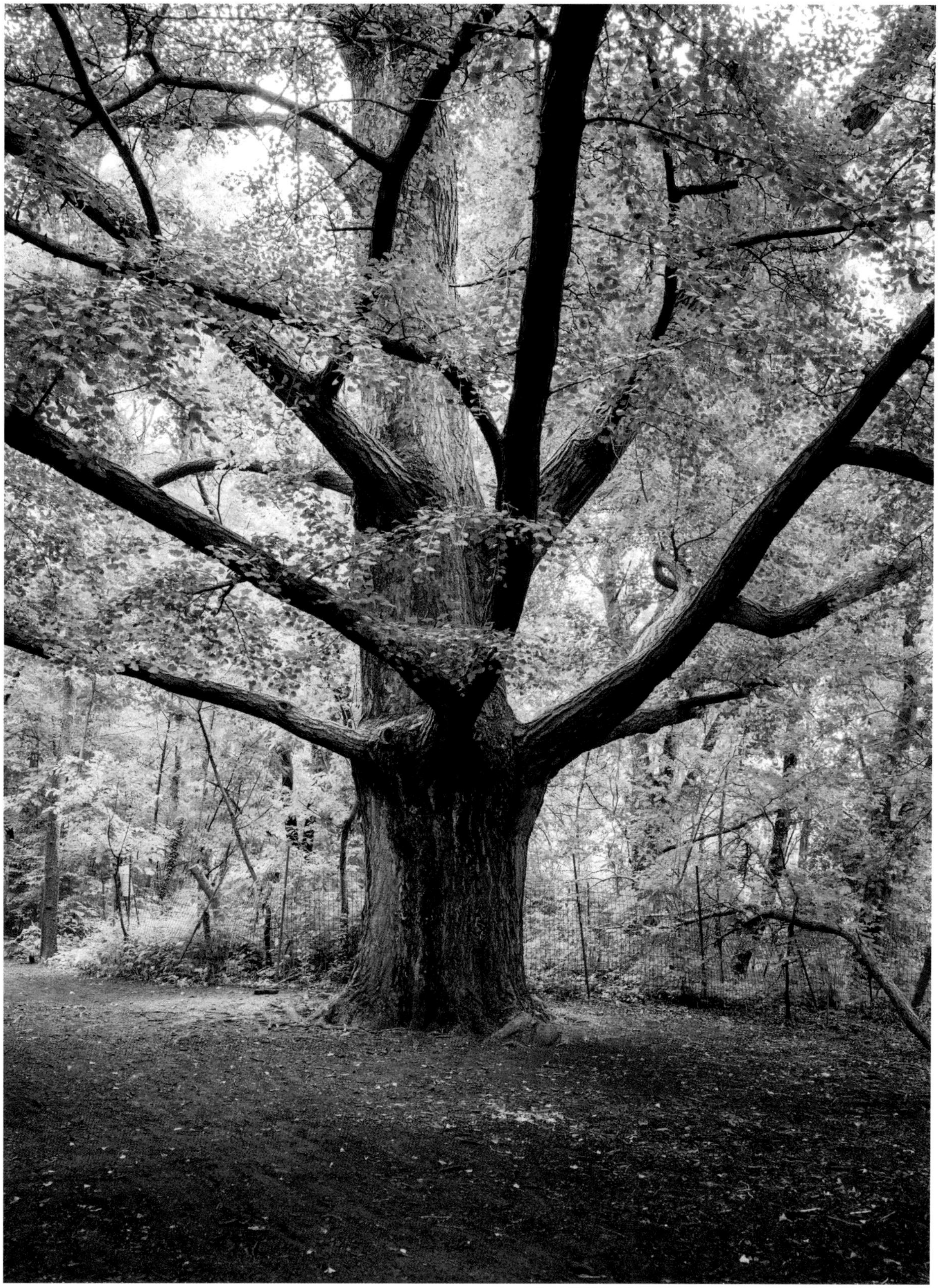

Ginkgo biloba, Ginkgo – Prospect Park, Brooklyn, New York, 2021

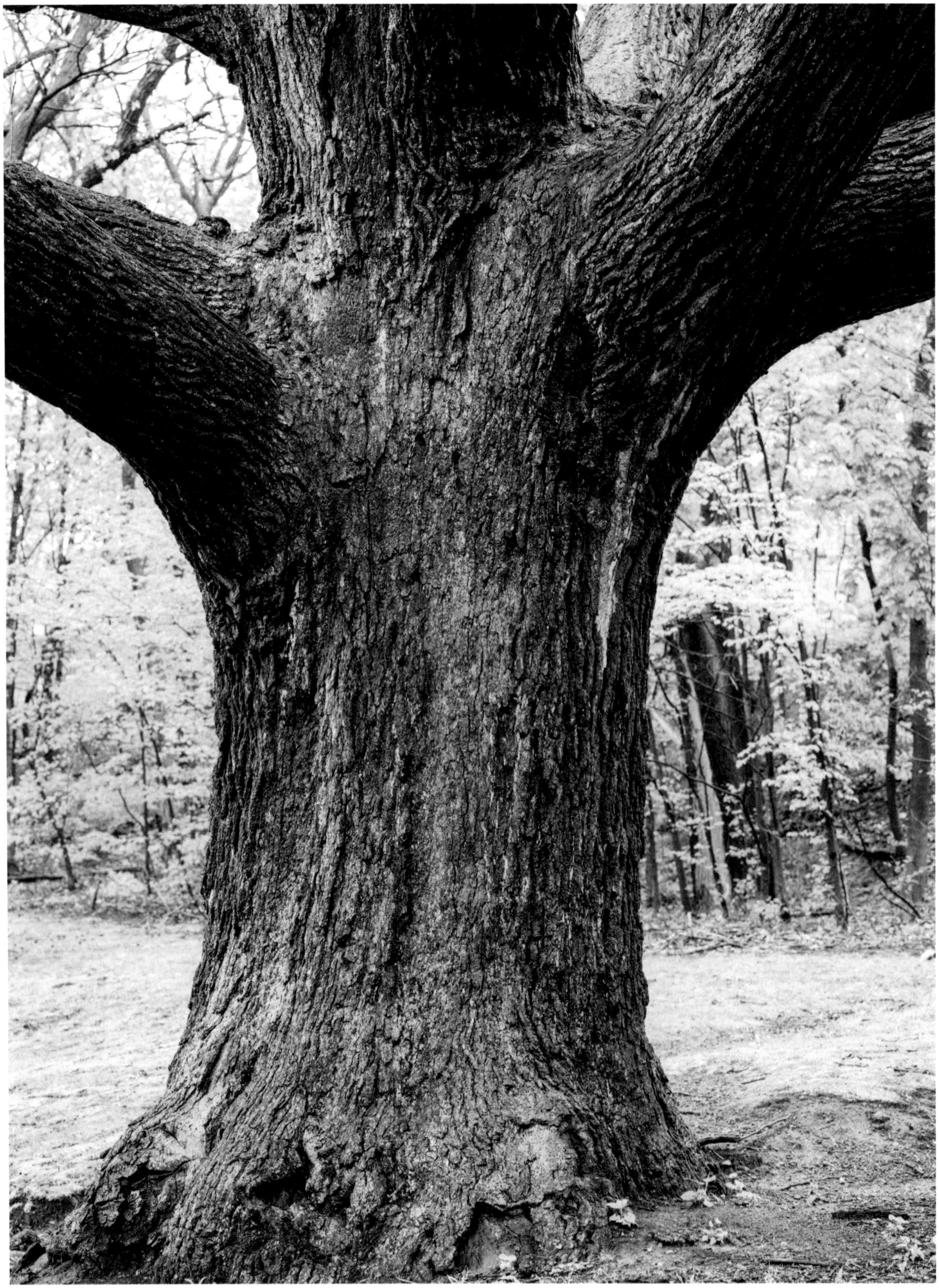

Quercus rubra, Northern Red Oak, Rot-Eiche – Riverway, Boston, Massachusetts, 2021

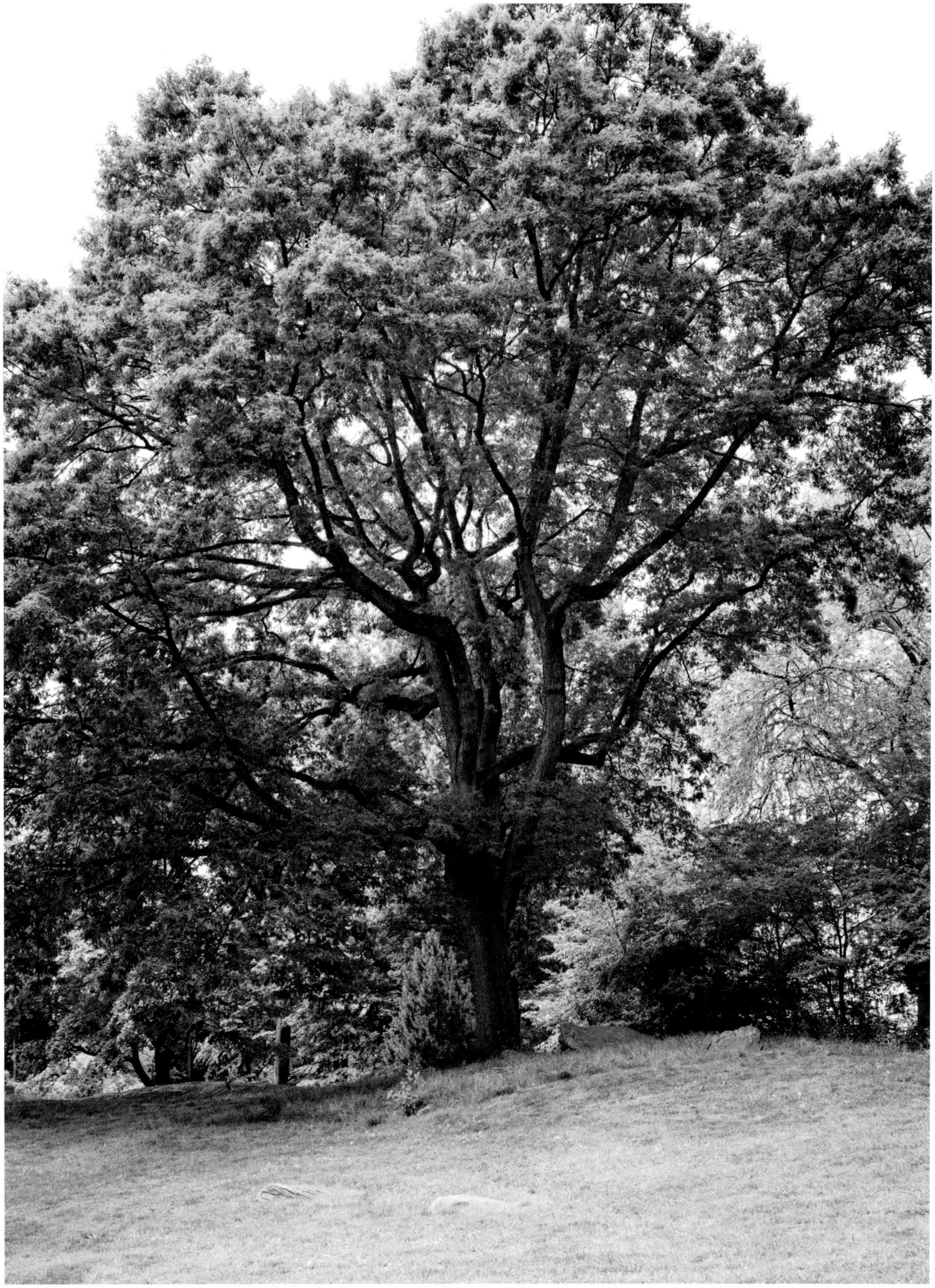

Quercus alba, White Oak, Amerikanische Weiß-Eiche – Central Park, New York, New York, 2021

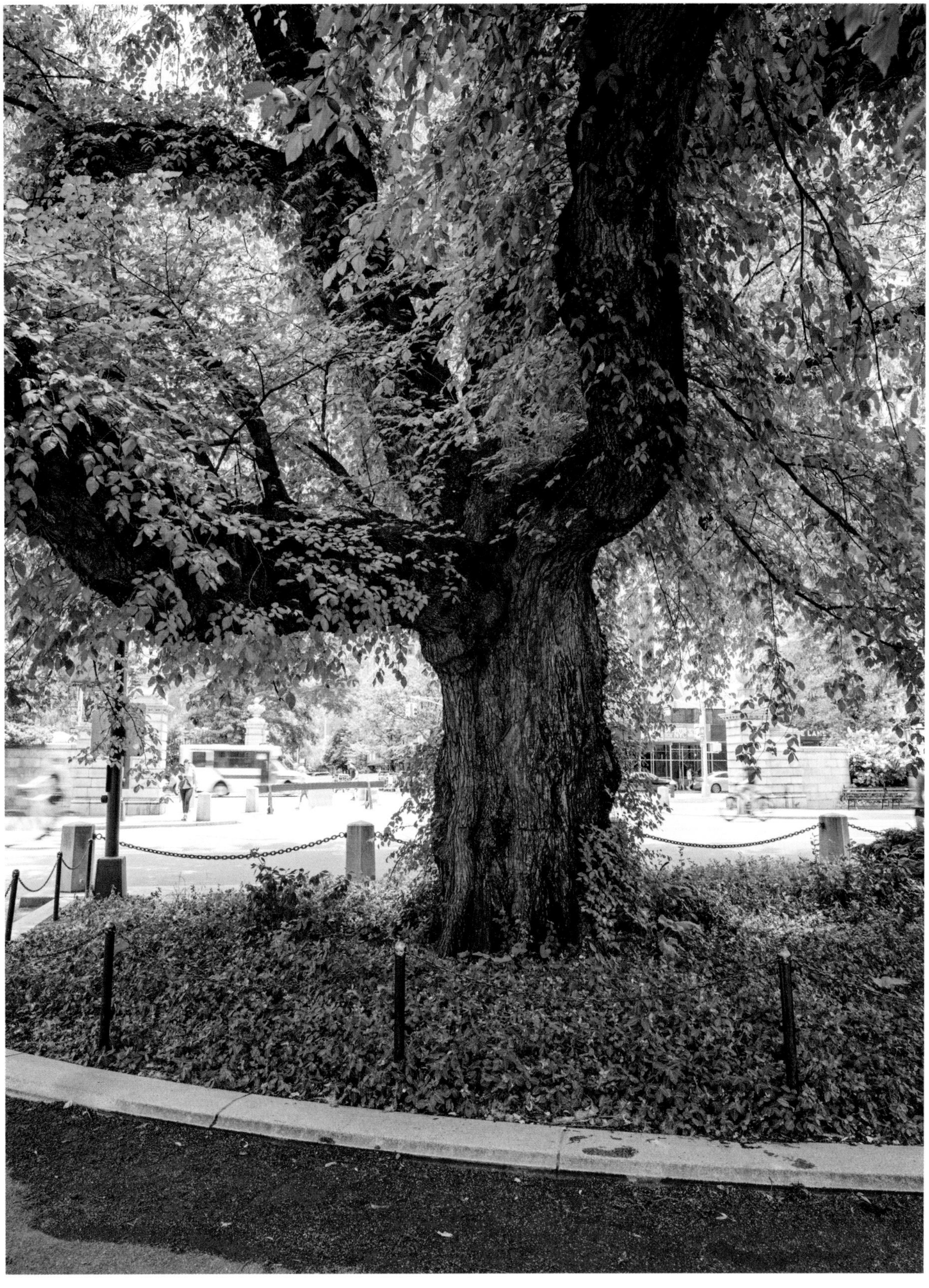

Ulmus minor, English Elm, Feld-Ulme – Central Park, New York, New York, 2021

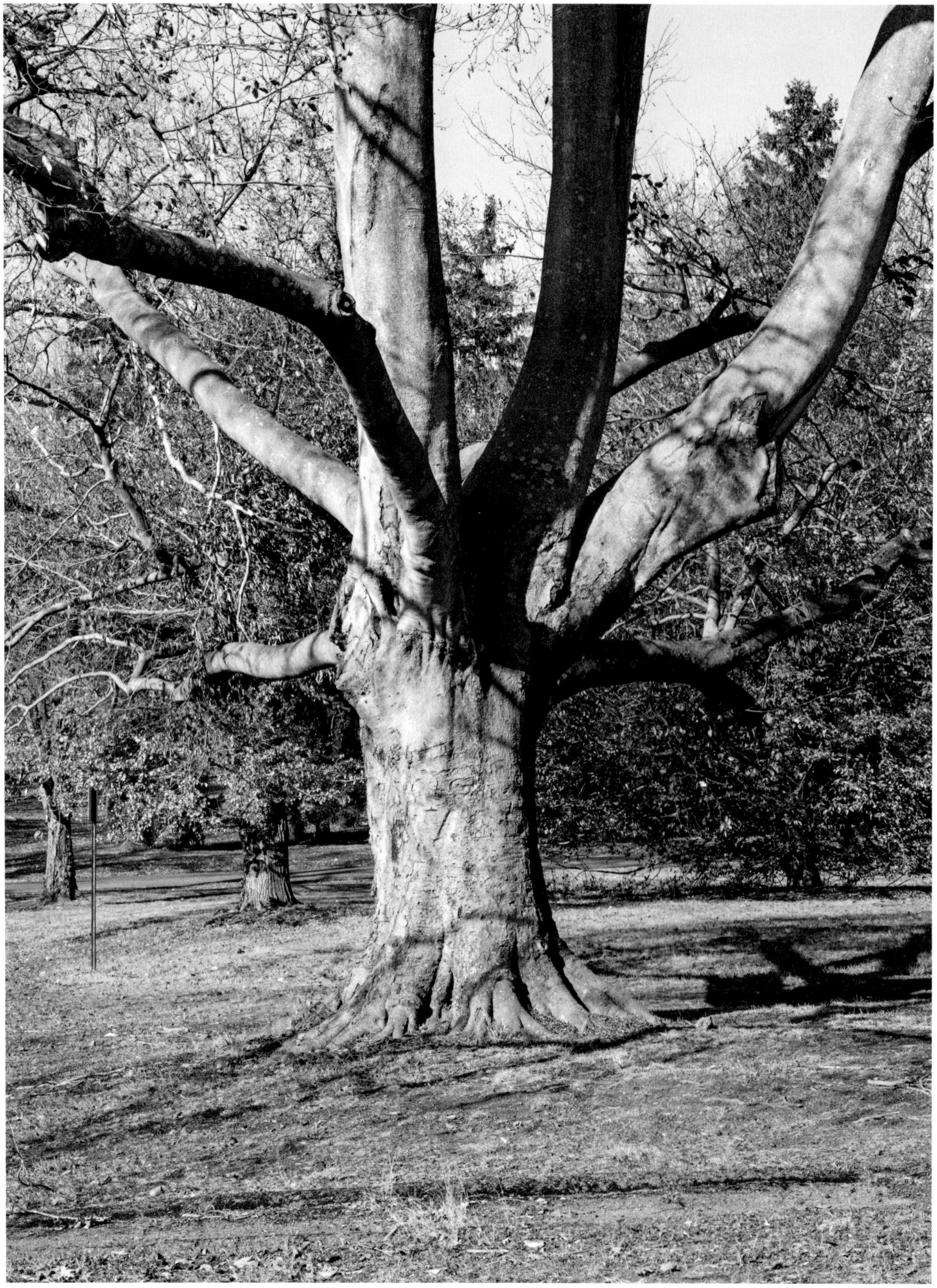

Fagus sp., Beech, Buche – Cadwalader Park, Trenton, New Jersey, 2019

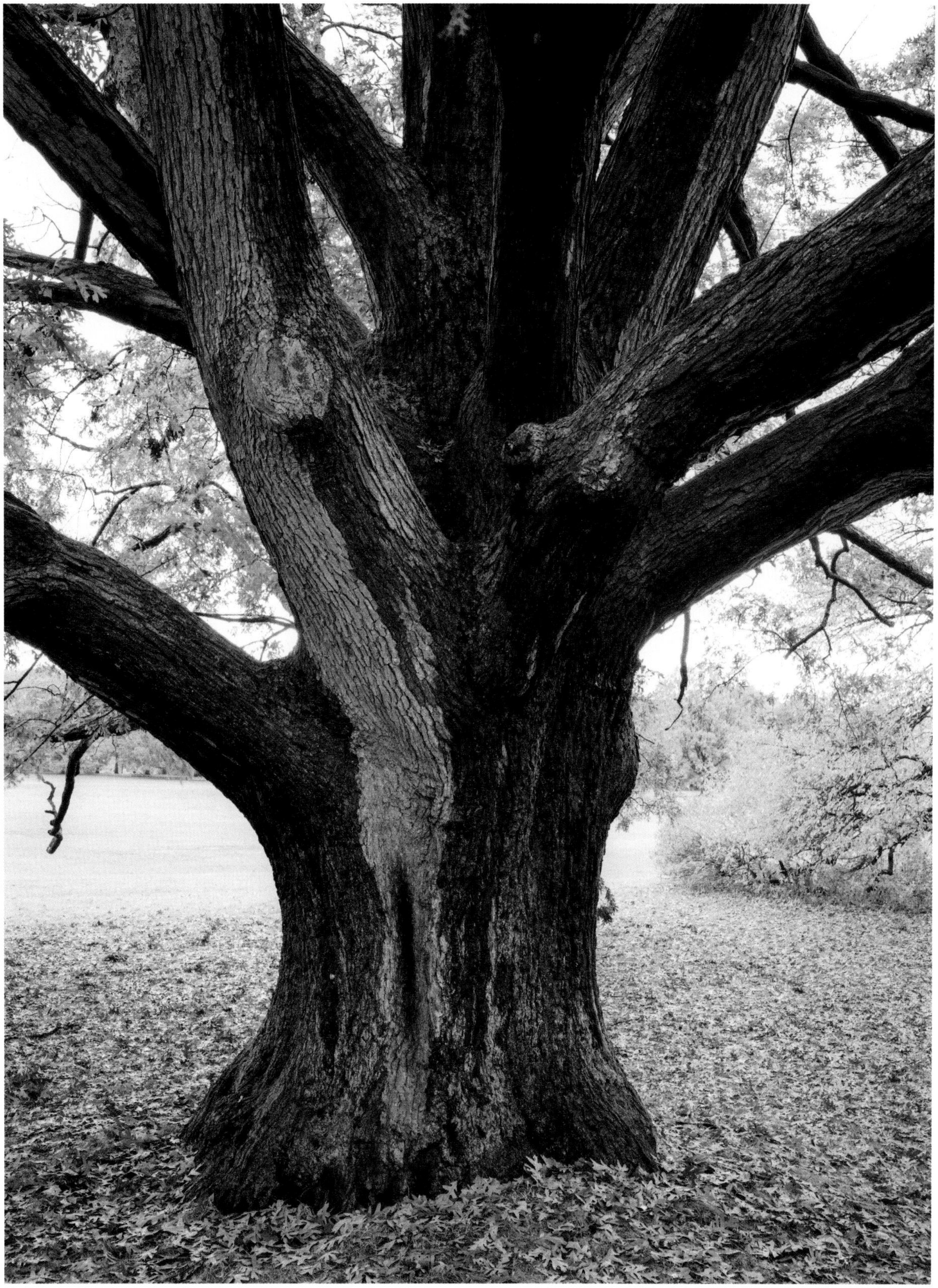

Quercus alba, White Oak, Amerikanische Weiß-Eiche – Genesee Valley Park, Rochester, New York, 2020

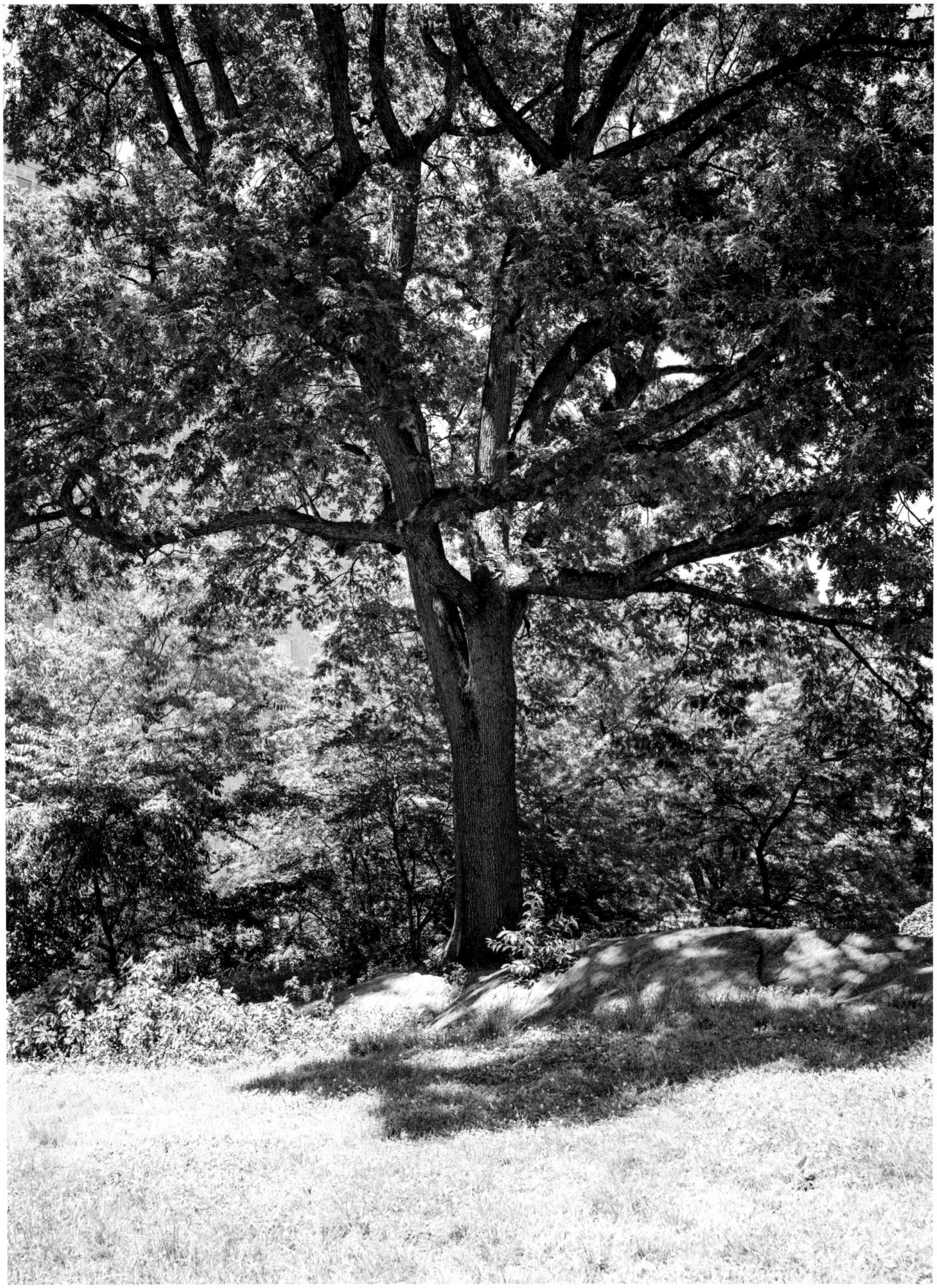

Quercus alba, White Oak, Amerikanische Weiß-Eiche – Central Park, New York, New York, 2021

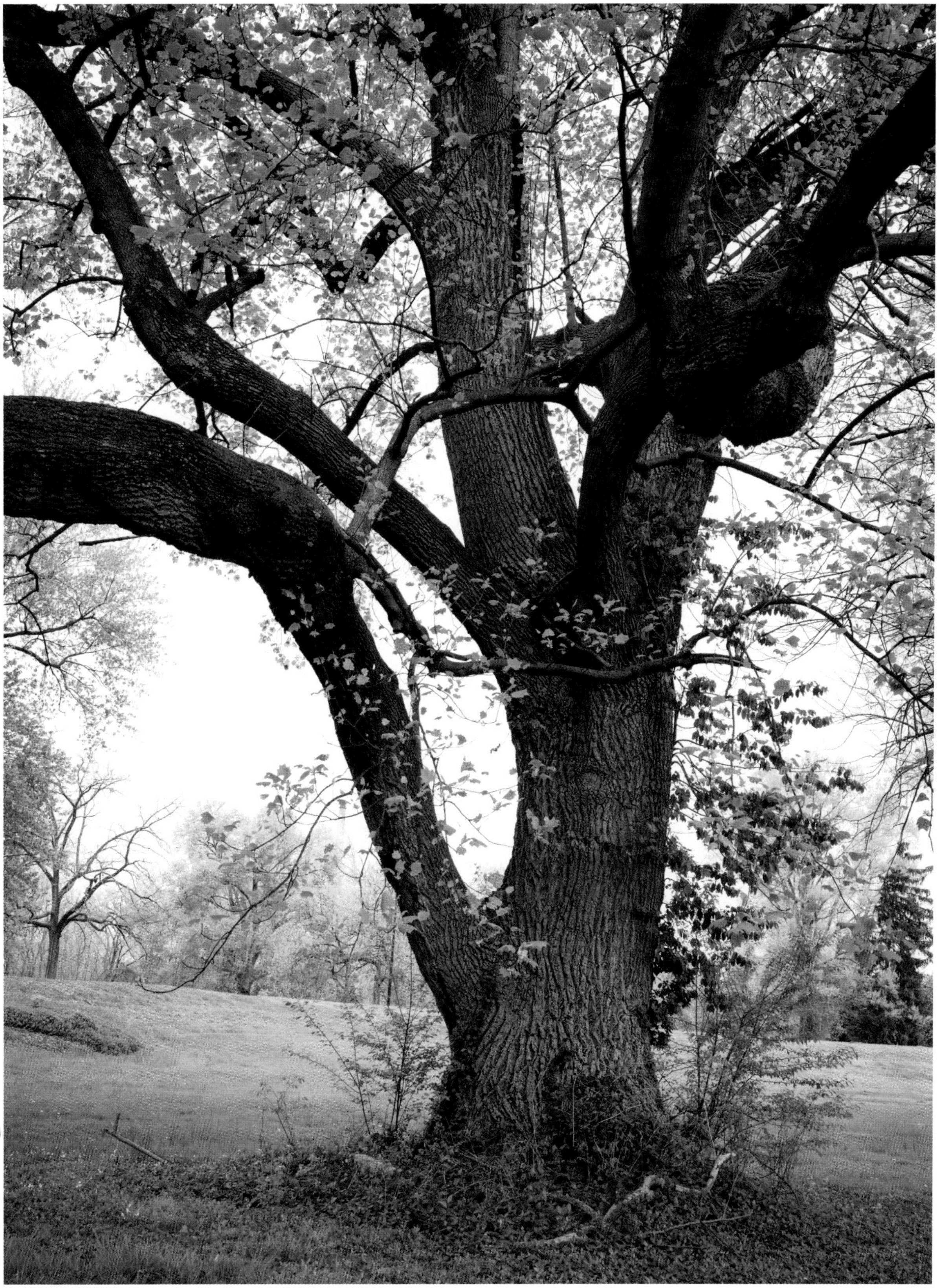

Liriodendron tulipfera, Tulip Tree, Tulpenbaum – Shawnee Park, Louisville, Kentucky, 2021

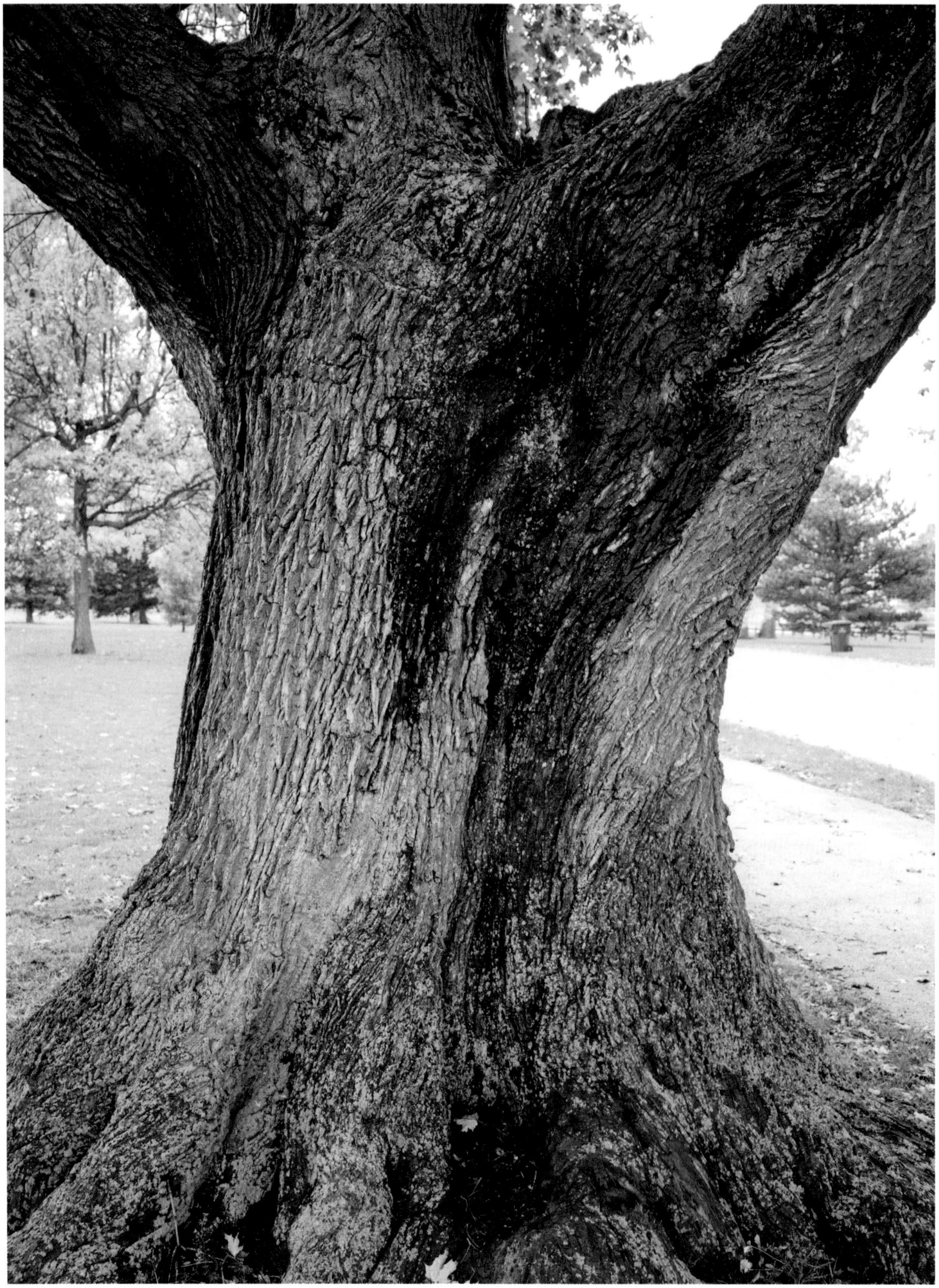

Acer saccharum, Sugar Maple, Zucker-Ahorn – Delaware Park, Buffalo, New York, 2020

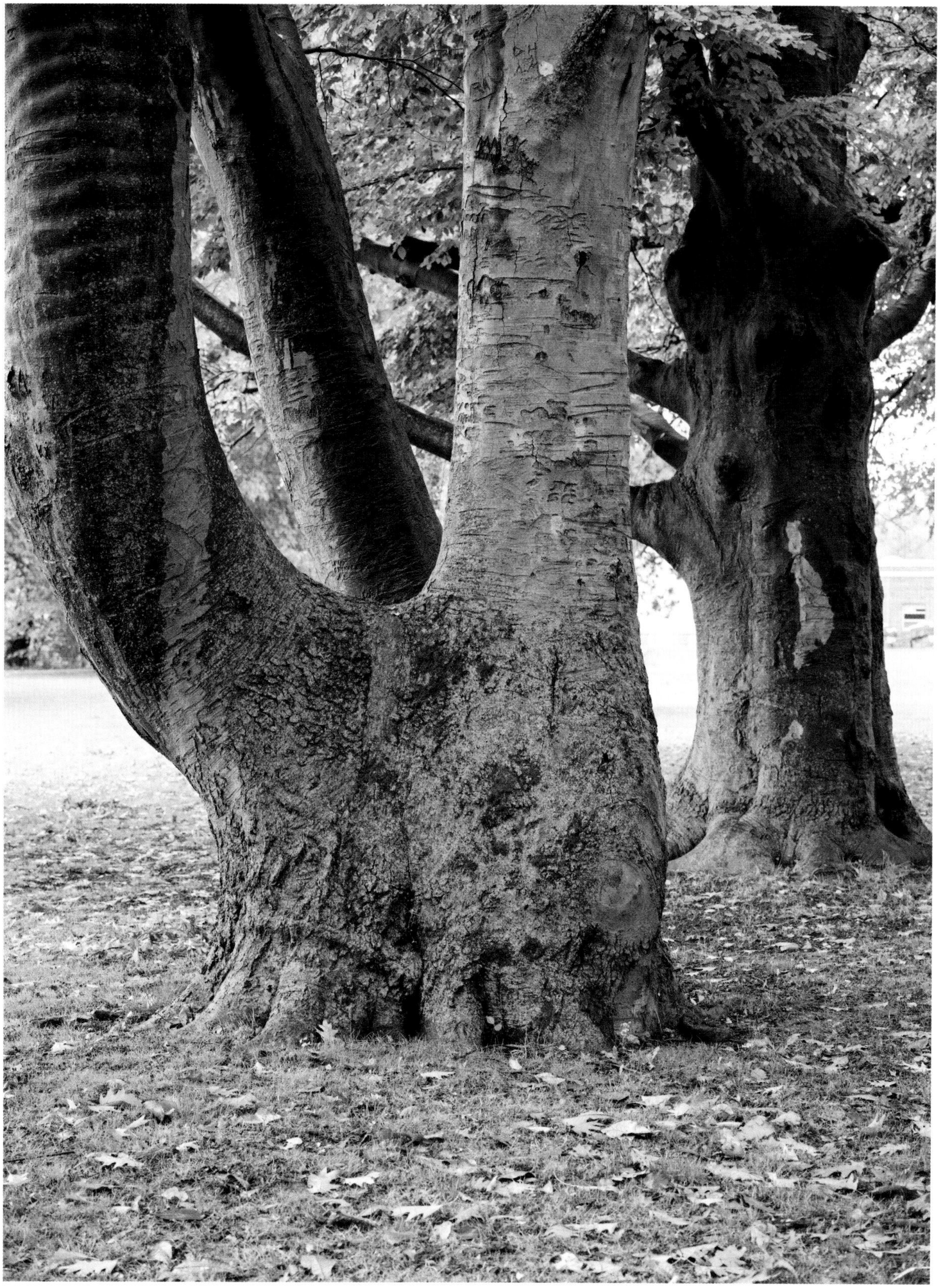

Fagus sp., Beech, Buche – South Park, Buffalo, New York, 2020

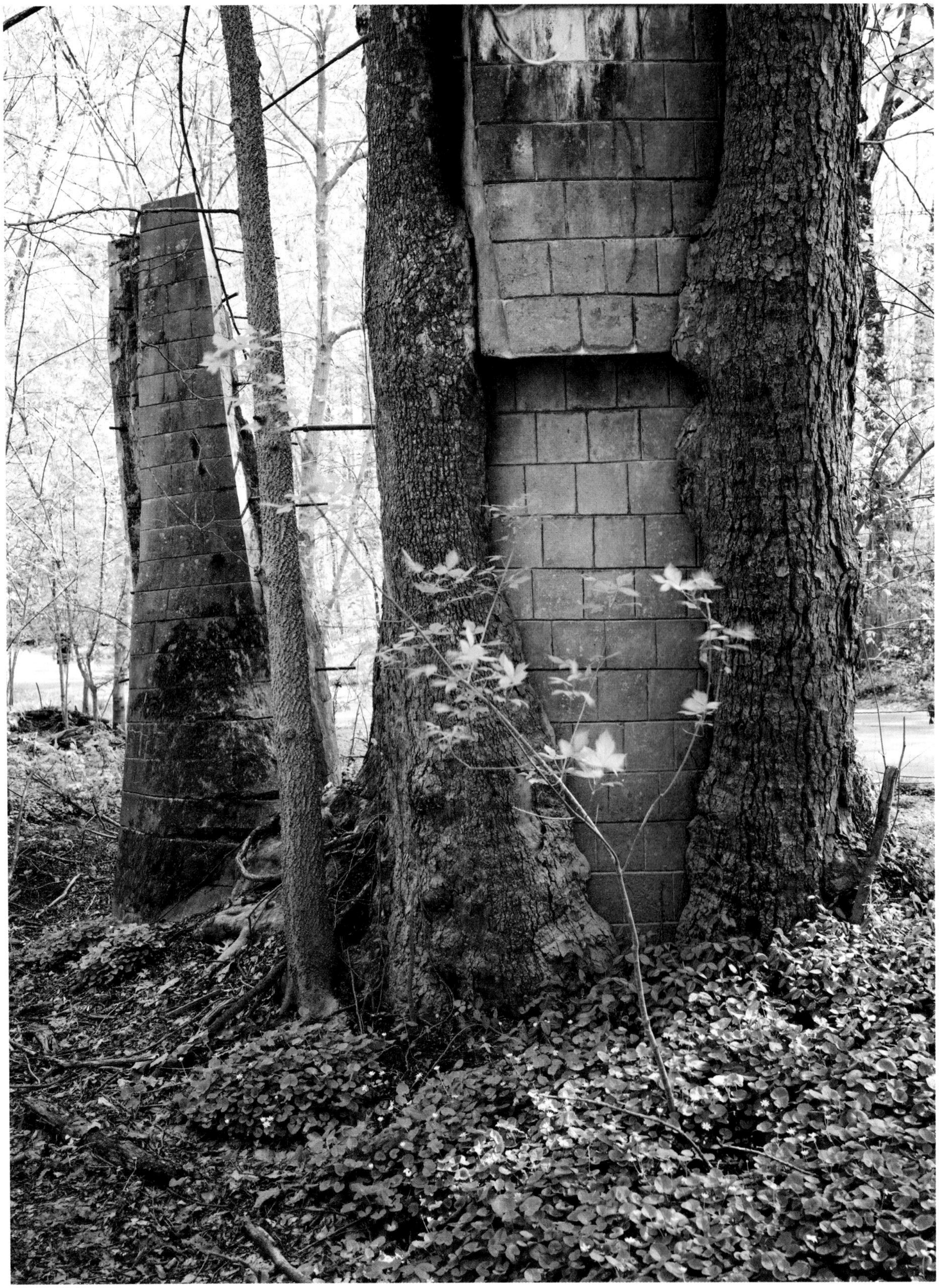

Platanus occidentalis, American Sycamore, Amerikanische Platane – Cherokee Park, Louisville, Kentucky, 2021

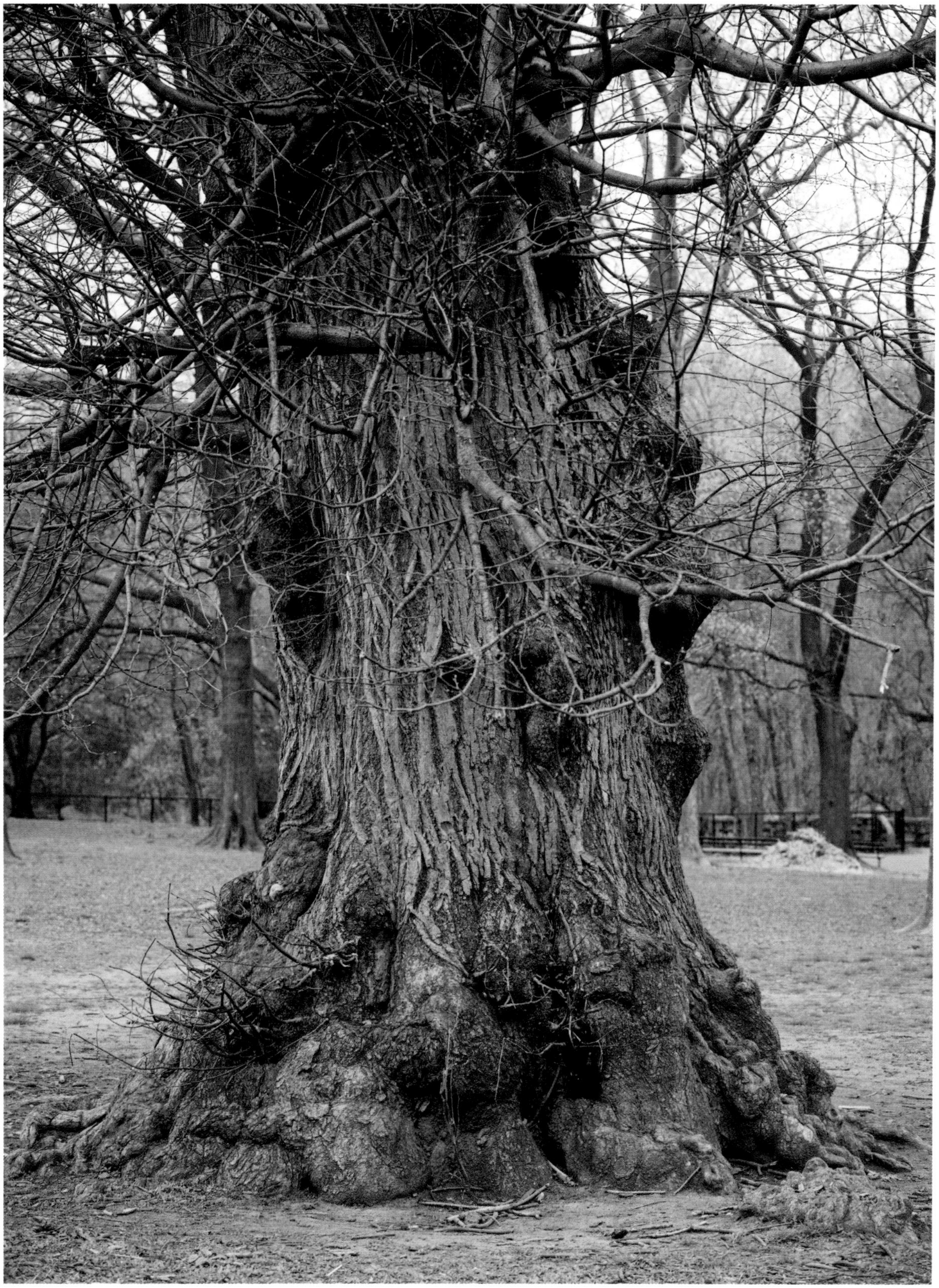

Tilia cordata, Little Leaf Linden, Winterlinde – Prospect Park, Brooklyn, New York, 2021

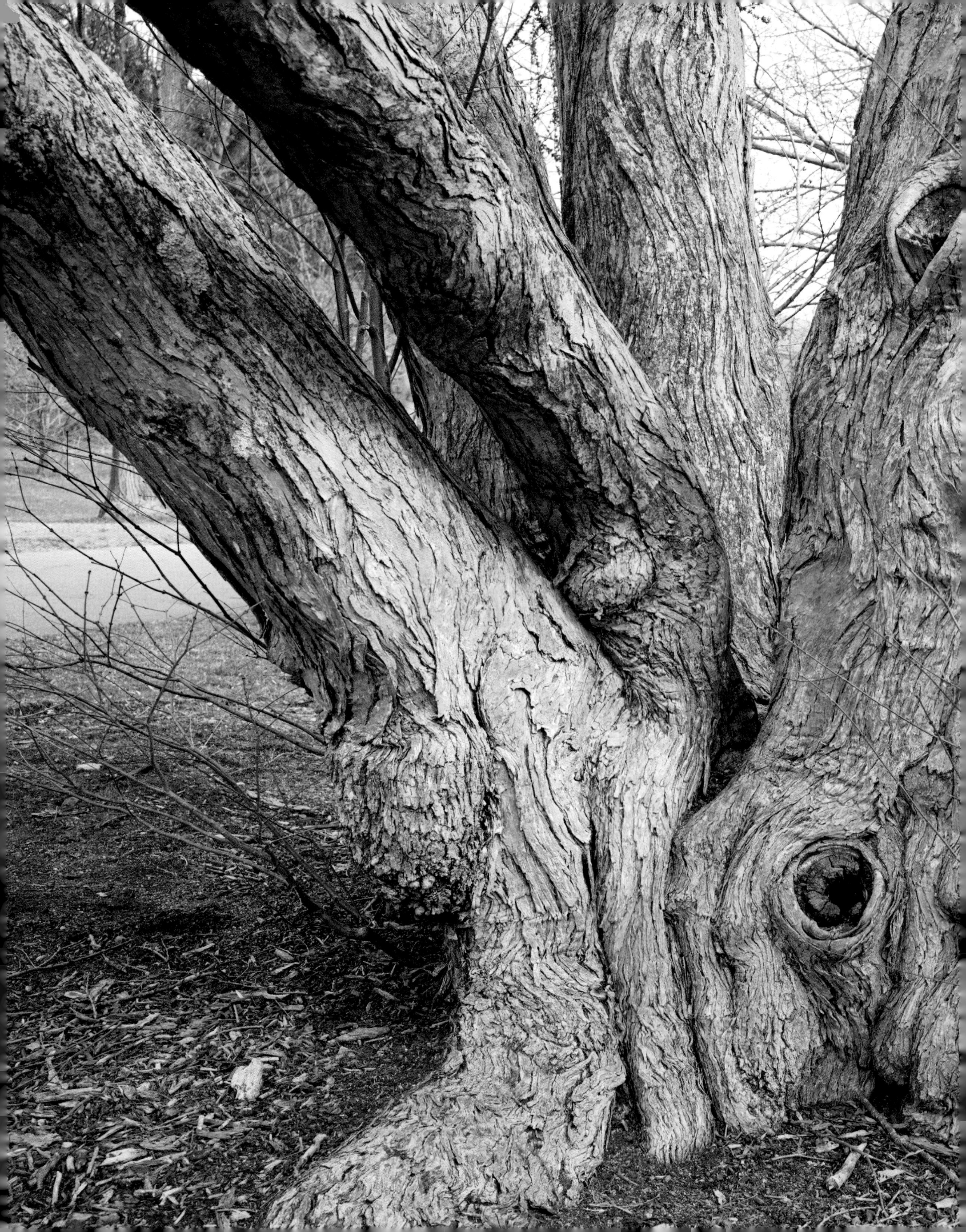

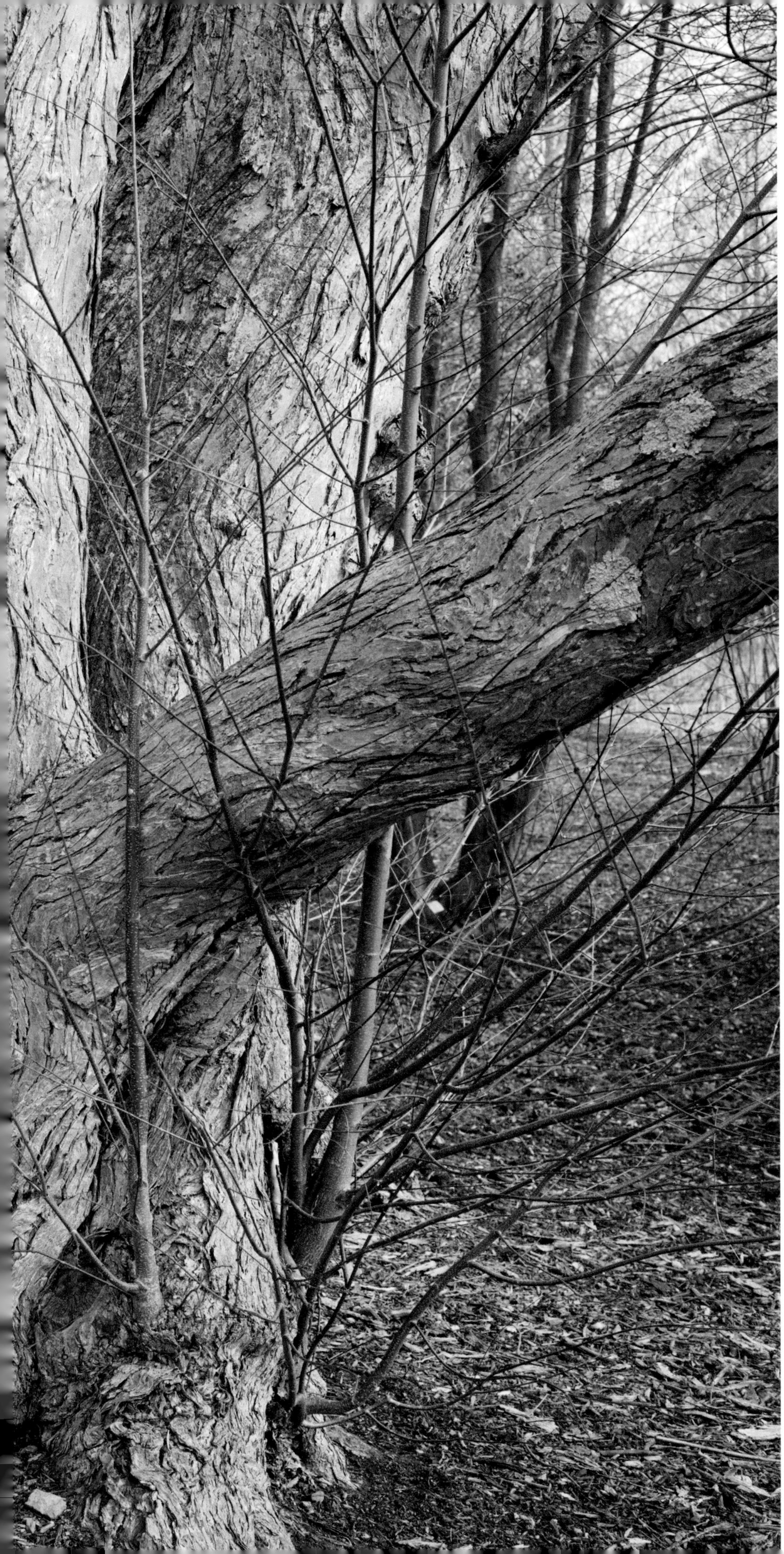

Cercidiphyllum japonicum,
Katsura Tree, Katsurabaum –
Arnold Arboretum, Boston,
Massachusetts, 2020

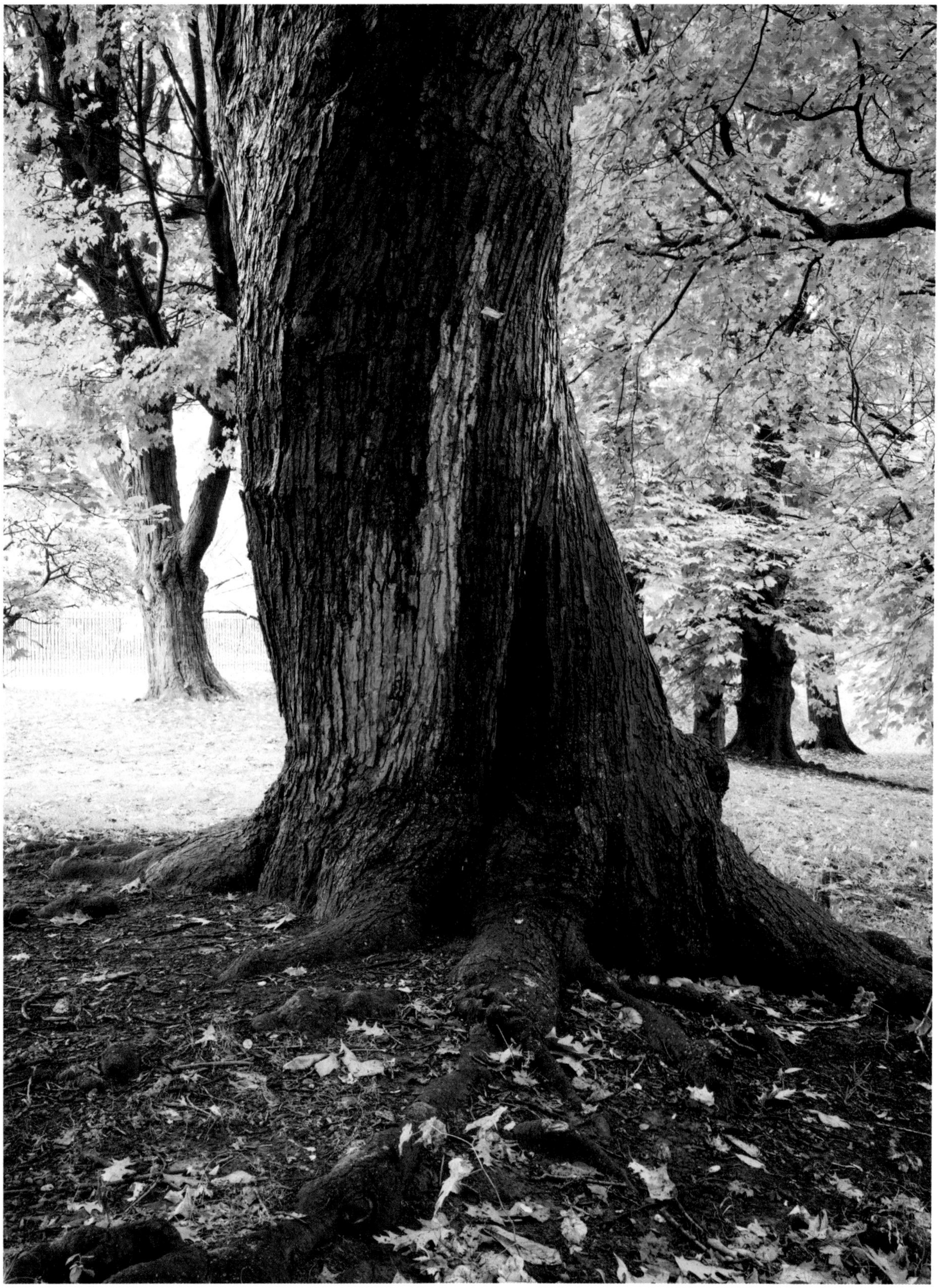

Acer saccharinum, Silver Maple, Silber-Ahorn – Highland Park, Rochester, New York, 2020

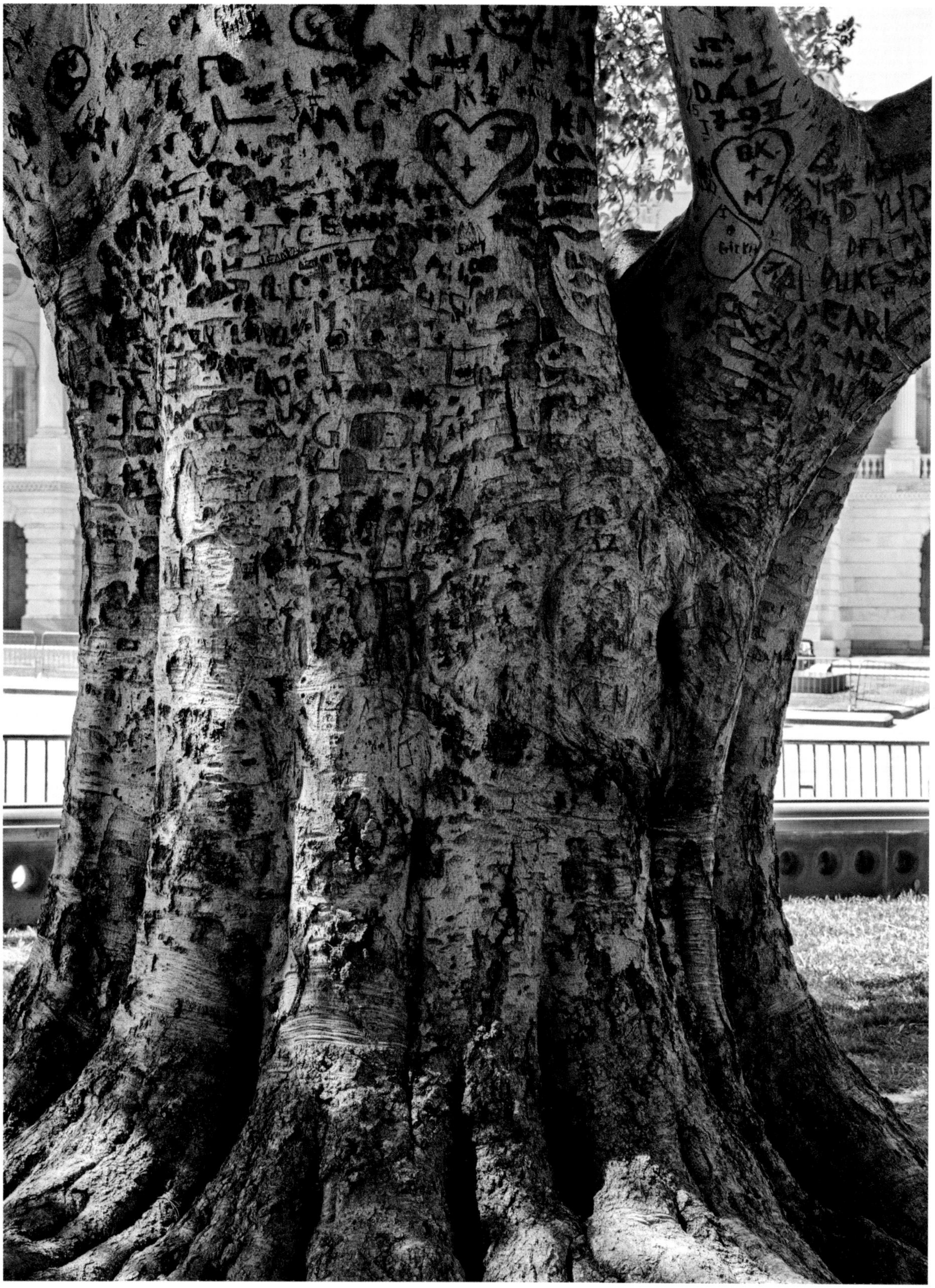

Fagus grandifolia, American Beech, Amerikanische Buche – US Capitol, Washington, DC, 2020

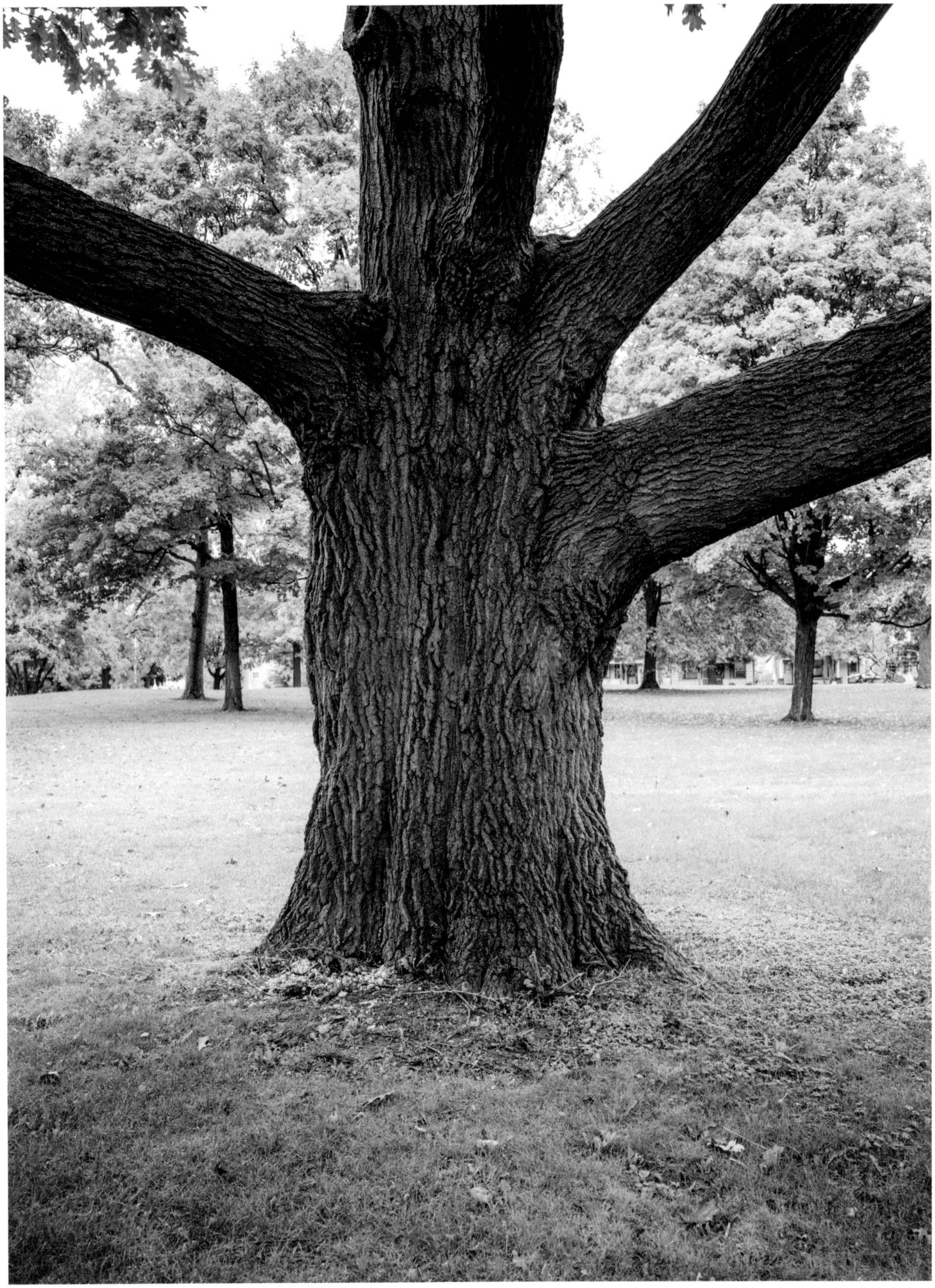

Quercus rubra, Northern Red Oak, Rot-Eiche – Washington Park, Milwaukee, Wisconsin, 2021

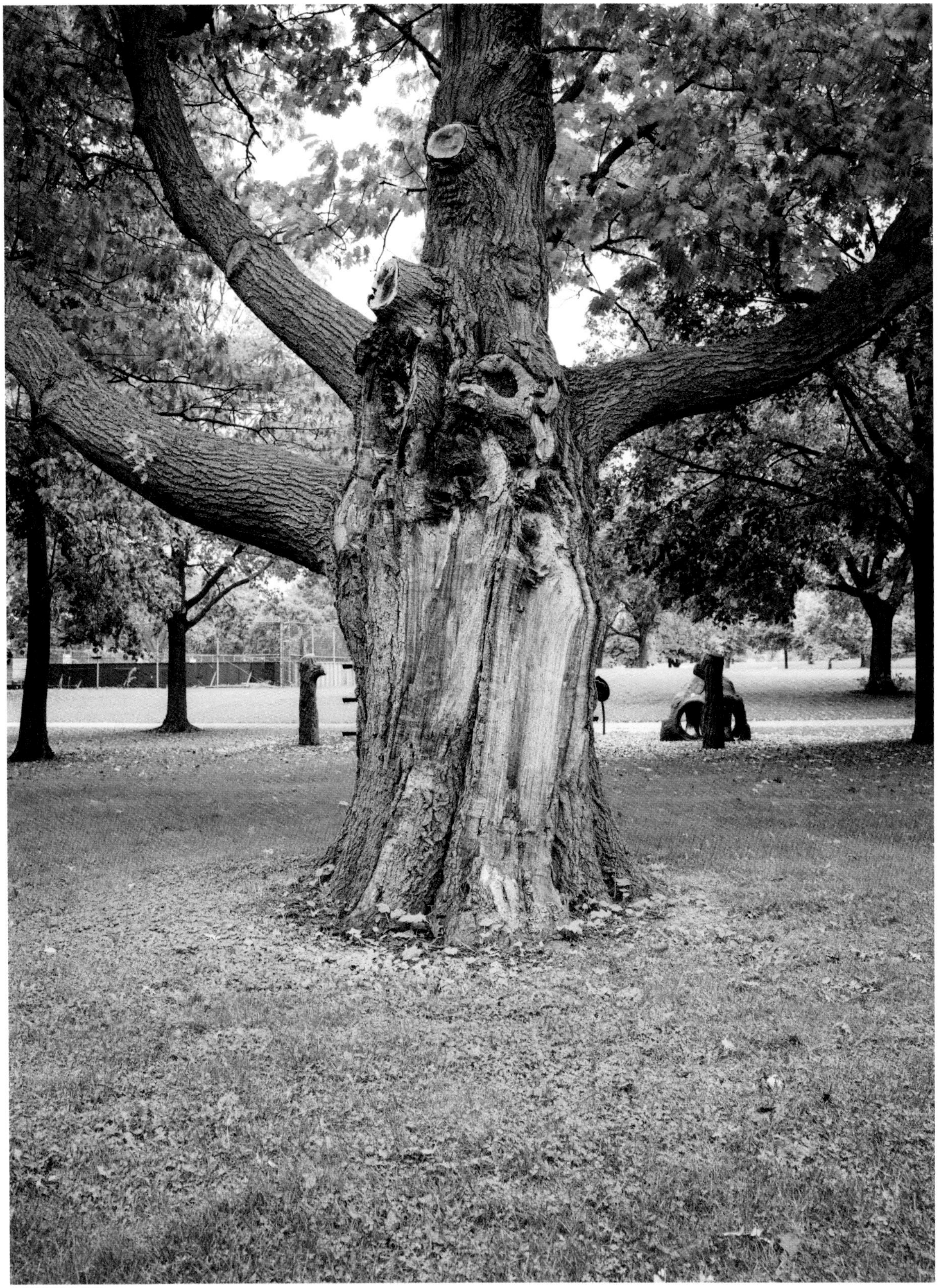

Quercus rubra, Northern Red Oak, Rot-Eiche – Washington Park, Milwaukee, Wisconsin, 2021

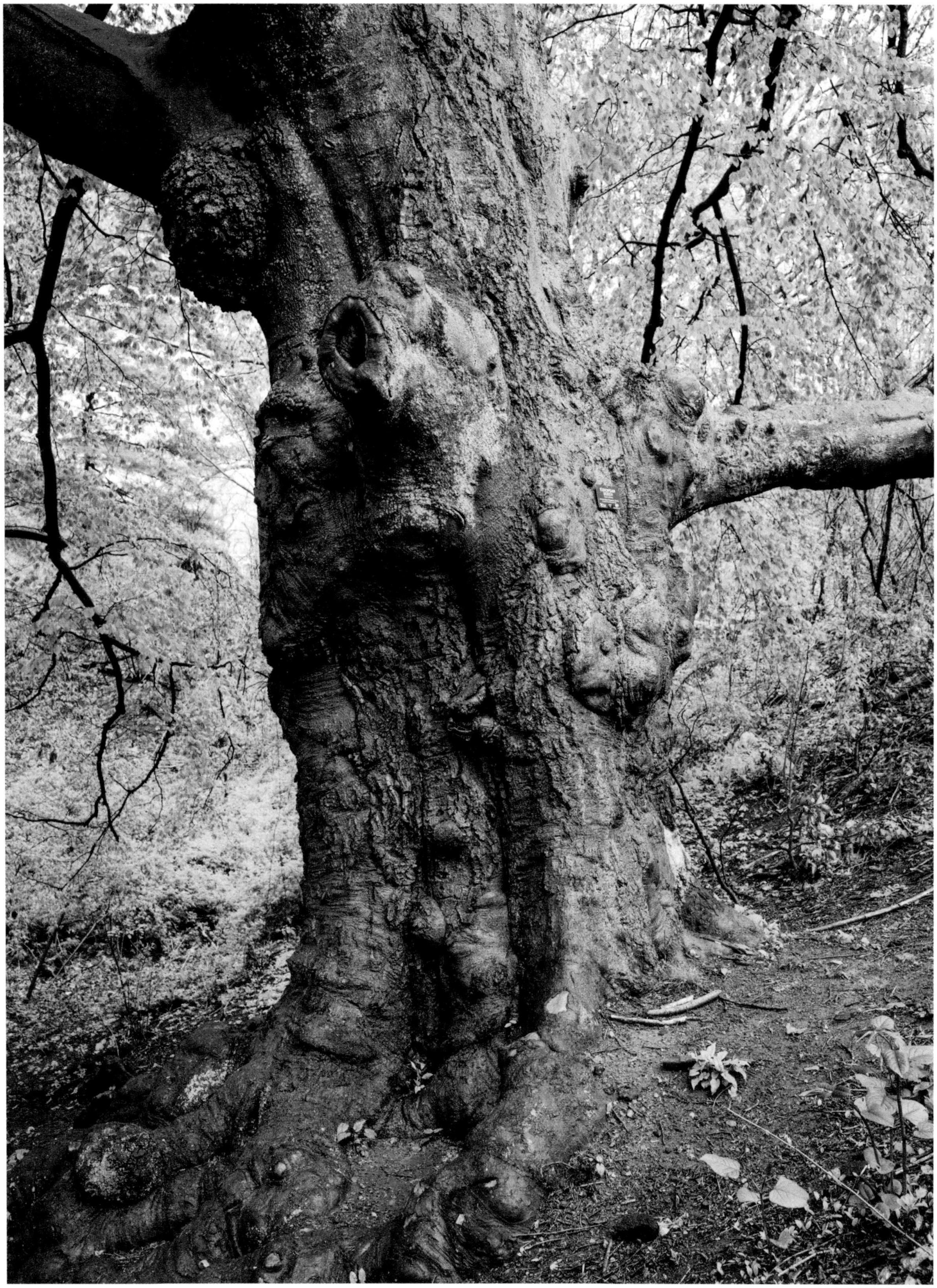

Fagus sylvatica, European Beech, Rot-Buche – Jamaica Pond, Boston, Massachusetts, 2021

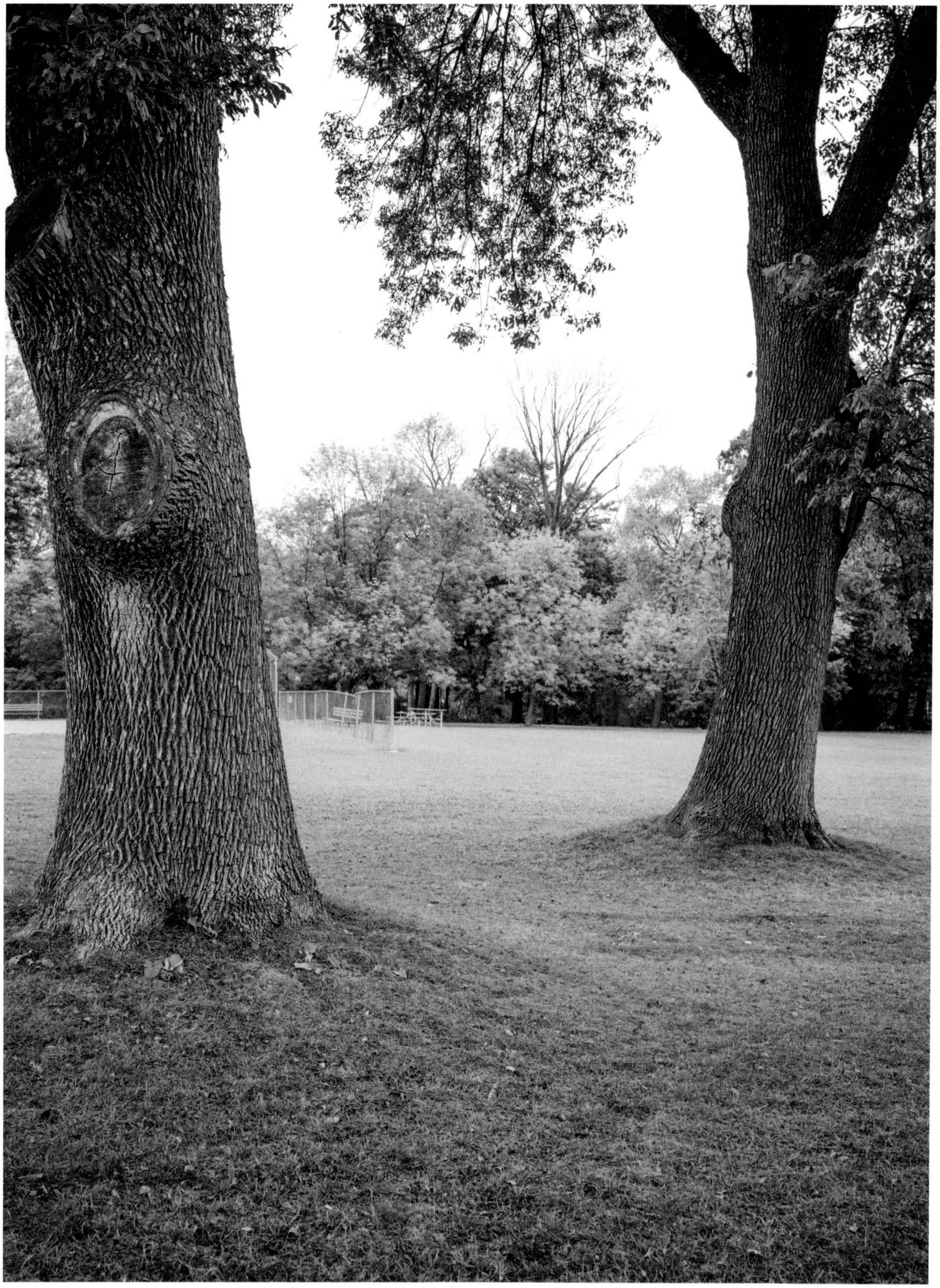

Fraxinus americana, White Ash, Weiß-Esche – Lake Park, Milwaukee, Wisconsin, 2021

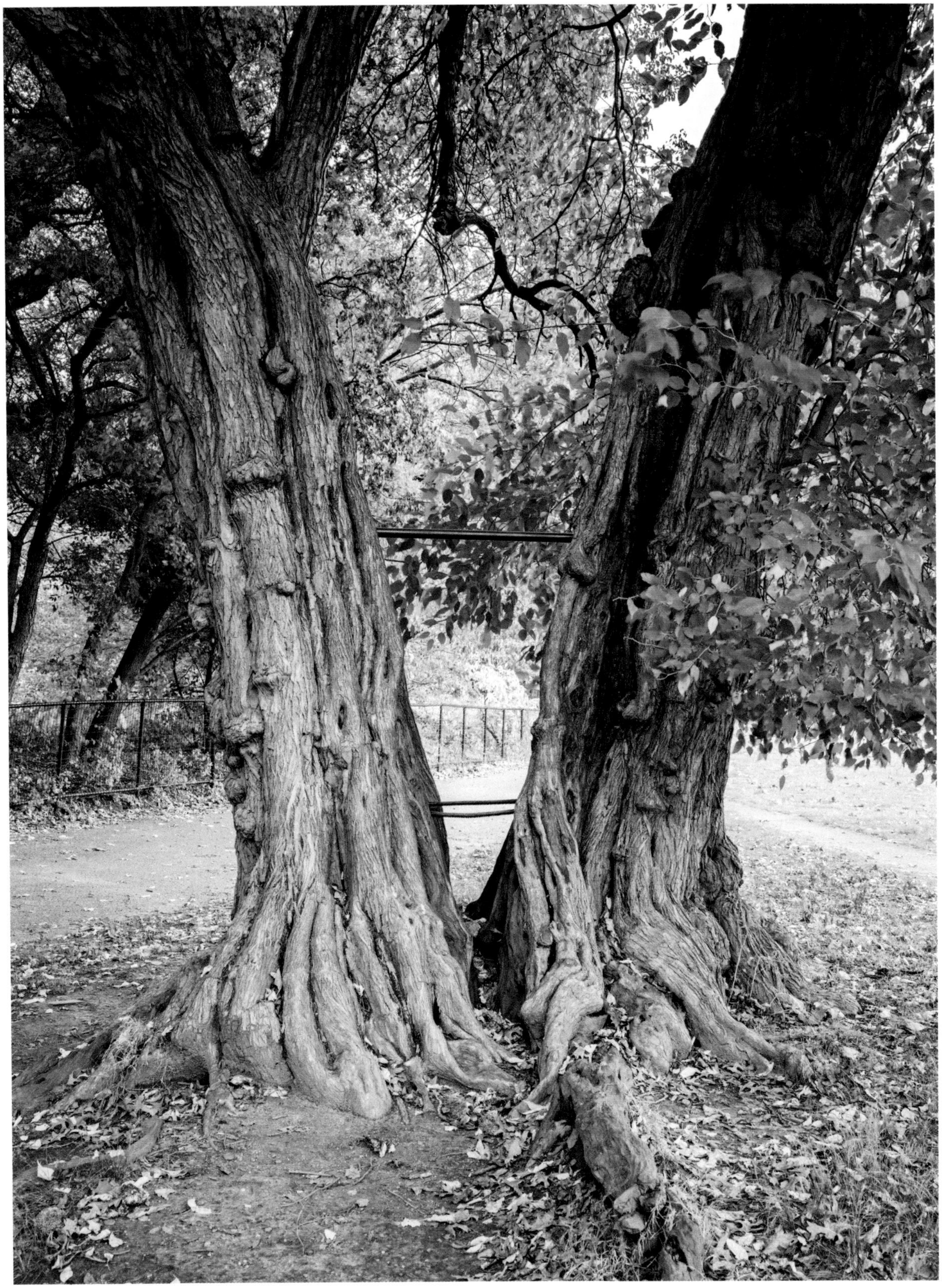

Maclura pomifera, Osage-Orange, Milchorangenbaum – Prospect Park, Brooklyn, New York, 2021

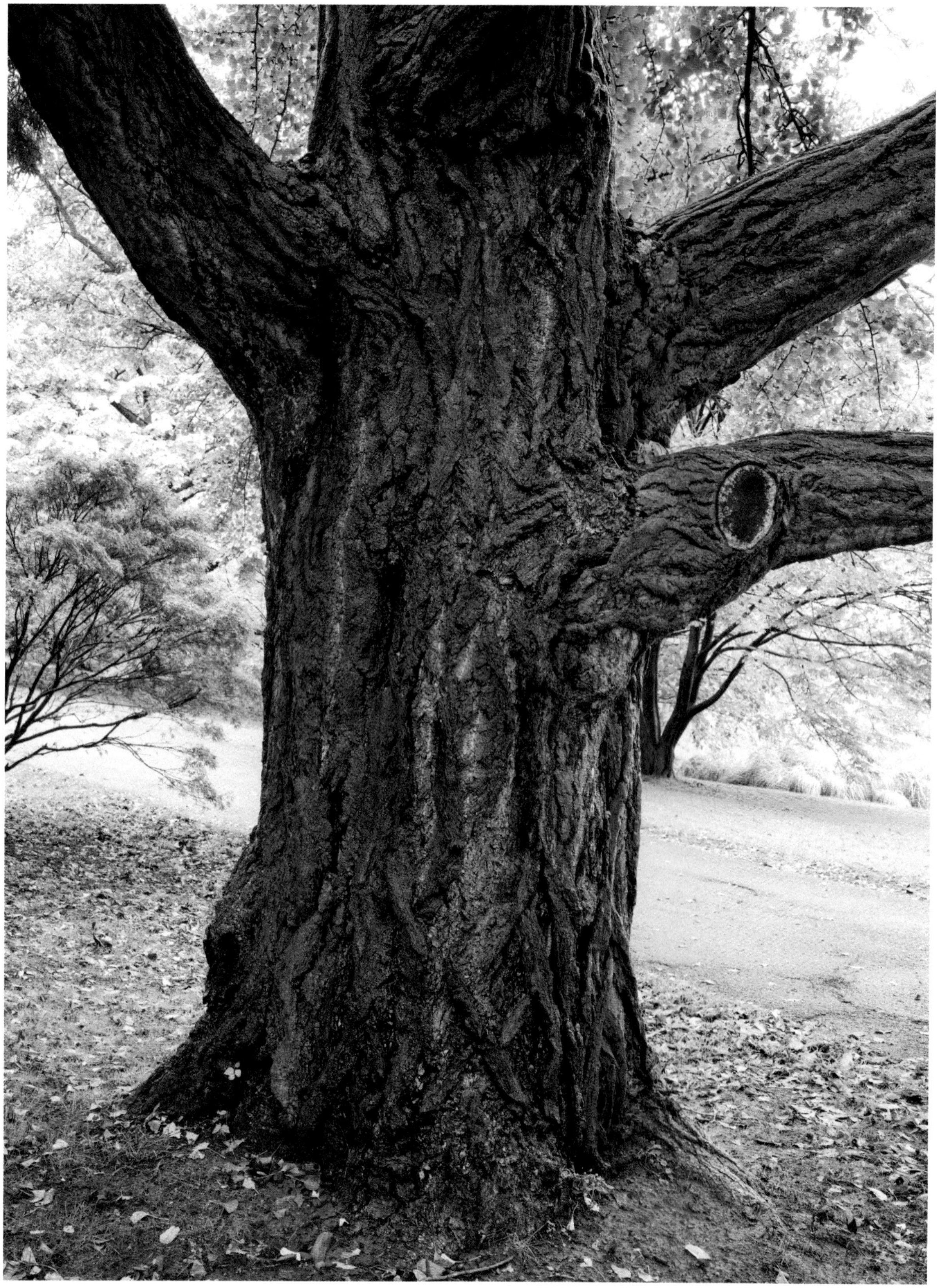

Ginkgo biloba, Ginkgo – Highland Park, Rochester, New York, 2020

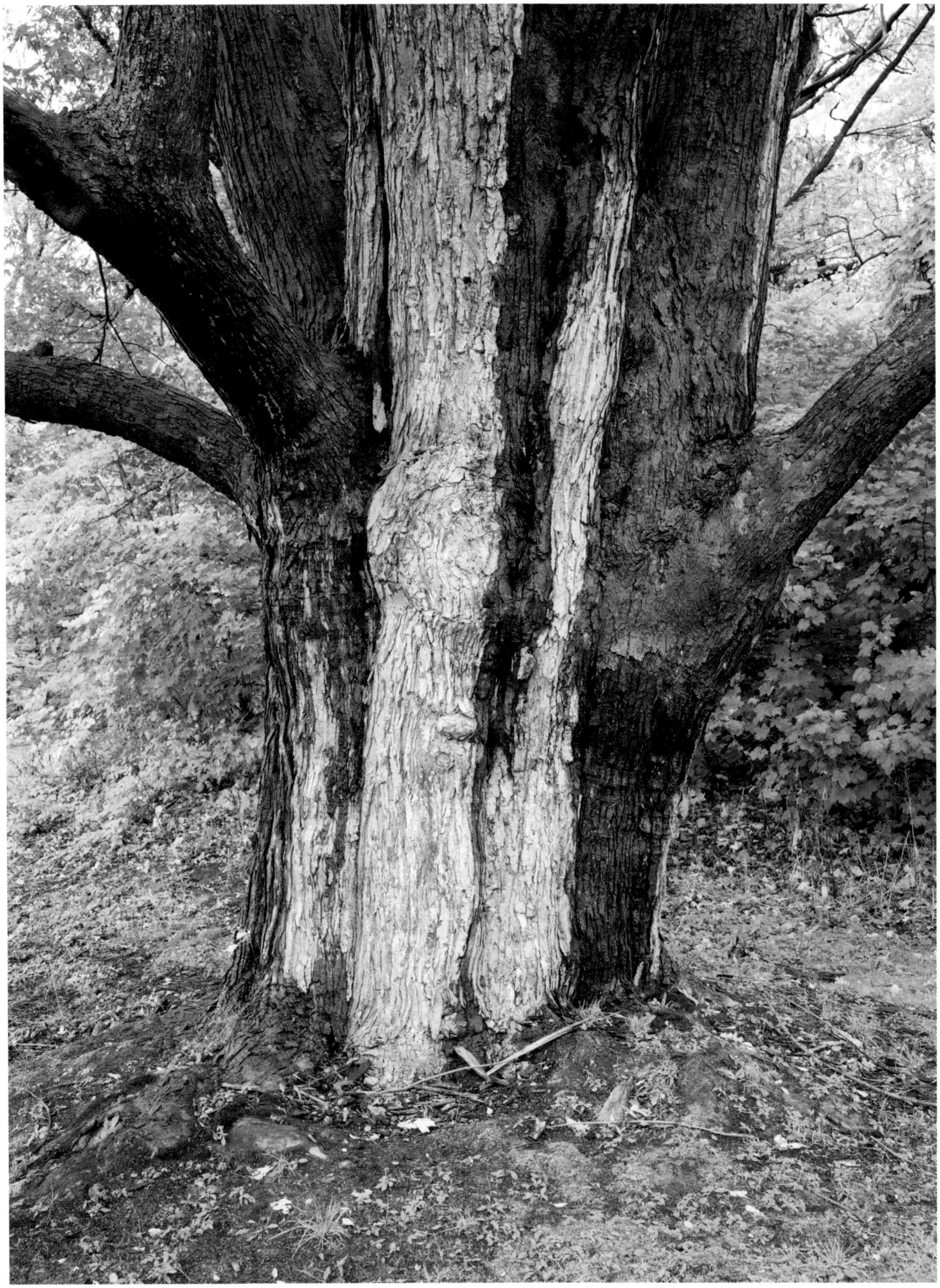

Acer rubrum, Red Maple, Rot-Ahorn – Highland Park, Rochester, New York, 2020

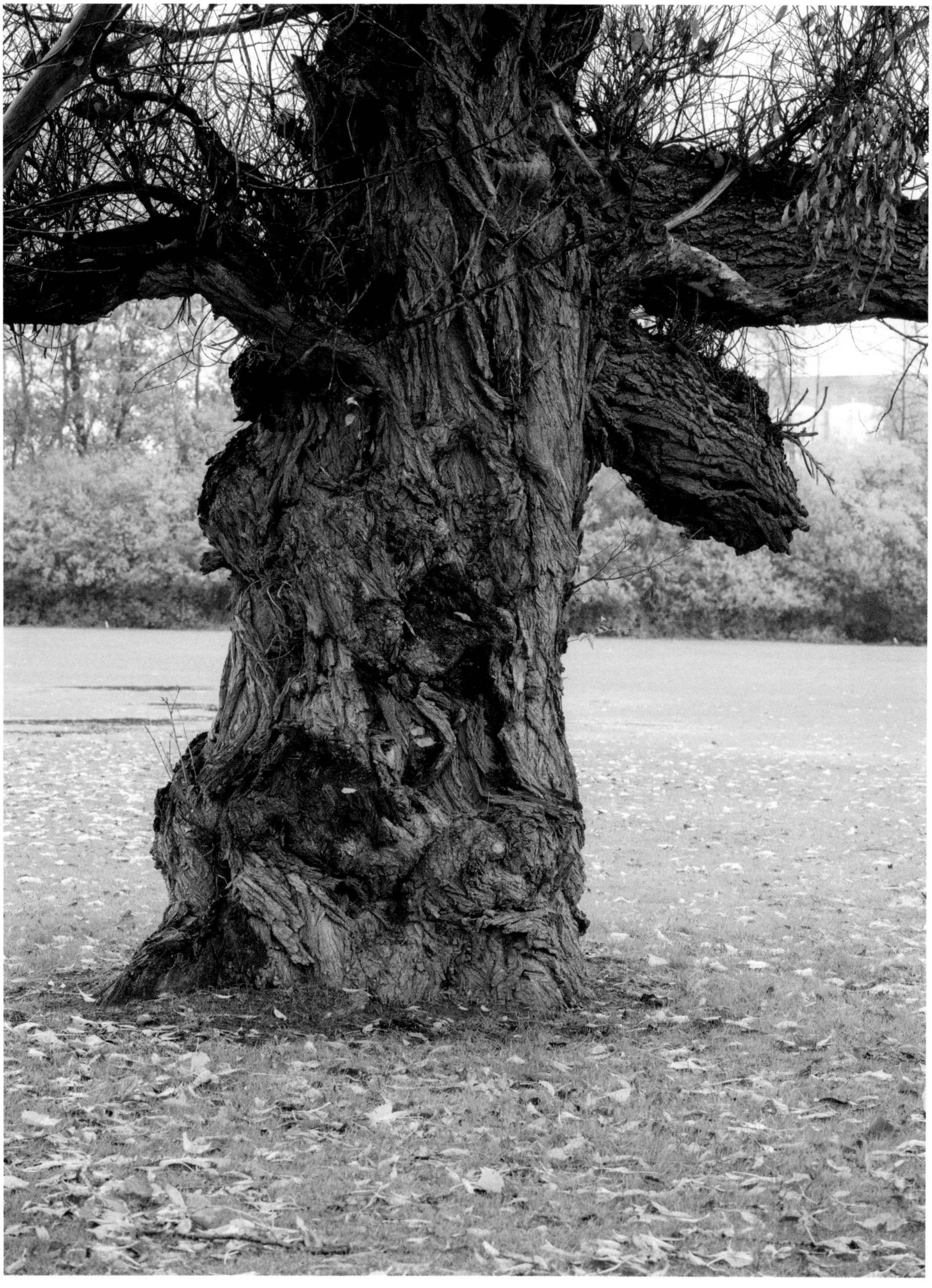

Populus deltoides, Eastern Cottonwood, Kanadische Schwarz-Pappel – South Park, Buffalo, New York, 2020

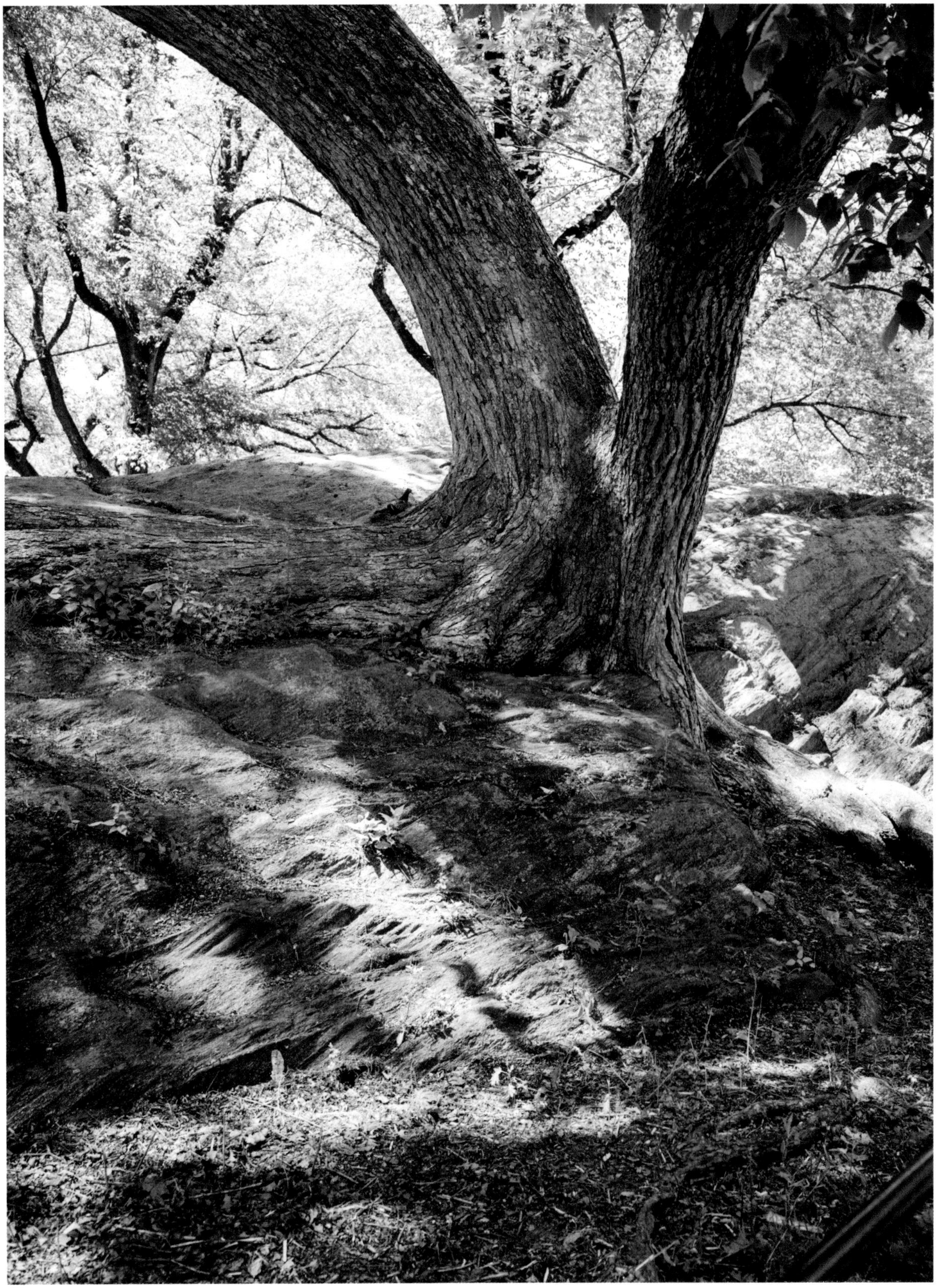

Ulmus americana, American Elm, Amerikanische Ulme – Central Park, New York, New York, 2021

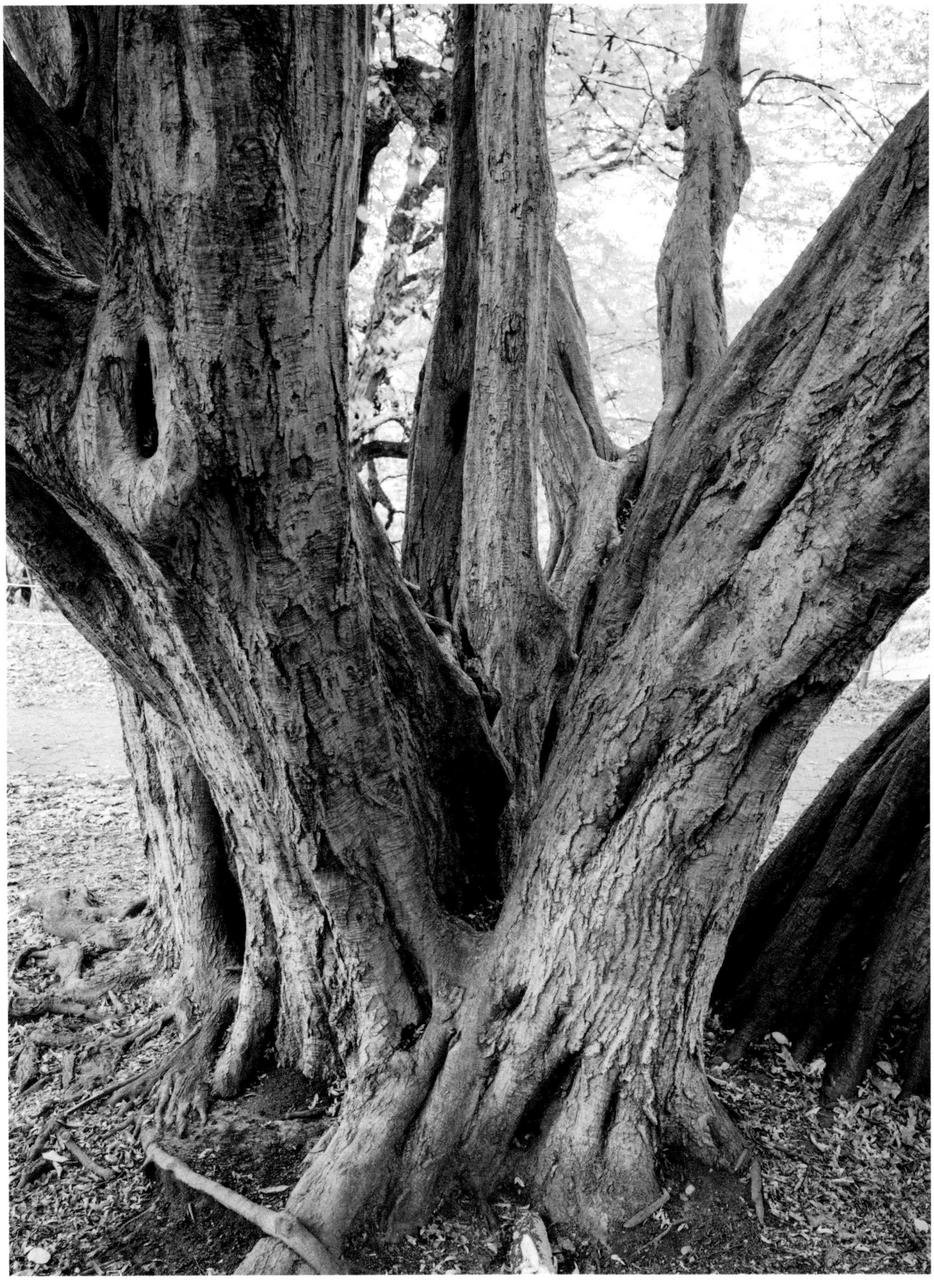

Carpinus betulus, European Hornbeam, Hainbuche – Prospect Park, Brooklyn, New York, 2021

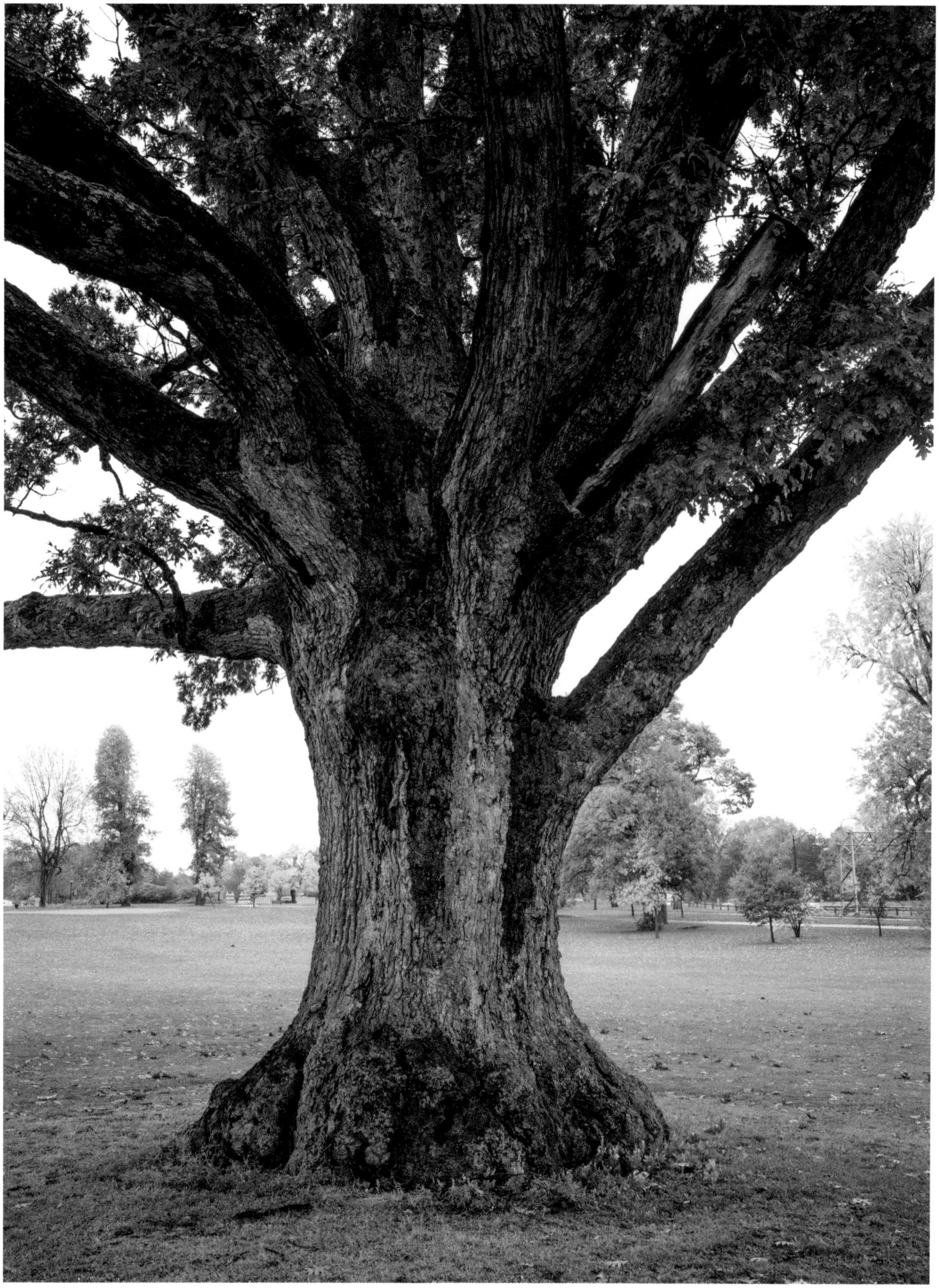

Quercus alba, White Oak, Amerikanische Weiß-Eiche – Delaware Park, Buffalo, New York, 2020

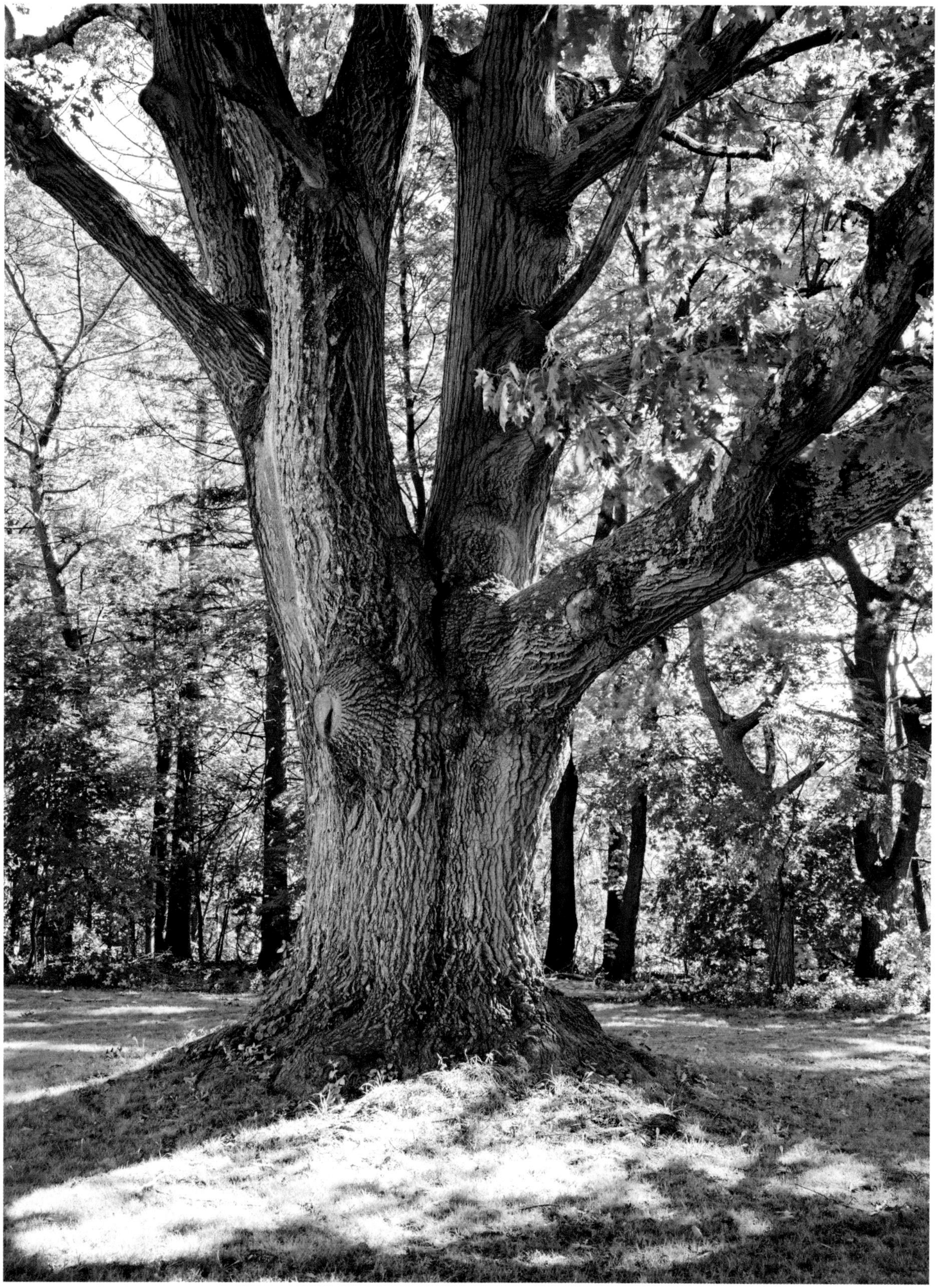

Quercus rubra, Northern Red Oak, Rot-Eiche – Walnut Hill Park, New Britain, Connecticut, 2021

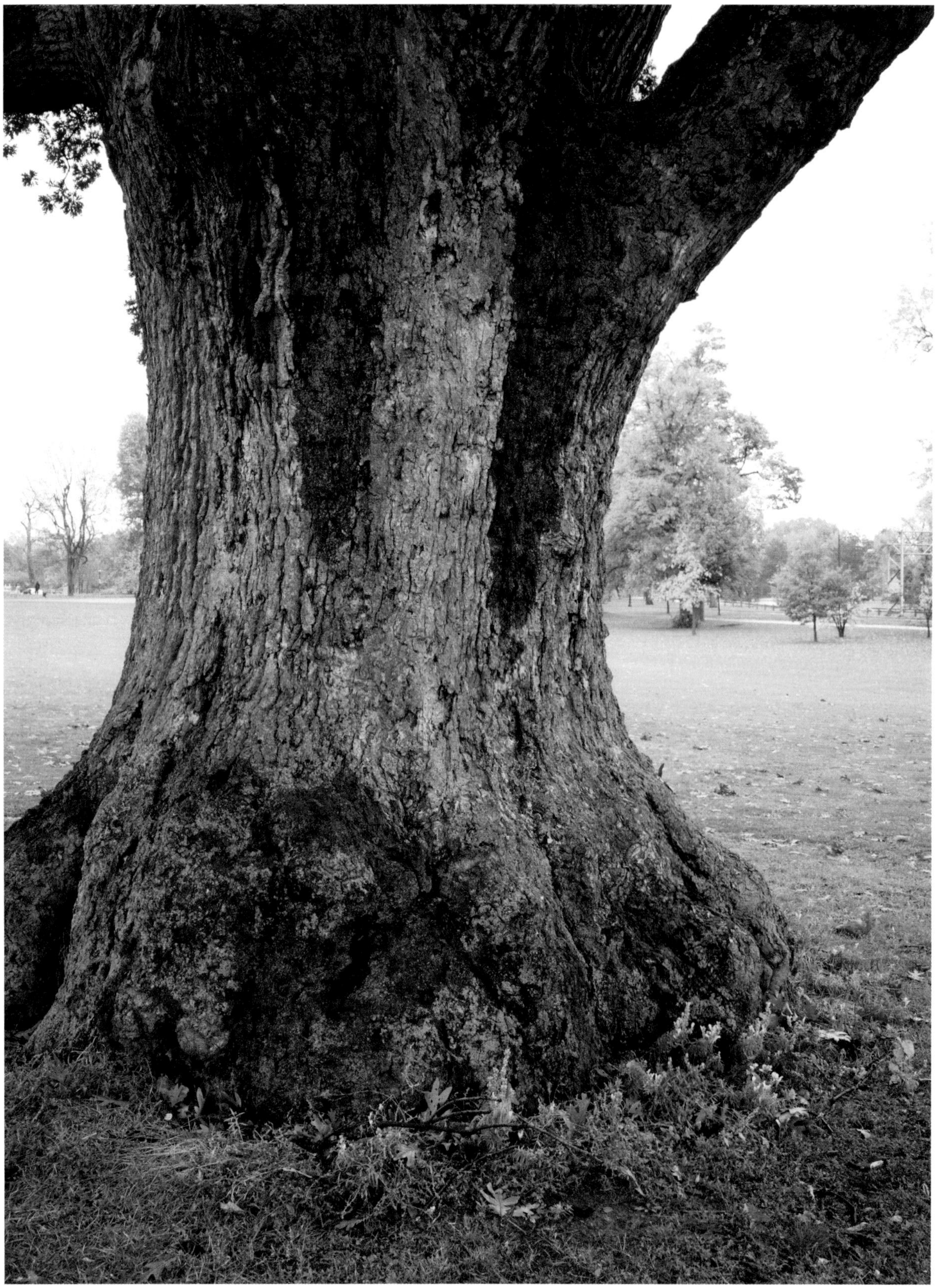

Quercus alba, White Oak, Amerikanische Weiß-Eiche – Delaware Park, Buffalo, New York, 2020

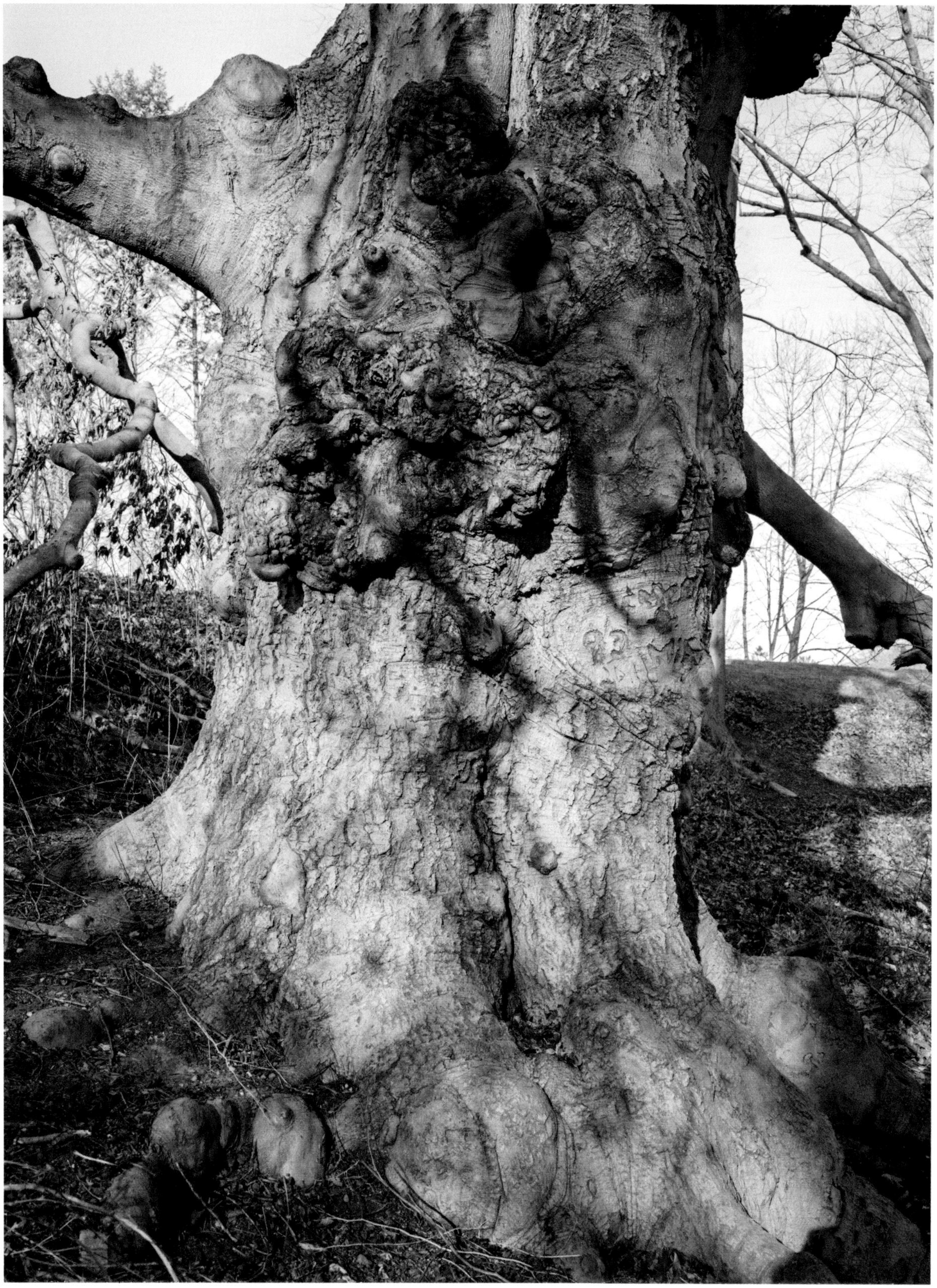

Fagus sylvatica, European Beech, Rot-Buche – Jamaica Pond, Boston, Massachusetts, 2020

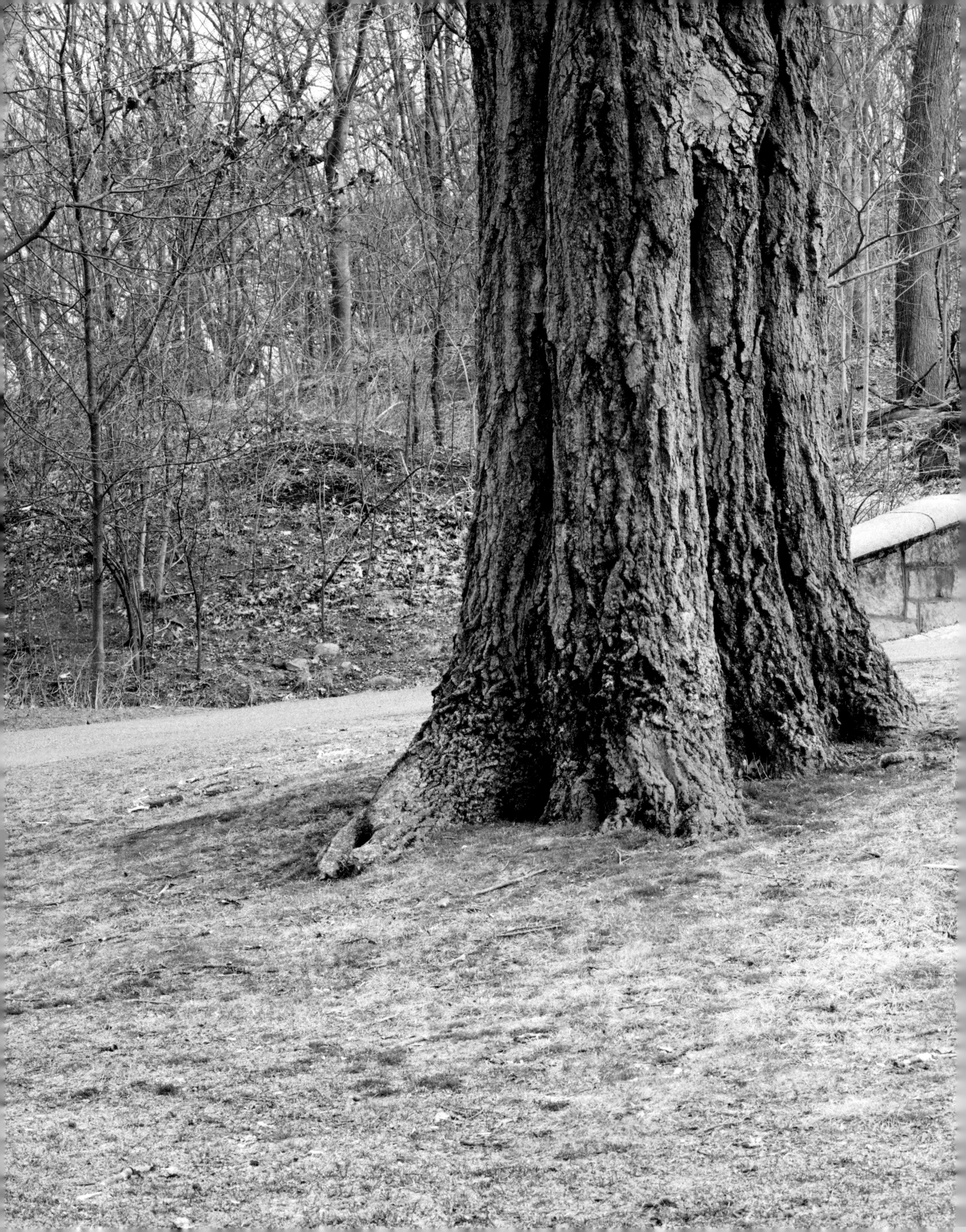

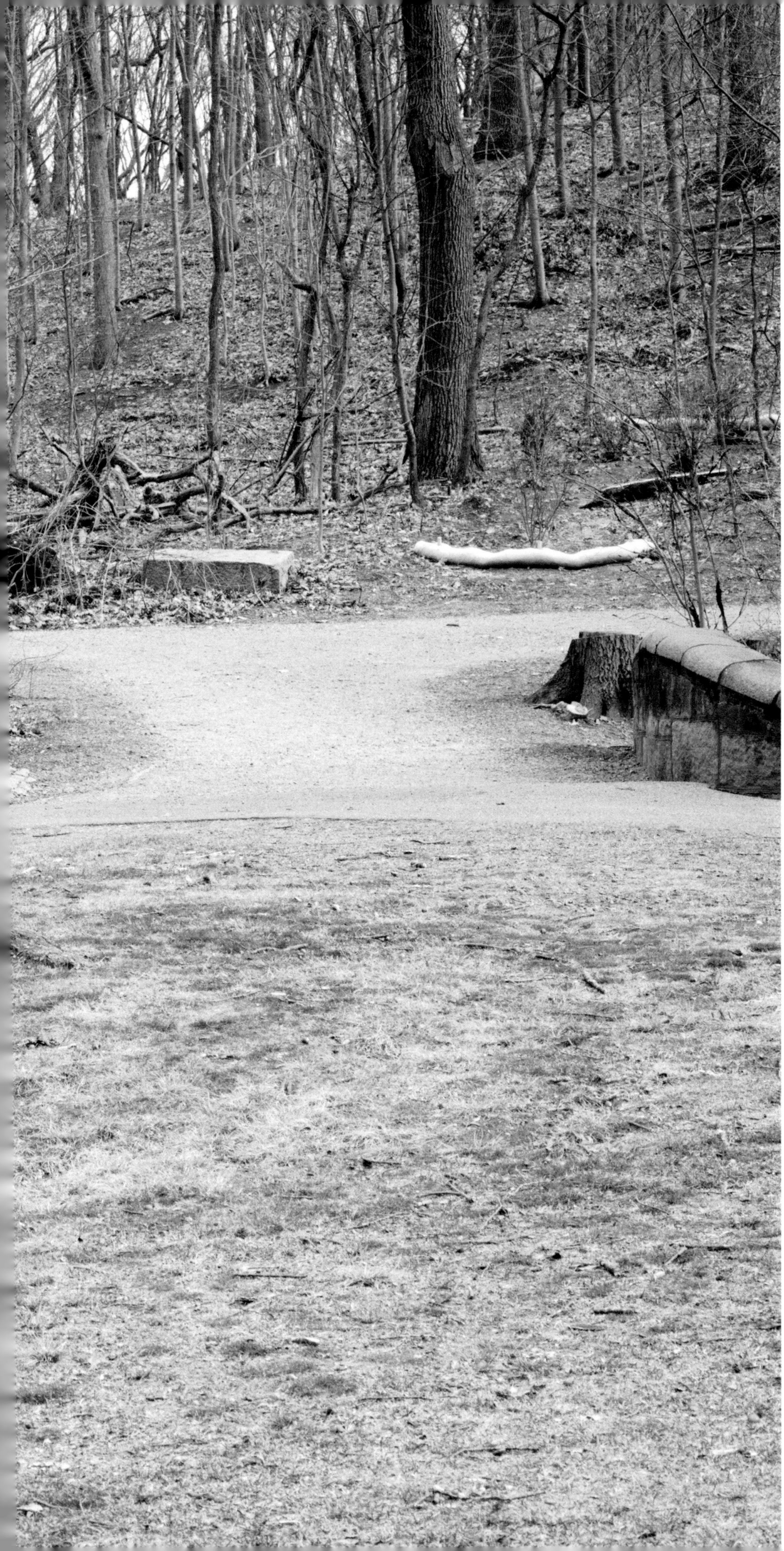

Quercus rubra,
Northern Red Oak, Rot-Eiche –
Olmsted Park, Boston,
Massachusetts, 2020

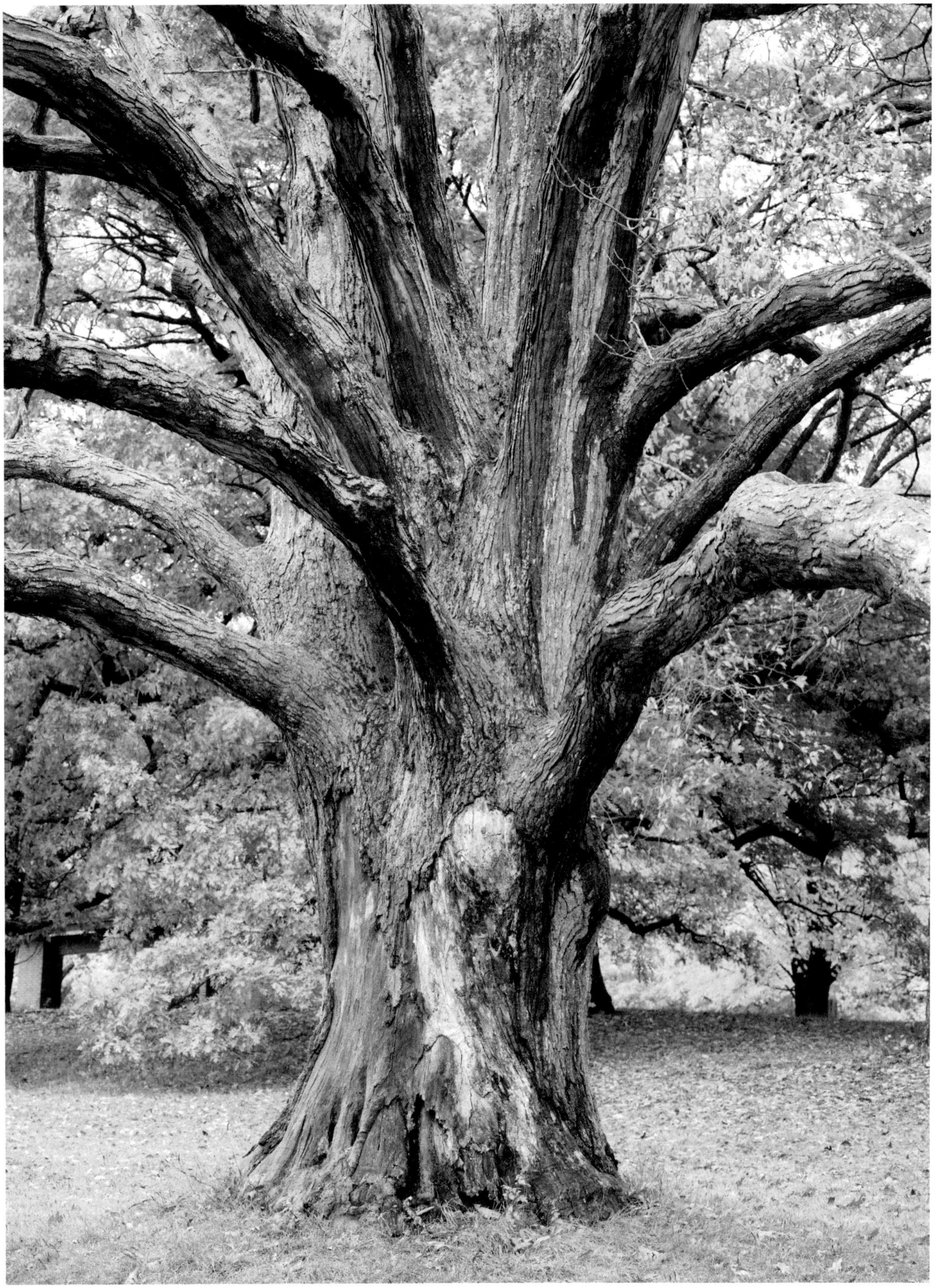

Quercus rubra, Northern Red Oak, Rot-Eiche – Genesee Valley Park, Rochester, New York, 2020

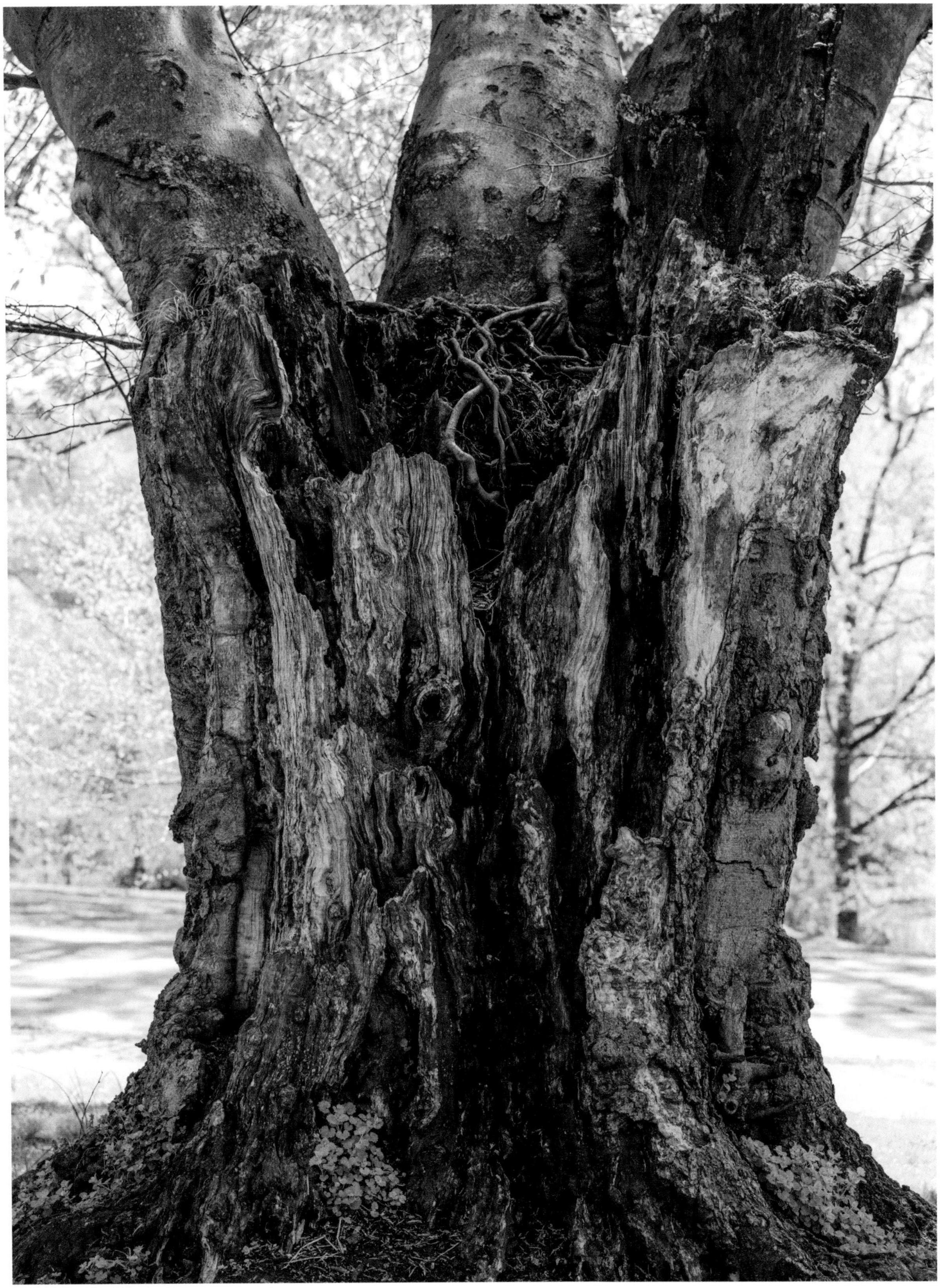

Fagus sp., Beech, Buche – Cherokee Park, Louisville, Kentucky, 2021

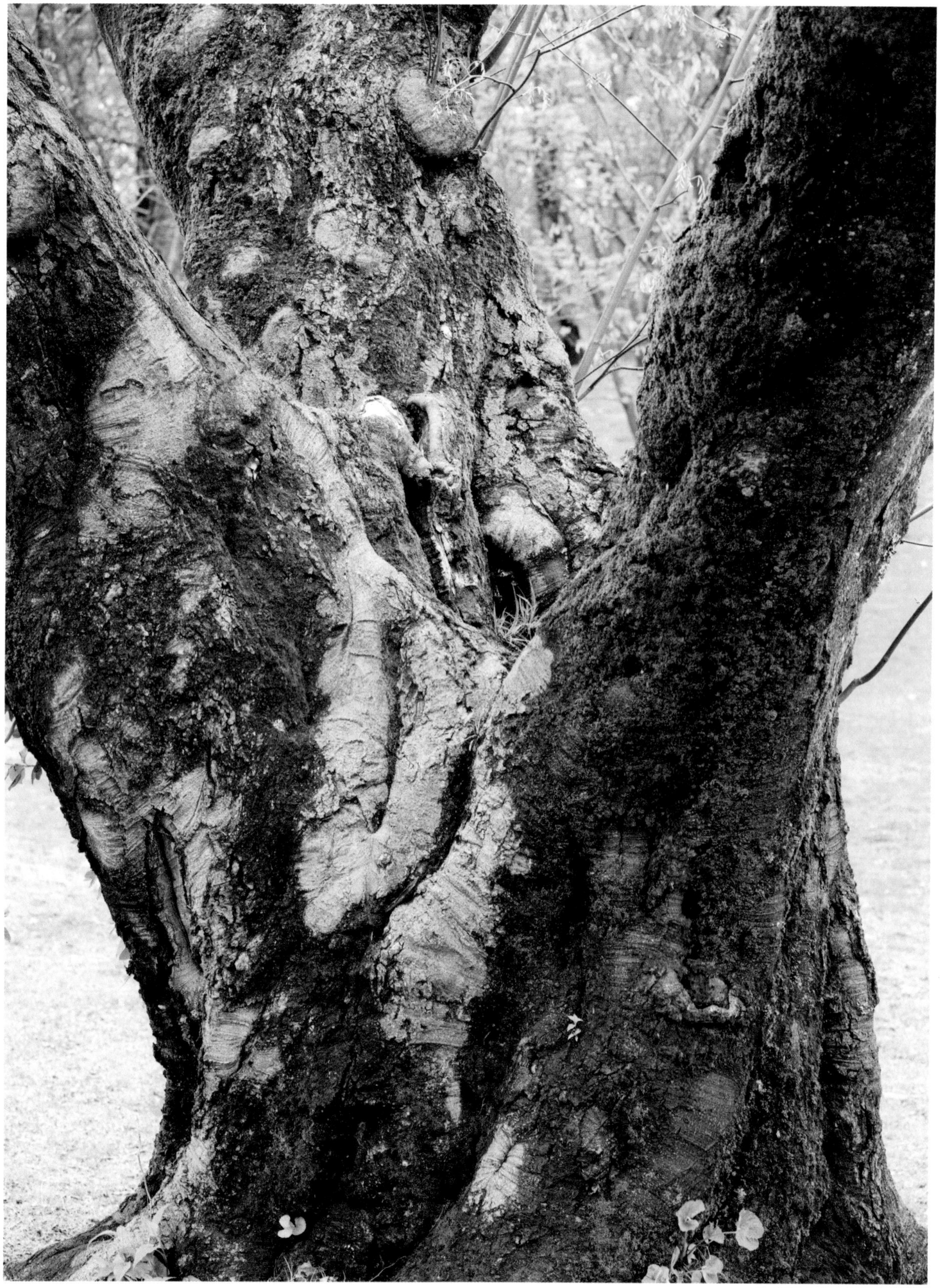

Cladrastis kentukea, Kentucky Yellowwood, Amerikanisches Gelbholz – Arnold Arboretum, Boston, Massachusetts, 2021

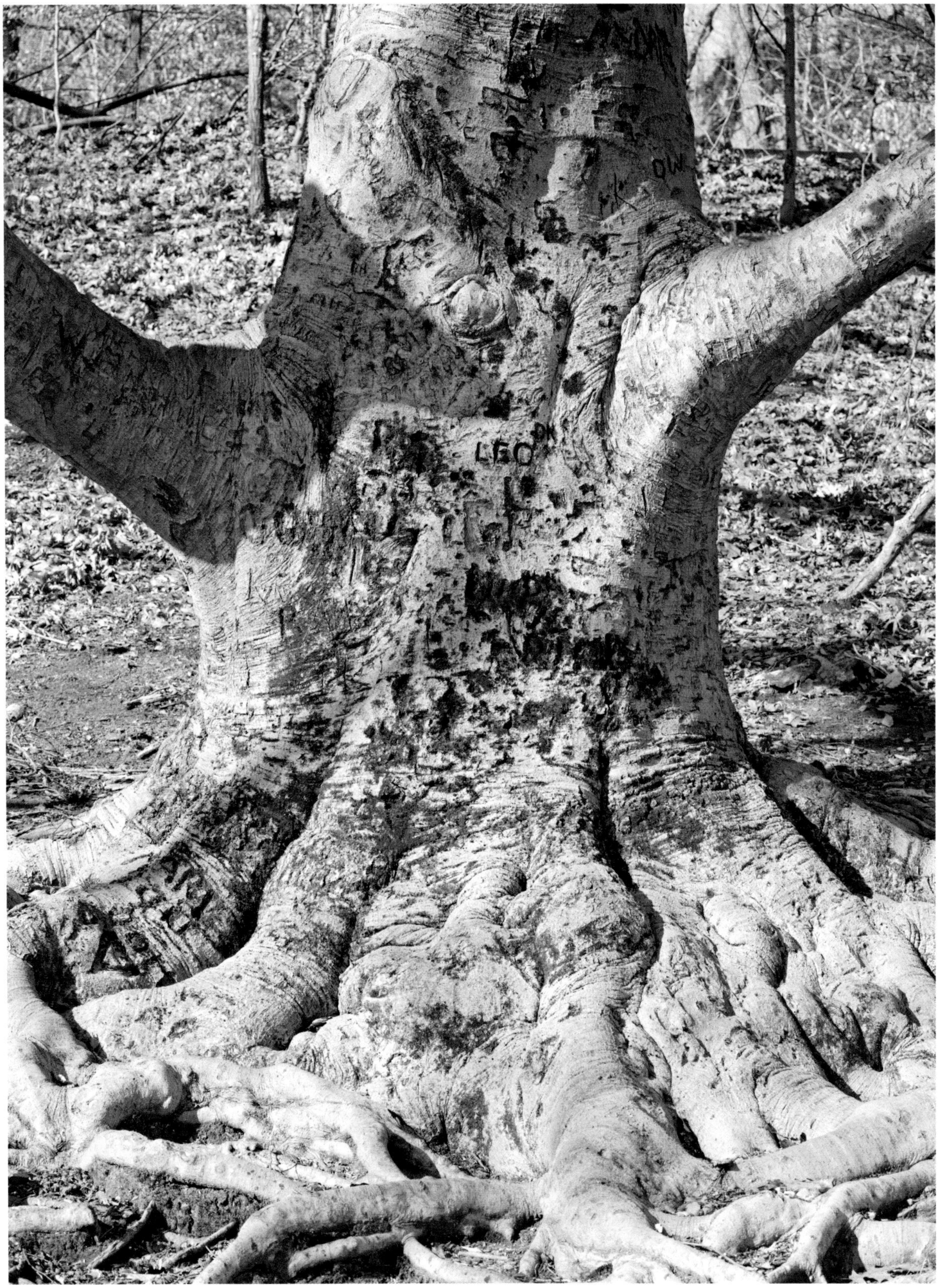

Fagus sylvatica, European Beech, Rot-Buche – Jamaica Pond, Boston, Massachusetts, 2020

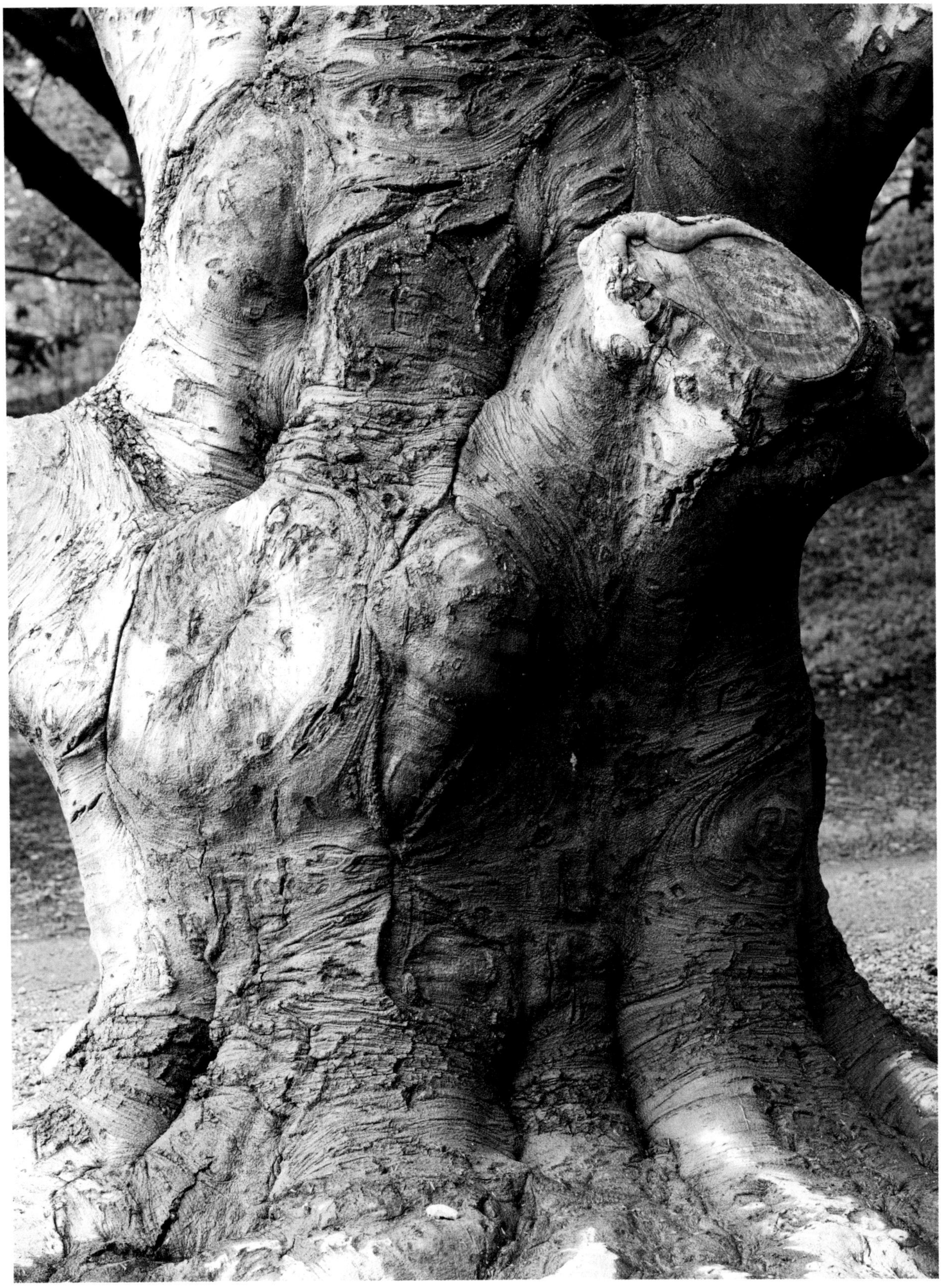

Fagus sylvatica "Asplenifolia," European Beech, Farnblättrige Rot-Buche – Arnold Arboretum, Boston, Massachusetts, 2021

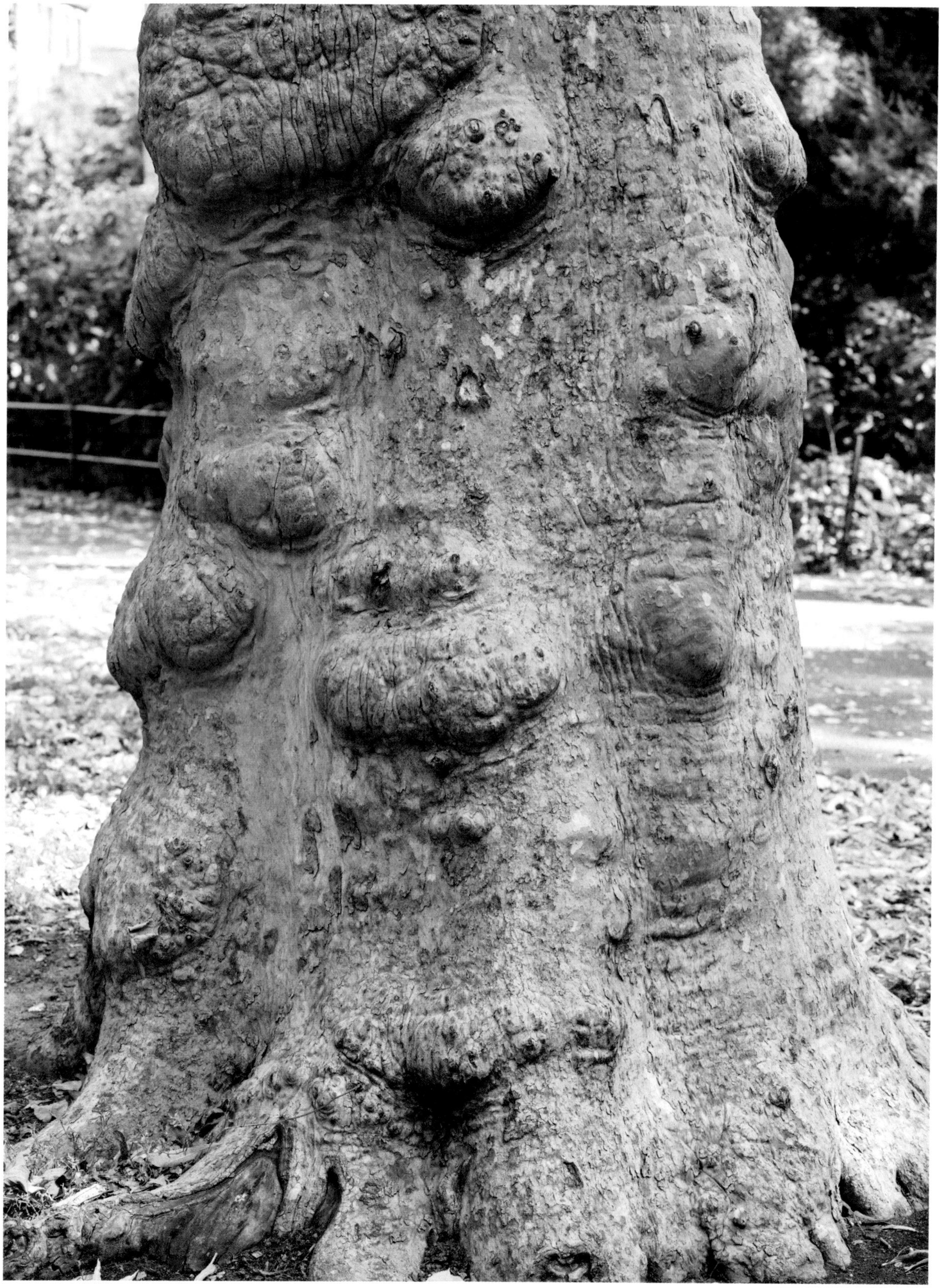

Platanus × acerifolia, London Plane, Ahornblättrige Platane – Herbert Von King Park, Brooklyn, New York, 2020

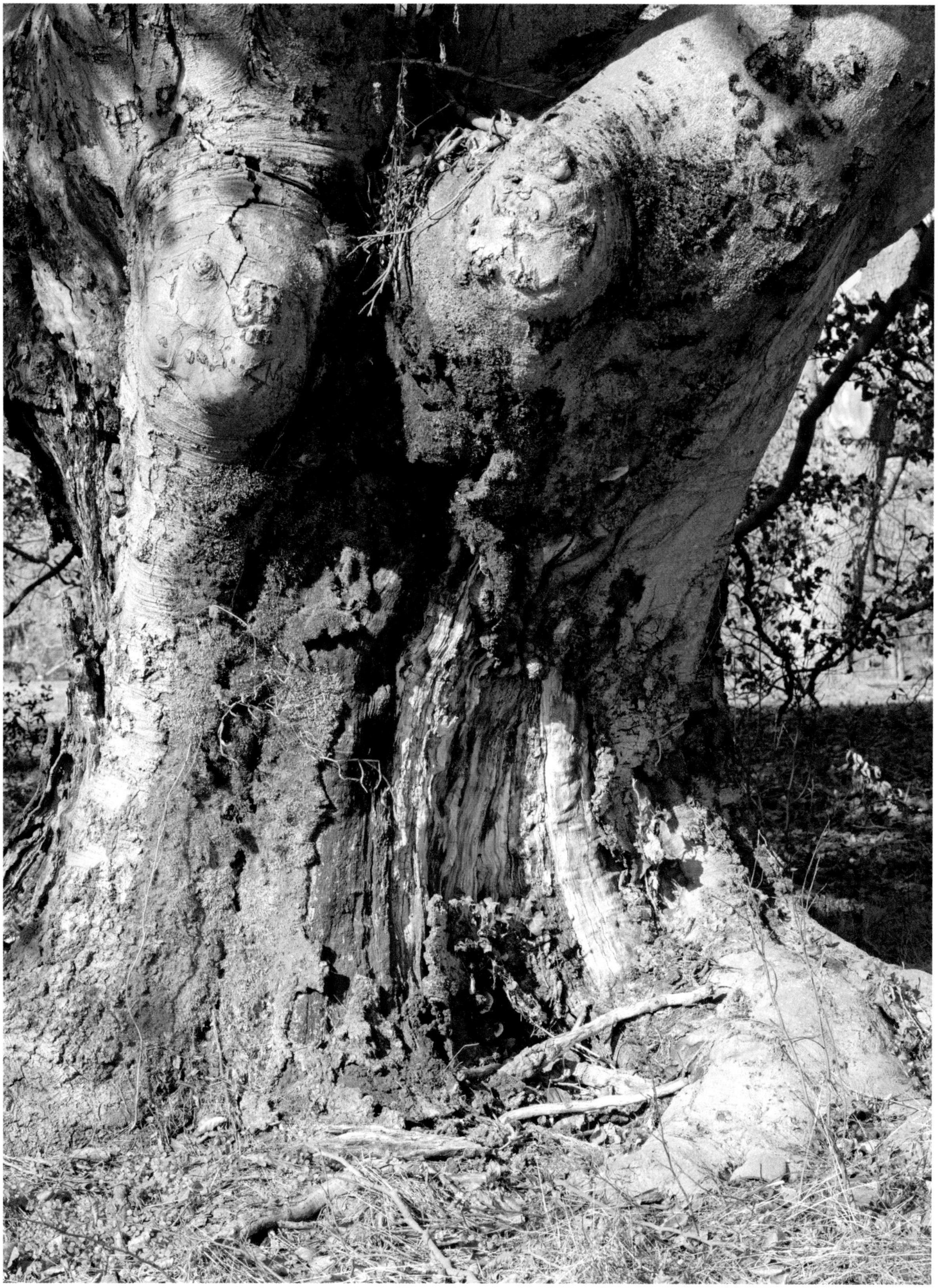

Fagus grandifolia, American Beech, Amerikanische Buche – Cadwalader Park, Trenton, New Jersey, 2019

Der Orange Park – wie Bindung an einen Ort entsteht

Mindy Thompson Fullilove

Als mich Stanley Greenberg bat, einen Essay für sein Buch über die Bäume in den Parkanlagen von Olmsted zu schreiben, fügte er seiner Anfrage eine seiner eindrucksvollen Fotografien bei. Die abgebildete Rinde und die sich windenden Äste riefen mir den Olmsted-Park in Erinnerung, in dem ich aufgewachsen bin: den Orange Park in Orange, New Jersey. Unser Park wurde von Olmsted Brothers gestaltet, dem Landschaftsarchitekturbüro der Brüder John Charles Olmsted und Frederick Law Olmsted Jr. Sie begannen mit der Gestaltung des Parks im Jahr 1898, drei Jahre, nachdem sich ihr Vater Frederick Law Olmsted Sr. zur Ruhe gesetzt hatte. Die Brüder übernahmen dabei den Ansatz ihres Vaters, einen ländlichen Kontrapunkt zum dichtbesiedelten urbanen Raum zu schaffen.[1]

Der Park wurde in einem sumpfigen Gelände angelegt und besaß einen Teich. Während meiner Kindheit umfasste er formal angelegte Gärten, weite Rasenflächen, akzentuiert durch alte Bäume, mit Baseballfeldern, einer Kirschbaumallee und besagtem Teich, von uns »Orange Pond« genannt. Dieser Teich war eine große Bereicherung des städtischen Lebens, er war die Seele des ganzen Parks. An seiner Südseite sah man noch das Schilf des einstigen Sumpflandes, dort stand das Wasser unbeweglich und trüb. Dieser Teil war nicht sonderlich attraktiv. Im Sommer roch es dort faulig und im Winter wollte das Wasser nicht zufrieren. Niemand »nutzte« diesen Abschnitt.

Am anderen Ende des Teichs gab es einen kleinen Damm, bestehend aus einem Ziegelfundament und einem darauf errichteten Eisengeländer. Das Wasser ergoss sich munter in den Abfluss am Fuß des Damms. Mein Vater, Ernest Thompson, stand gerne dort, lehnte sich gegen das Geländer, stützte einen Fuß auf die Ziegel und dachte über seine Arbeit als Community Organizer nach. Dabei sinnierte er über all die Machtverhältnisse in der Stadt und wie man Fortschritte erzielen könnte. Überlegene Organisation schlägt überlegene Kräfte, so lautete sein oft wiederholtes Credo, und der »Orange Pond« war der Ort, an dem er seine siegreichen Strategien entwickelte.[2]

An der Ostseite des Teichs standen einige Nadelbäume, deren Wurzeln sich am Ufer verknoteten und für mich eine Art Kai zu bilden schienen. Dort saß ich oft und setzte

1 Jeanne Kolva, Olmsted Parks in New Jersey, Atglen, PA, 2011.

2 Ernest Thompson und Mindy Thompson Fullilove, Homeboy Came to Orange: A Story of People's Power, New York 2018.

Orange Park and the Making of Attachment

Mindy Thompson Fullilove

When Stanley Greenberg asked me to write an essay for his book on the trees of Olmsted parks, he included one of his stunning photographs. The bark and twisting limbs took me back to the Olmsted park in which I grew up, Orange Park, in Orange, New Jersey. Our park was designed by the firm Olmsted Brothers, established by John Charles Olmsted and Frederick Law Olmsted, Jr. They started the design of the park in 1898, three years after the retirement of Frederick Law Olmsted, Sr. The Olmsted Brothers adopted their father's style for creating a pastoral counterpoint to the dense urban space.[1]

The park was built on marshy land that had a small lake. When I was growing up, Orange Park had formal gardens, wide lawns dotted with mature trees, baseball diamonds, an allée of cherry trees, and the lake, known to us as "Orange Pond." The pond was a particularly powerful addition to urban life, the organizing point of the whole park. The southern end of the pond hosted the grasses of its former days as a marsh, and the waters were still and slightly funky. That end of the pond was not particularly attractive. It smelled in summer and refused to freeze in winter. It was not "useful" to anyone.

At the other end of the pond stood a small dam, a brick foundation set with a small length of iron fence. Water flowed swiftly down the drain at the foot of the dam. My father, Ernest Thompson, liked to stand there, one foot resting on the bricks, leaning on the metal fence, to think about his work as a community organizer, considering all the power relations of the city to find the way forward. He always said that superior organization could defeat superior force, and Orange Pond was where he developed his winning strategies.[2]

In between the poles, on the eastern side, was a stand of evergreens, whose roots intertwined at the water's edge to form a dock, as I liked to think of it. I often sat there to push small boats of acorn caps off into the water. In my adolescence, the hovering trees were a shelter, as I pondered my own power relations, smaller in scale than those that troubled my father but no less gripping.

The western bank, which sloped gently down to the water, was a favorite spot for fishing. There were carp and other fish in the pond, and catching them proved of endless

1 Jeanne Kolva, *Olmsted Parks in New Jersey* (Atglen, PA: Schiffer Publishing, 2011).

2 Ernest Thompson and Mindy Thompson Fullilove, *Homeboy Came to Orange: A Story of People's Power* (New York: New Village Press, 2018).

kleine Boote aus Eichelkappen ins Wasser. Als Jugendliche boten mir dann die über mir schwebenden Baumkronen Schutz, wenn ich über meine eigenen Machtverhältnisse nachdachte, die nicht so ausufernd waren wie die meines Vaters, die mich aber nicht weniger beschäftigten.

Das Westufer, das sanft zur Wasserfläche abfiel, war ein beliebter Angelplatz. Es gab Karpfen und andere Fische. Die Jungs meines Viertels waren leidenschaftliche Angler. Auch Enten hielten sich gerne auf dieser Seite des Teichs auf, sie watschelten ins Wasser hinein oder heraus. Ausladende Bäume spendeten Schatten über dem Angelplatz und boten ein gemütliches Plätzchen, um dort einen Nachmittag zu verbringen.

Der Teich, der in seinem Grundriss einem Oval glich, lud auch zu einem Spaziergang ein. Dabei schlenderte man vorbei an den vielen kleinen Besonderheiten dieses Ökosystems und den Menschen, die sich daran erfreuten. Viele Jahre hielt ich mich beinahe jeden Tag dort auf, sodass zahlreiche meiner Erinnerungen mit diesem Teich verbunden sind. Wenn jemand davon spricht, dass etwas »Kreise zieht«, fallen mir die Kiesel ein, die ich in den »Orange Pond« geworfen habe. Kommt die Rede auf den Klimawandel, erinnere ich mich ans Schlittschuhlaufen auf dem »Orange Pond«.

Es muss nur jemand erwähnen, dass er ertrinkt, sei es real oder im übertragenen Sinne, dann denke ich ebenfalls an den »Orange Pond«, habe ich doch einmal erlebt, wie Jungs einer trächtigen Katze eine Schnur um den Hals banden und sie tatsächlich im Teich zu ertränken suchten. Völlig außer mir sprang ich hinterher und rettete sie. Ich nahm sie mit nach Hause, wo sie sich zu unserem Hund und den zwei anderen Katzen gesellte, und bald fünf Katzenjunge warf, die mein Bruder und ich nach unseren Lieblingsbüchern benannten. Das Muttertier und die Kleinen kamen schließlich ins Tierheim, und vielleicht haben sie nicht überlebt, doch davon erfuhr ich nichts, und wenn, hätte ich es sicherlich verhindert.

Diese dynamische Welt aus Tieren, der Bewegung des Wassers, den Menschen, die Kontakt zueinander suchten, den Bäumen, die Wache hielten, all dies hat sich in mein Herz eingebrannt. Doch gewiss ist damit die starke körperliche Beziehung, die ich zu diesem Park und diesem Teich habe, noch lange nicht erschöpft. Meine Füße erinnern sich an das mal glatte, mal holprige Eis. Vor meinen Augen erscheint immer noch das bunte Kaleidoskop der Blätter im Herbst, deren Farben noch durch ihre Reflektionen im Wasser verstärkt wurden. Meine Ohren kennen noch das Geräusch jedes Steins, der ins Wasser flog und Kreise zog, und meine Hand fühlt immer noch die Kiesel, die ich so gerne ins Wasser warf.

Genau das verstehe ich unter Bindung an einen Ort, nämlich, dass unser Geist und unser Körper von den Interaktionen mit einem Ort erfüllt sind und mit dem, was uns dort begegnet, von Enten bis zu Eichen. So verinnerlichen wir, während sich der Horizont unseres Lebens mit den Jahren erweitert und wir von Ort zu Ort wechseln, eine lange Folge von Geschichten und physischen Erinnerungen. Ich habe mit einer Fähre den Bosporus überquert und einen Teich in Kyoto besucht; so weit entfernt diese Orte von Orange sein mögen, meine Erfahrungen am »Orange Pond« sind stets Referenz all meiner Gedanken

interest to the boys of the neighborhood. Ducks liked that side of the pond, too, walking into and out of the water as they went about their own fishing. Several broad trees provided shade over the fishing bank and made it a comfortable place to spend a summer afternoon.

The pond, because of its roughly oval shape, was also good for a short walk: one walked by so many different little moments of the pond's ecosystem and the people participating in it. Because I was there nearly every day for many years, I have whole banks of memory associated with the pond. If someone says, "like ripples in the water," it is the pond that comes to mind. If someone talks about ponds and climate change, it is ice skating on Orange Pond that comes to mind.

If someone says, "we'll have to drown the kittens," it is Orange Pond that comes to mind, specifically an occasion on which several boys tied a rope around the neck of a pregnant cat and threw it into the pond to drown. I was hysterical and jumped into the pond to rescue the cat. I took it home, where it joined our dog and two cats, and soon added five kittens that my brother and I named after our favorite books. Mama and babies went off to the animal shelter, and perhaps they did not survive there, but that happened out of my sight, as I certainly would have stopped it otherwise. That eight cats were too many for our house was not particularly a concern of mine.

This dynamic world of wildlife, moving water, people seeking to connect, and trees standing sentinel is nestled in my heart, yes, but that is a wholly inadequate way to describe the whole-body connection I have with the park and its pond. My feet remember the ice when it was smooth and when it was pockmarked or bumpy. My eyes remember the kaleidoscope of colors as the leaves turned and their colors were intensified by their reflections in the water. My ears remember the sound of a stone falling into the water, causing ripples, and my hand remembers the feel of the stones that I liked to cast.

This is what place attachment is about: that our minds and bodies fill with interactions in a place, interactions with whatever or whoever is there, from ducks to oak trees. We integrate a long succession of place stories and body memories as we go from place to place, as our circle of life broadens throughout the years. I have taken a ferry on the Bosphorus and visited a pond in Kyoto; these places are far from Orange, but it is knowing Orange Pond that is the beginning of all my thoughts about bodies of water, with their flows and their inhabitants and their offerings. When I discovered Northern Manhattan's Highbridge Park, with its abandoned forest and views of the Harlem River, it was Orange Park that was the source of my new love.

In childhood I had a great belief that where I was living had always been there and would always be there. I didn't think to ask, "Why is there a pond opposite my house?" Or if I did, the answer that would have worked for me was, "My mother bought a house facing the park." That the park was built and then some decades later the house was built: these were concepts far outside my understanding. It took many decades before

zu Gewässern, ihrem Fließen, ihren Bewohnerinnen und Bewohnern und deren Möglichkeiten. Auch als ich den Highbridge Park im Norden Manhattans mit seinem menschenleeren Wald und seinen Ausblicken auf den Harlem River entdeckte, war letztlich der Orange Park Basis und Ausgangspunkt für diese neue Liebe meinerseits.

Als Kind war ich fest davon überzeugt, dass der Ort, an dem ich lebte, immer schon da gewesen war und immer bleiben würde. »Warum liegt ein Teich gegenüber meinem Haus?«, war keine Frage, die mir jemals in den Sinn gekommen wäre. Oder falls doch, hätte mir als Antwort genügt: »Deine Mutter hat ein Haus mit Blick auf den Park gekauft.« Dass der Park einst angelegt worden war und einige Jahrzehnte später das Haus gebaut wurde: Solche Gedanken lagen mir damals fern. Jahrzehnte vergingen, ehe die Anlage der Stadt, des Parks und der Bau unseres Hauses mein Interesse weckten. Mein Vater sagte oft, die einzige Konstante sei die Veränderung. Ich habe darüber gespottet, wie über so viele seiner Weisheiten – was ich heute bedaure.

Orange war in den 1890er-Jahren eine blühende Industriestadt, und die wohlhabenden Bürgerinnen und Bürger wollten ihre Stadt verschönern. In dieser Zeit entwarf Standford White seine Bibliothek, die Brüder Olmsted den Park und unweit davon ein Viertel für die Wohlhabenden: Seven Oaks. Laut Jeanne Kolva reservierte man die sumpfige Senke für einen Park, als man dort um 1850 die Straßen anlegte.[3] In den 1890er-Jahren war dies ein umstrittenes Unterfangen. Die zuständigen Vertreter von Essex County scheuten die Kosten für den Landerwerb, die Bürgermeister von Orange und East Orange sowie die Bewohnerinnen und Bewohner waren hingegen Feuer und Flamme für den Park.

Ihre Bemühungen trugen Früchte: 1898 begann man mit der Anlage. Die Brüder Olmsted bezogen beim Entwurf den vorhandenen alten Baumbestand mit ein. Weil es bereits zu beiden Seiten des Parks Straßen gab, wollten sie zunächst eine Durchgangsstraße in der Mitte vermeiden. Da diese aber schon vorhanden war, lenkten sie schließlich ein. Bei der Anlage wurde das Gelände begradigt und entwässert, der vorhandene Teich erweitert. Nach drei Jahren Bauzeit wurde der Park mit einem Konzert im Pavillon eingeweiht. Er lockte damals mit anmutigen Wegen, großen Bäumen und Blumenrabatten, und der vergrößerte Teich bekam einen flachen Bereich, in den man barfuß hineingehen konnte.

Verglichen mit anderen Parkanlagen der Olmsteds war der Orange Park eher klein, hatte aber eine angemessene Größe für die Stadt. Seine »Freiräume«, wie Landschaftsarchitekten gerne die von ihnen gestalteten Areale bezeichnen, boten Platz für Ballspiele und Blumen, Angeln und geselliges Beisammensein. Er lud Menschen aller Art ein, auch wenn die Errichtung eines Zauns an der den Armenvierteln zugewandten Seite nicht gerade eine Willkommensgeste darstellte. Ich konnte nicht einfach aus dem Haus gehen und den Park betreten, wie es den Leuten auf der östlichen Seite der Anlage möglich war. Ich musste das Tor passieren oder unter dem Zaun hindurchkriechen, wie es alle Kinder aus dem Stadtviertel taten. Dennoch vermittelte mir der Zaun nie die Botschaft »Du bist hier unerwünscht«, und um was für eine befremdliche Barriere es sich dabei handelte, erkannte ich erst, als ich über Jahrzehnte hinweg die Zeichen der Segregation in amerikanischen

3 Kolva 2011 (wie Anm. 1).

the construction of the city, its park, and my home became a subject of interest to me, or even a subject at all. My father used to tell me that change was the only constant. I scoffed at that, as I did at much of my father's wisdom, I report with much chagrin.

Orange was a thriving manufacturing town in the 1890s, and the wealthy citizens wanted to decorate their city. In that era, Stanford White designed the library and the Olmsted Brothers designed both the park and a nearby enclave for the wealthy, known as Seven Oaks. According to Jeanne Kolva, when the roads of the area were laid out in 1850, the marshy bottom land was set aside for a park.[3] In the 1890s, the building of the park was a contentious process. Essex County parks commissioners disagreed about spending the money for the land; the mayors of Orange and East Orange, and the area's residents, were vociferous in their support for a park.

Those advocacy efforts paid off, and in 1898 the building began. The Olmsted Brothers designed the park to take advantage of mature trees that were already there. Because there were roads on either side of the park, they wanted to avoid a drive through the middle. However, as that was already in place, they conceded the point. The development of the site involved grading and drainage, and the development of the small lake into a larger water feature. After three years of construction, the park opened with a concert in the bandstand. At that time there were gracious paths, mature trees, and flower gardens, while the enlarged lake included a small wading area.

Though small by comparison with many Olmsted parks, Orange Park was of a good size for the city. Its outdoor "rooms," as landscape designers like to think of the spaces they define, offered space for ballgames and blossoms, fishing and fellowship. It has provided a welcome for people of all kinds, though the erection of a fence along the lengths of the park that faced the city's ghetto neighborhoods was certainly a "not so much." I couldn't walk out of my house and enter the park, as people on the eastern side of the park could. I had to go in the gate, or go under the fence, which all the children in the neighborhood preferred to do. I never once read the fence as "YOU keep out," and I didn't even recognize its oddity until I'd spent decades decoding signs of segregation in other American cities. Instead, what I thought I had at my front door was a playground of possibility and a pond.

Now in my seventies, I return to the park often. I never walk through the park without trying to decide how I might start a Friends of Orange Park organization to ensure that it gets the attention it needs. The bedraggled trees need surgery, the pond's dam needs brick work, the paths need resurfacing, and the grading needs attention. When I fell in love with Highbridge Park, I was able to join with friends to create City Life Is Moving Bodies (CLIMB) to advocate for reinvestment in all the cliffside parks to which Highbridge is linked. We wanted to fix all that had collapsed from neglect. We estimate that, since we started in 2004, $150 million has gone into those parks, reanimating them and reweaving them into the fabric of the city. There is no question in my mind but that I cared so deeply about those parks because of my love for Orange Park.

3 Kolva, *Olmsted Parks*.

Städten erforscht und dekodiert hatte. Für mich lagen da vor meiner Haustür einfach ein Spielplatz voller Möglichkeiten und ein Teich.

Jetzt, in meinen Siebzigern, kehre ich oft in den Park zurück. Immer wenn ich dort spazieren gehe, überlege ich, wie ich einen Verein der Freunde des Orange Parks gründen könnte, damit der Park endlich die Aufmerksamkeit bekommt, die er verdient. Die vernachlässigten Bäume benötigen Zuwendung, der Damm des Teichs muss repariert, die Wege erneuert und das ganze Gelände besser gepflegt werden. Als ich mich in den Highbridge Park verliebte, rief ich mit Freunden CLIMB (City Life Is Moving Bodies) ins Leben, um uns für die Aufwertung der an den Hängen gelegenen Parkanlagen, die mit der Highbridge verbunden sind, einzusetzen. Seit 2004, als wir mit unserer Arbeit begannen, sind schätzungsweise 150 Millionen Dollar in diese Parks geflossen, um sie zu beleben und wieder in das Stadtgefüge zu integrieren. Ich habe keinerlei Zweifel daran, dass mich meine Liebe zum Orange Park zum Engagement für diese Parkanlagen anregte.

Und so fühlte ich mich unter alten Freunden, als ich Stanley Greenbergs Fotos von Bäumen sah, Freunden, deren Rinde ich während all der Jahre meines Aufwachsens gestreichelt hatte, deren Wurzeln meine Sitzgelegenheit und deren Blätter mein Farbkasten gewesen waren. Ein Stadtpark ist eine ganz besondere und wunderbare Anlage. Frederick Law Olmsted und seinen Söhnen ist es mit ihrem tiefen Verständnis für die Elemente eines Ortes gelungen, Räume zu schaffen, in denen wir groß werden und unsere Vorstellungen entwickeln können. Und es ist dieses Angebot an Möglichkeiten, das Ausgangspunkt wird für unsere Liebe zu einem Park und unsere Verbundenheit mit ihm.

And this meant that when I saw Stanley Greenberg's photographs of trees, I felt like I was with old friends, friends whose bark I had petted through all the years of my growing up, whose roots had been my chairs and leaves my paintbox. A city park is a very particular and very glorious place, and it is the Olmsteds' profound understanding of the elements of place that created spaces within which we might grow and imagine, and it is that offering of possibility that is the source of our love and attachment to the park itself.

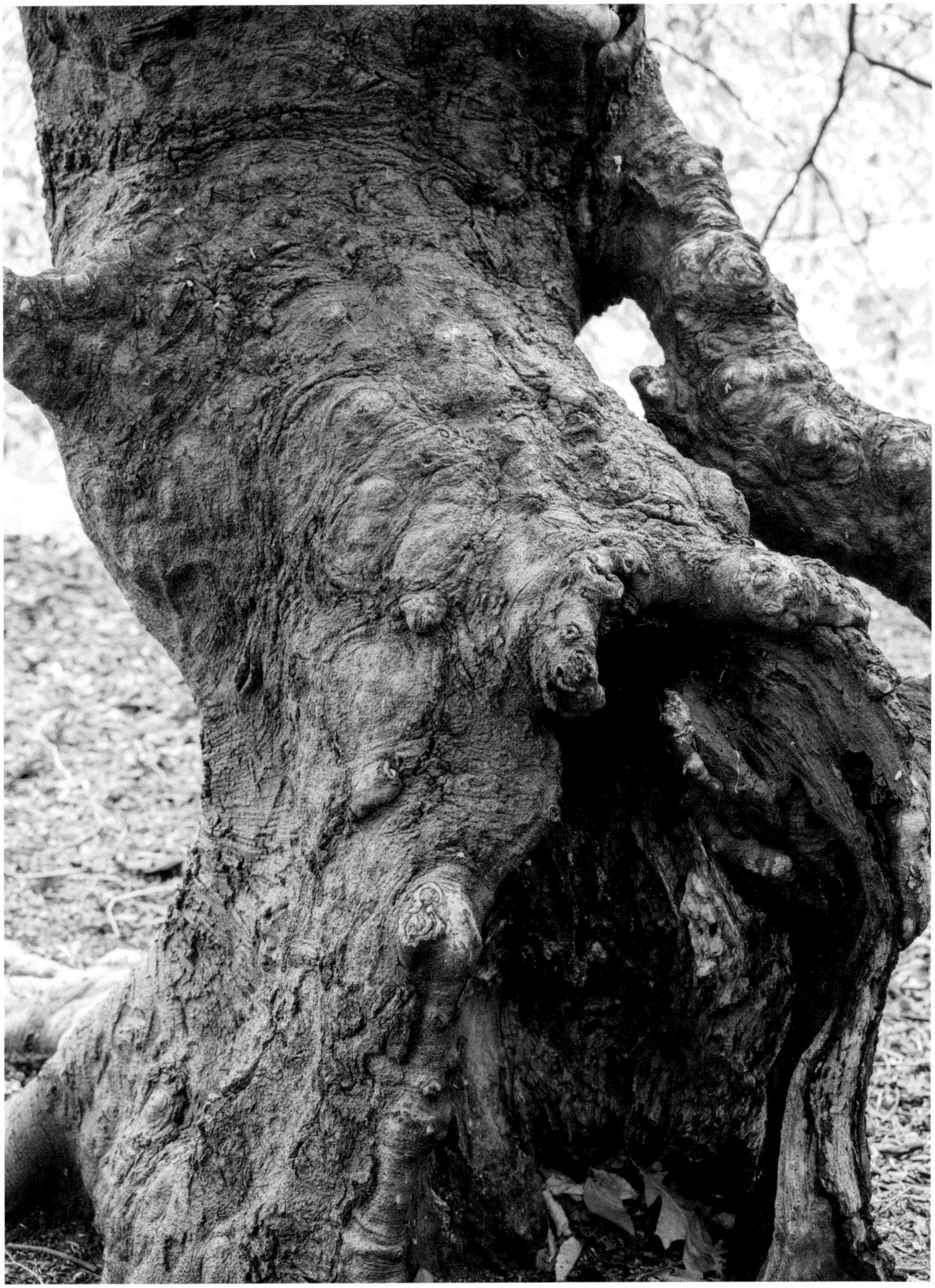

Fagus sylvatica "Tortuosa," European Beech, Rot-Buche – Arnold Arboretum, Boston, Massachusetts, 2021

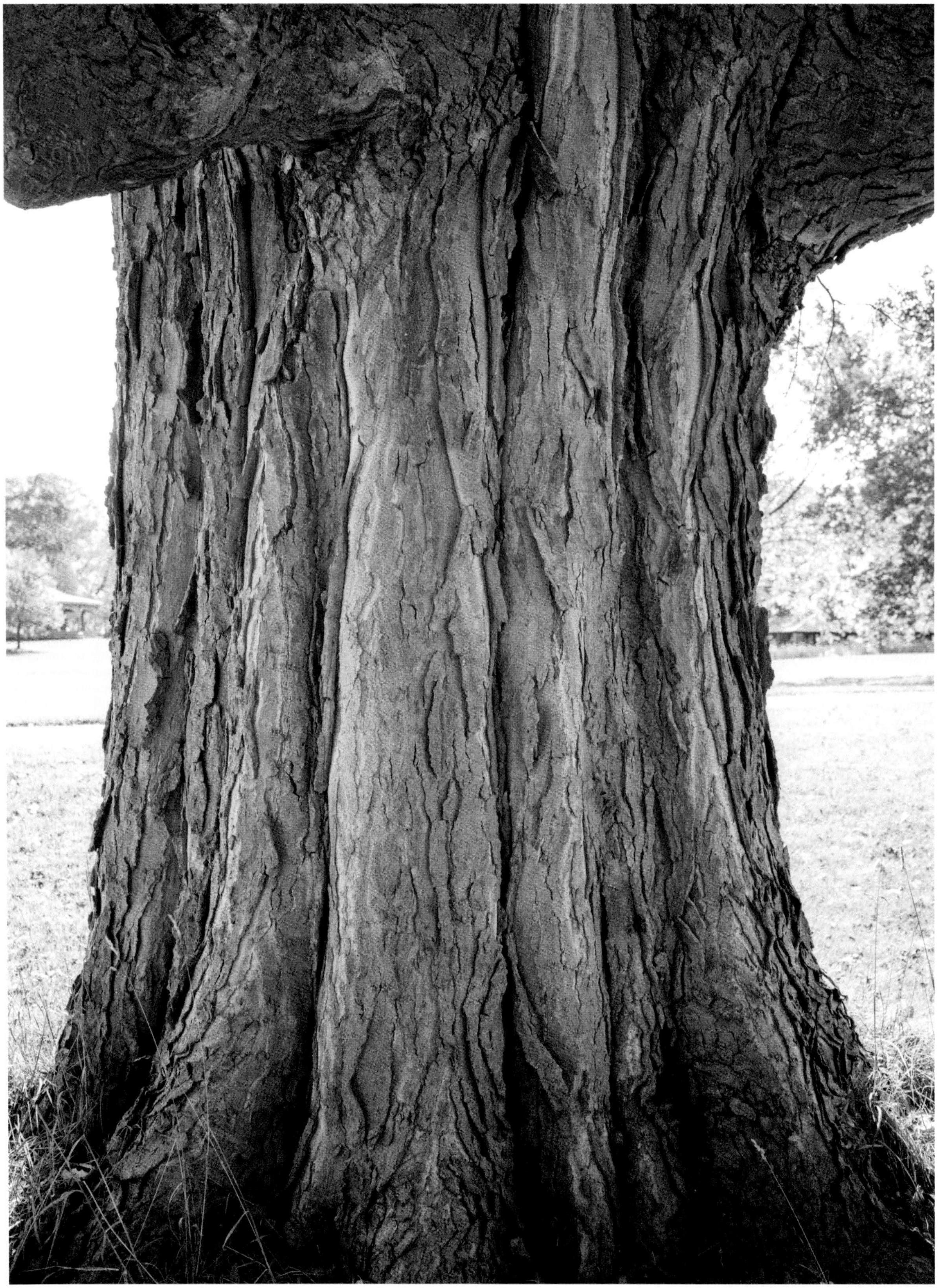

Ulmus americana, American Elm, Amerikanische Ulme – Genesee Valley Park, Rochester, New York, 2020

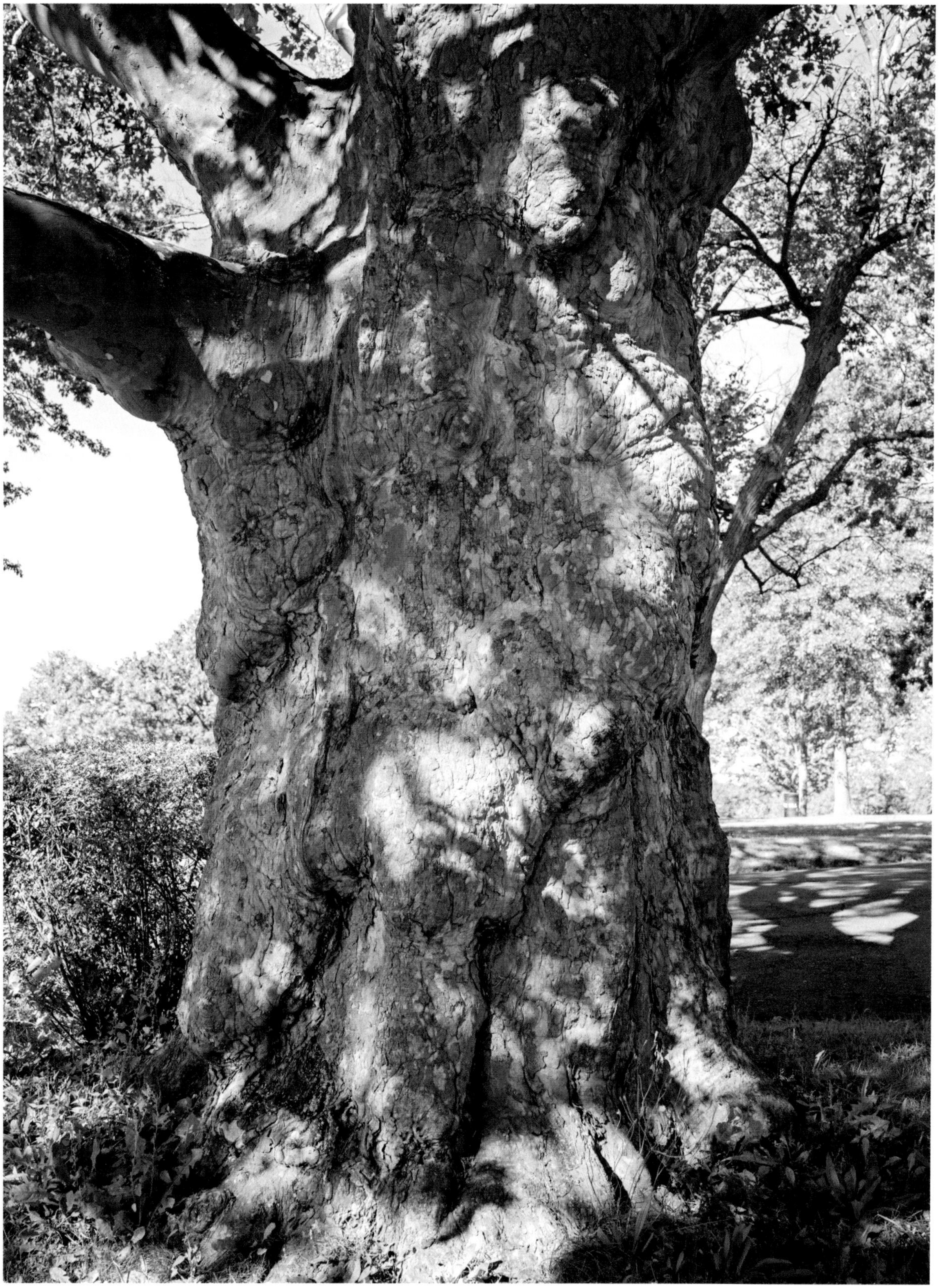

Platanus × acerifolia, London Plane, Ahornblättrige Platane – Walnut Hill Park, New Britain, Connecticut, 2021

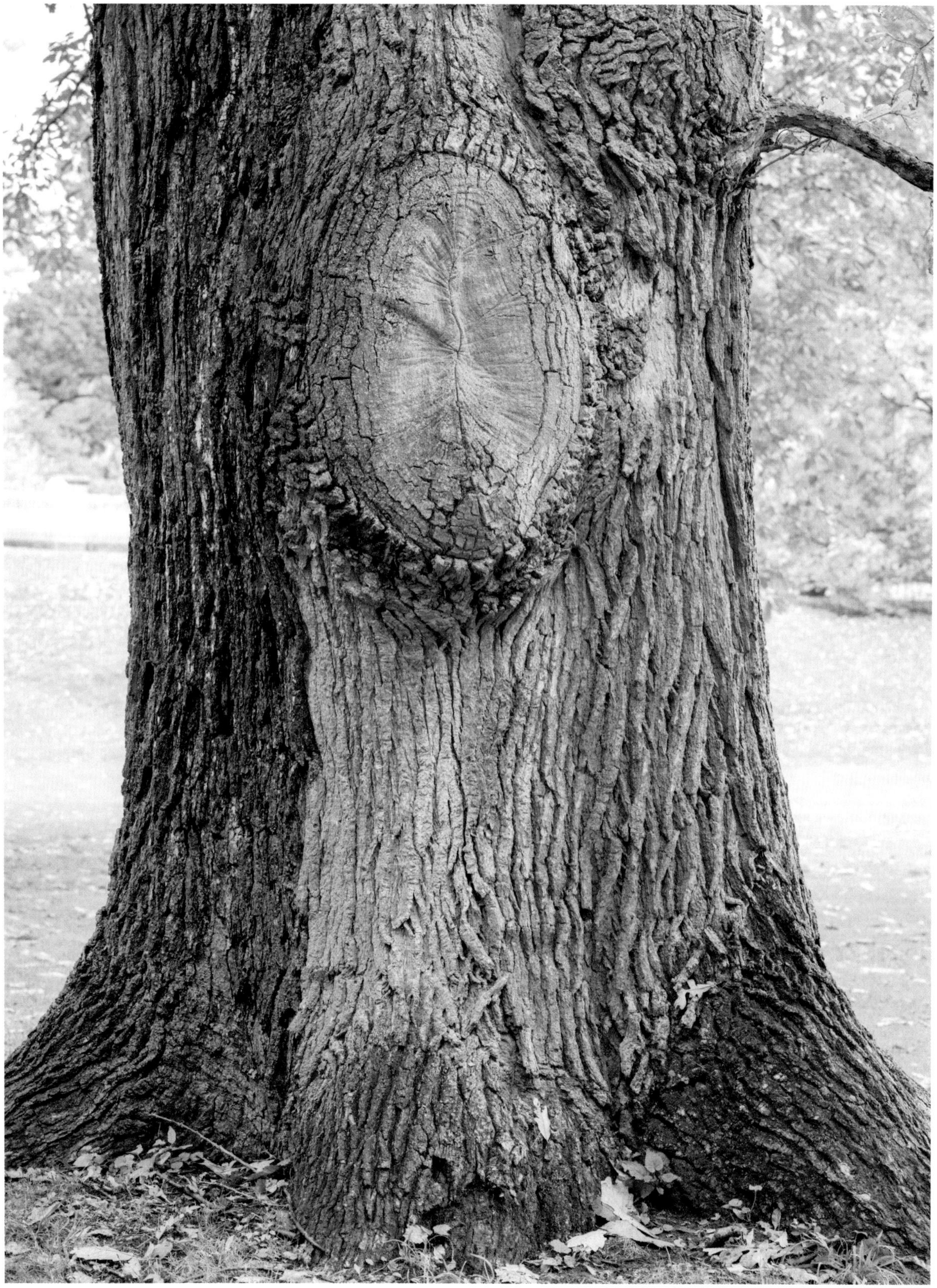

Quercus montana, Chestnut Oak, Kastanien-Eiche – Highland Park, Rochester, New York, 2020

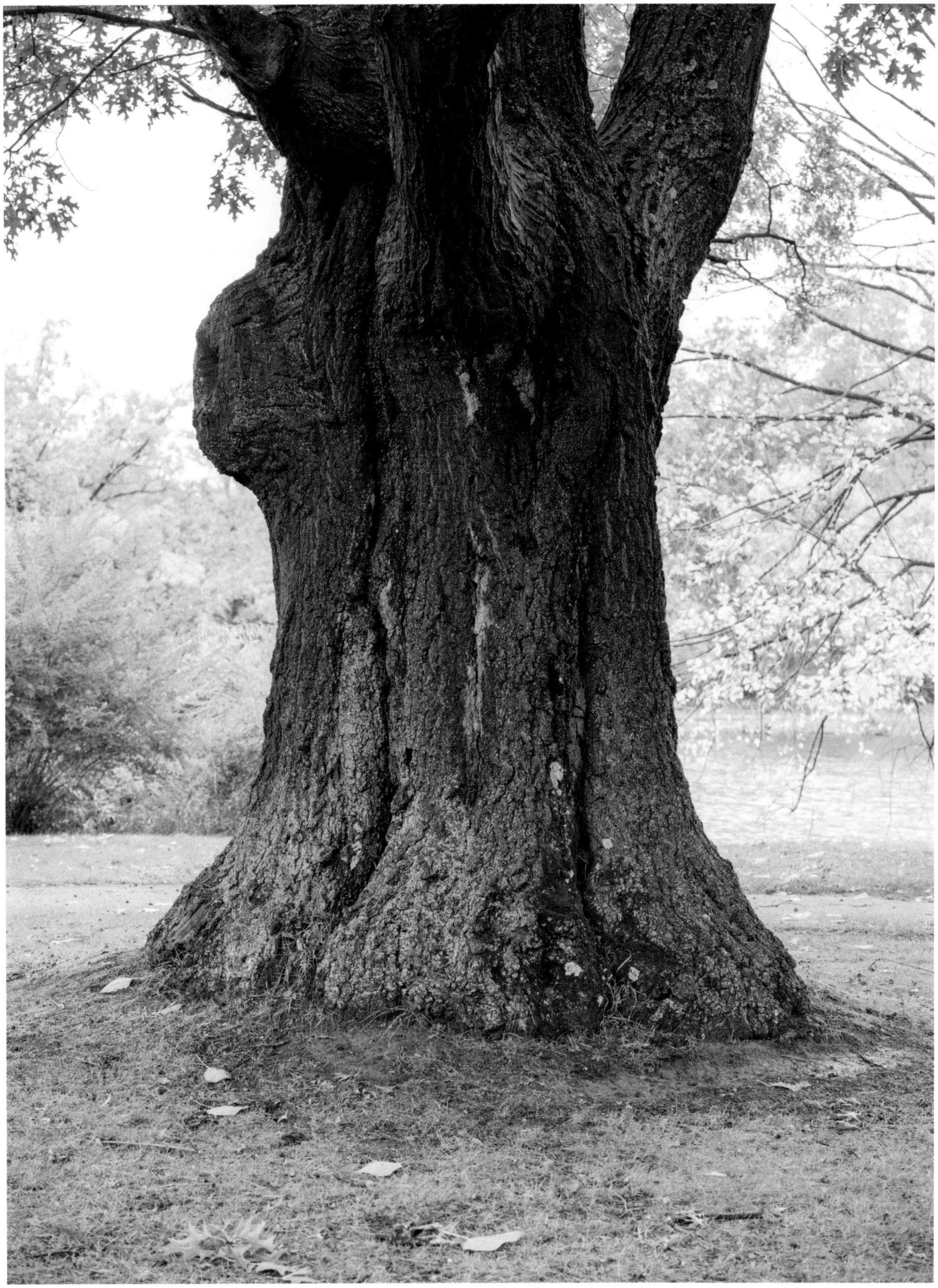

Quercus coccinea, Scarlet Oak, Scharlach-Eiche – Seneca Park, Rochester, New York, 2020

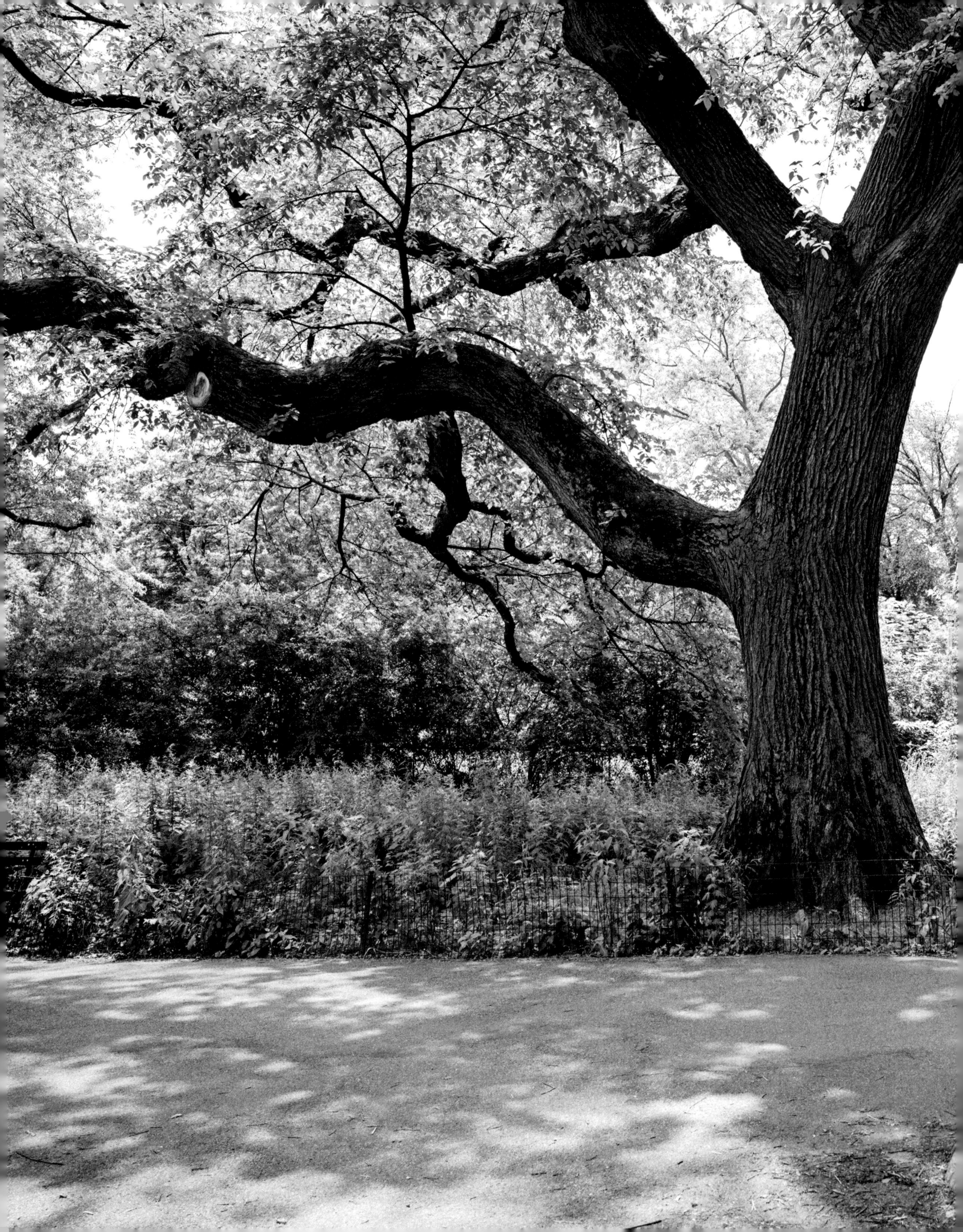

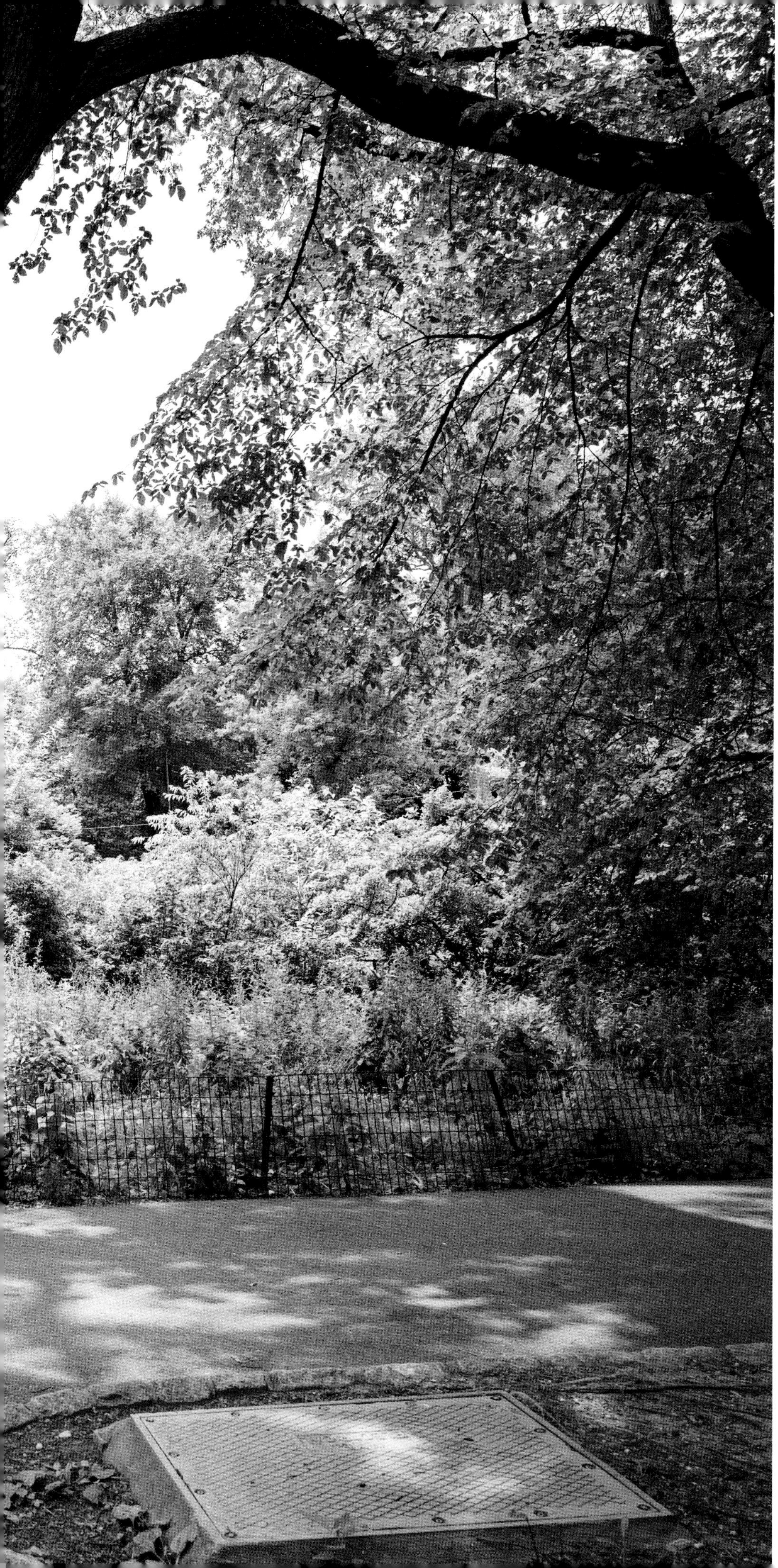

Ulmus americana,
American Elm, Amerikanische Ulme –
Central Park, New York,
New York, 2021

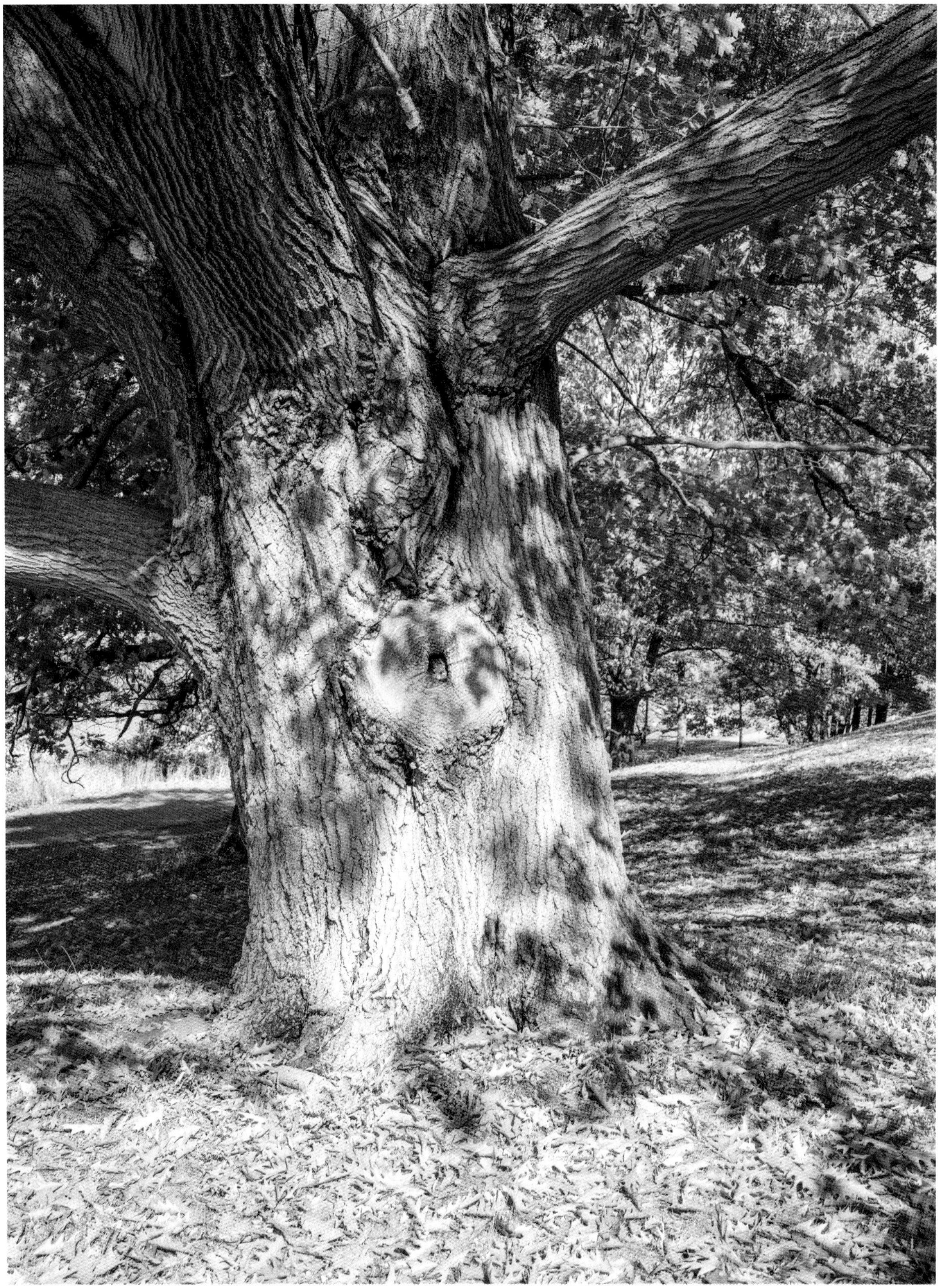

Quercus rubra, Northern Red Oak, Rot-Eiche – Genesee Valley Park, Rochester, New York, 2020

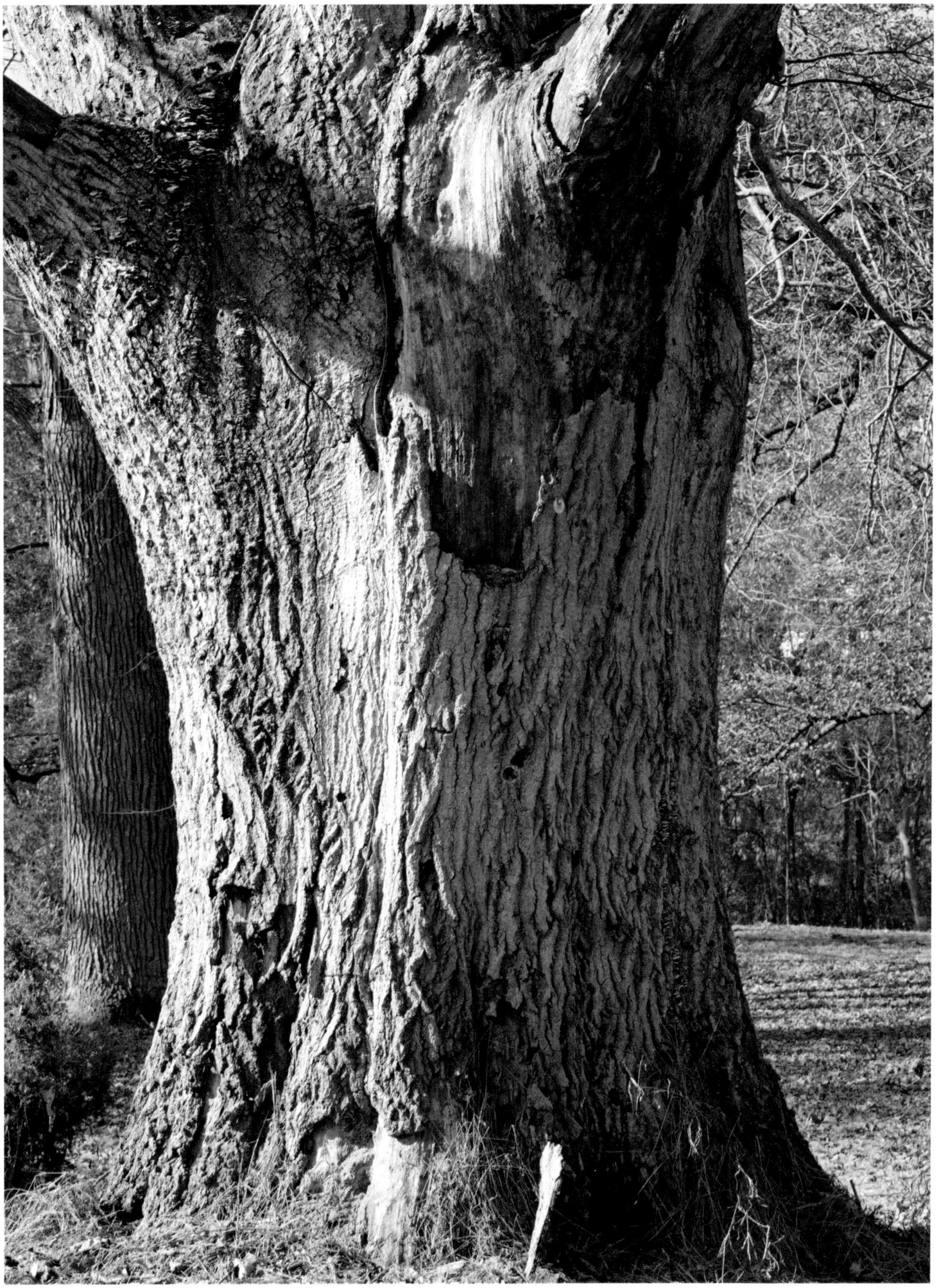

Tilia sp., Linden, Linde – Cadwalader Park, Trenton, New Jersey, 2019

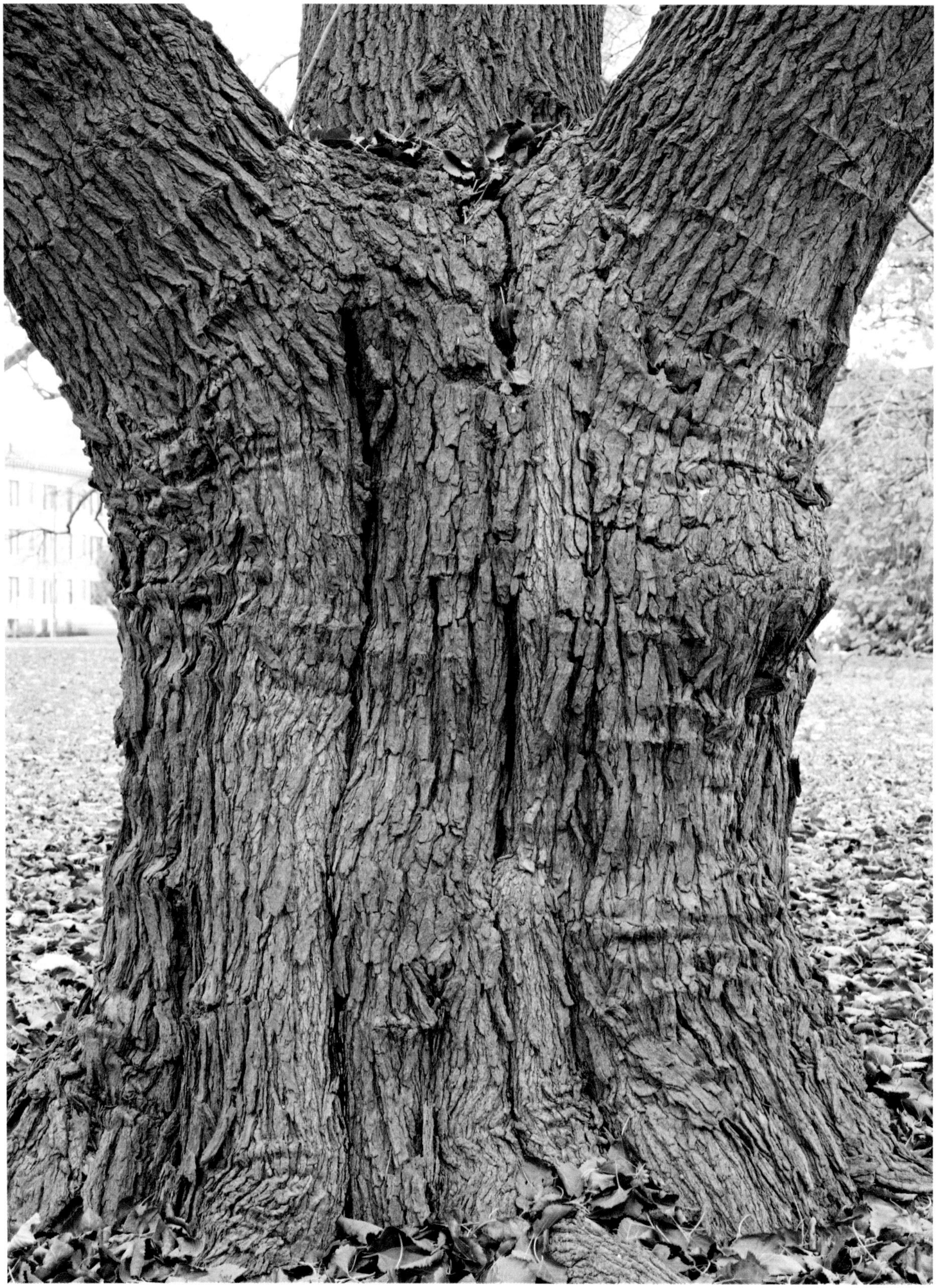

Morus sp., Mulberry, Maulbeere – Washington Park, Chicago, Illinois, 2019

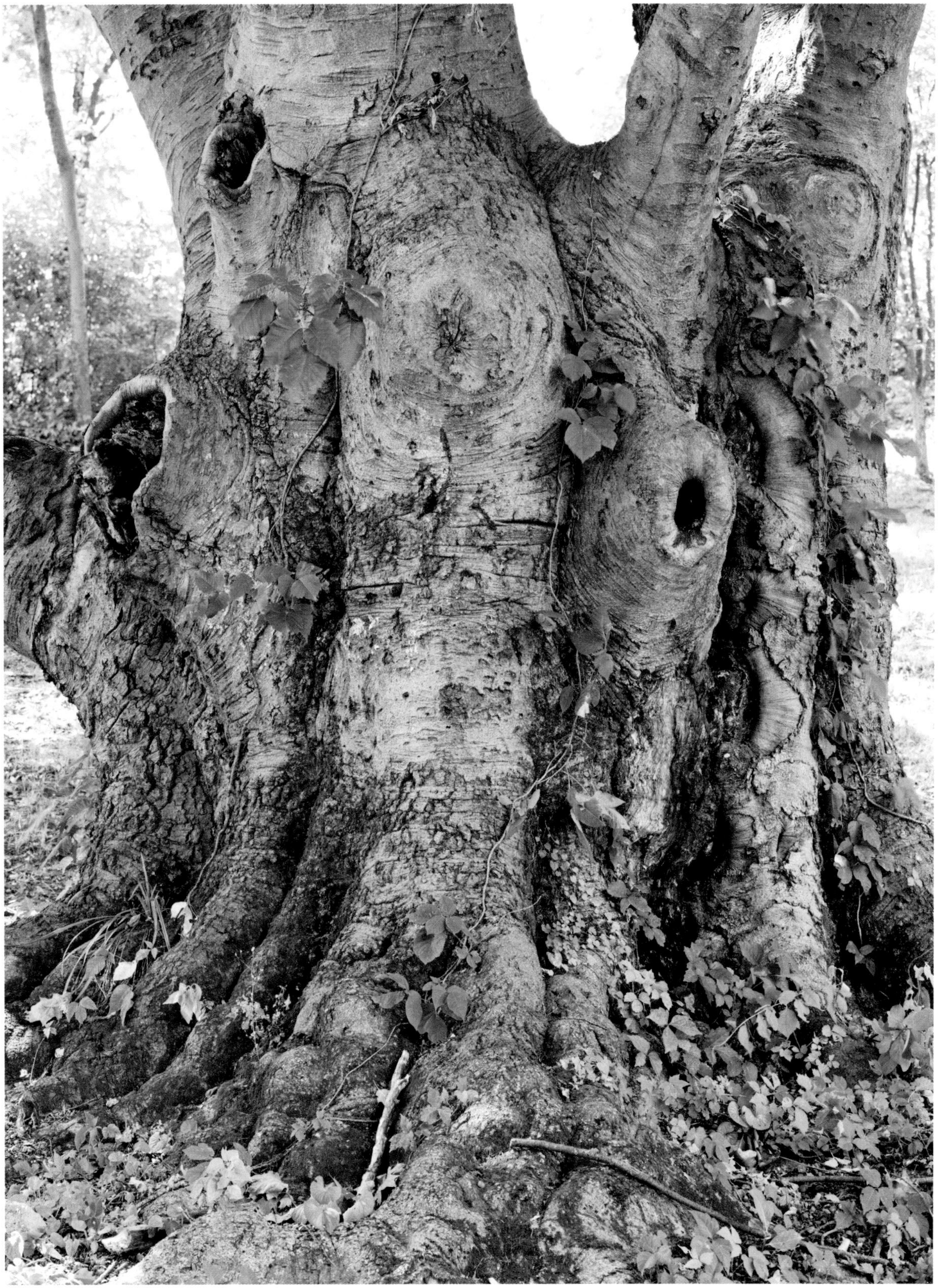

Fagus grandifolia, American Beech, Amerikanische Buche – Downing Park, Newburgh, New York, 2020

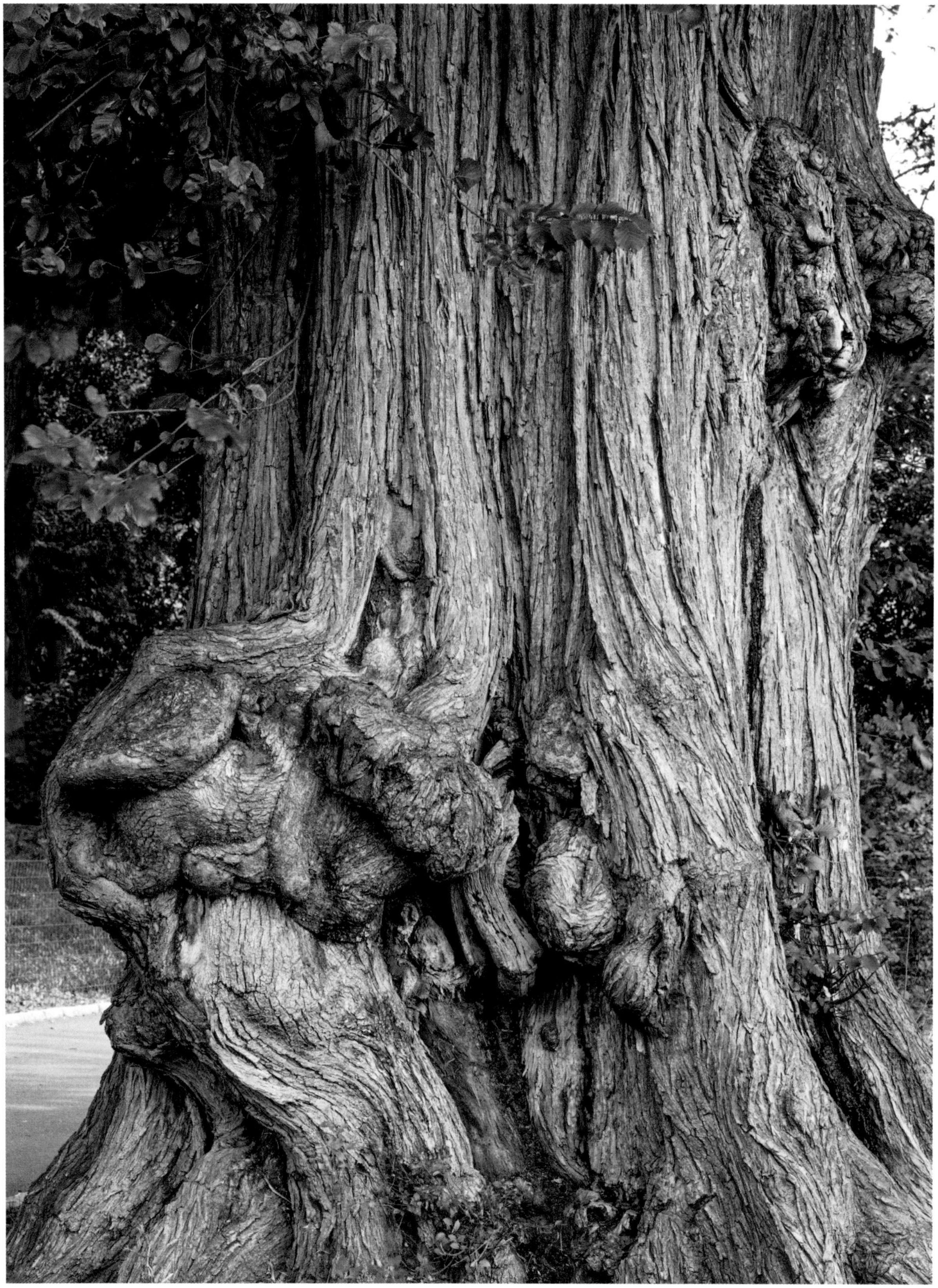

Ulmus americana, American Elm, Amerikanische Ulme – Fort Greene Park, Brooklyn, New York, 2019

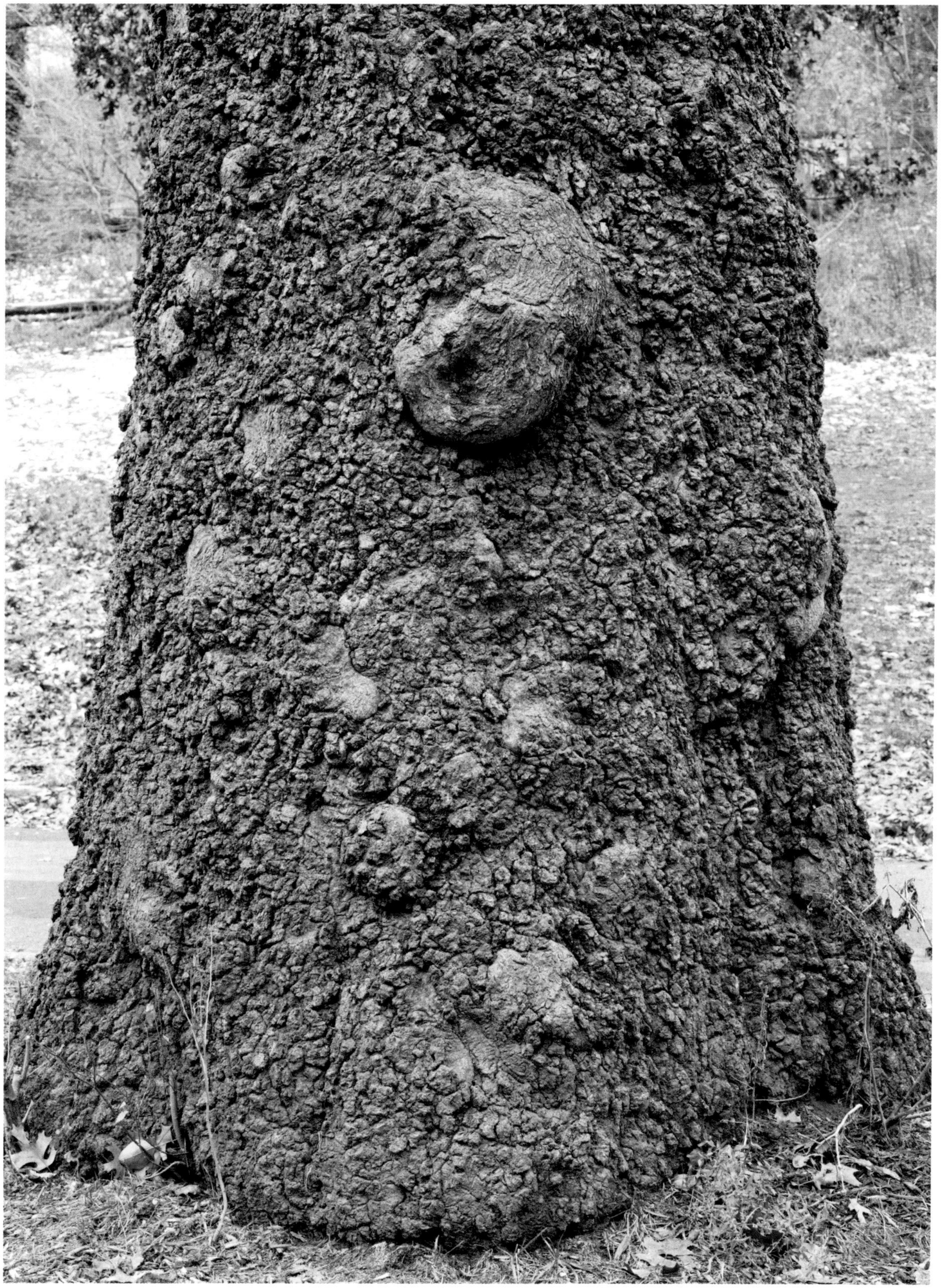

Quercus palustris, Pin Oak, Sumpf-Eiche – Morningside Park, New York, New York, 2019

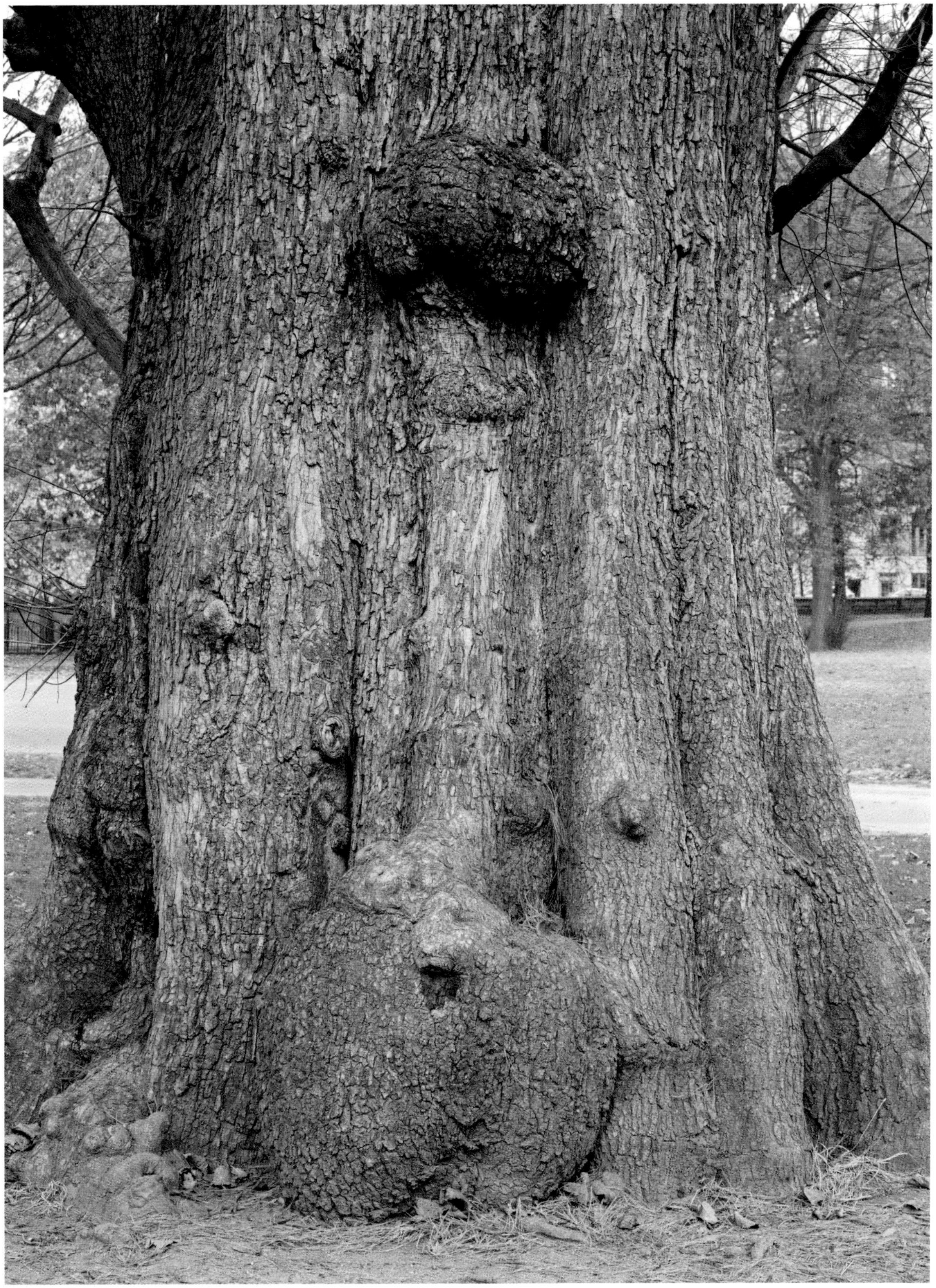

Ulmus americana, American Elm, Amerikanische Ulme – Prospect Park, Brooklyn, New York, 2019

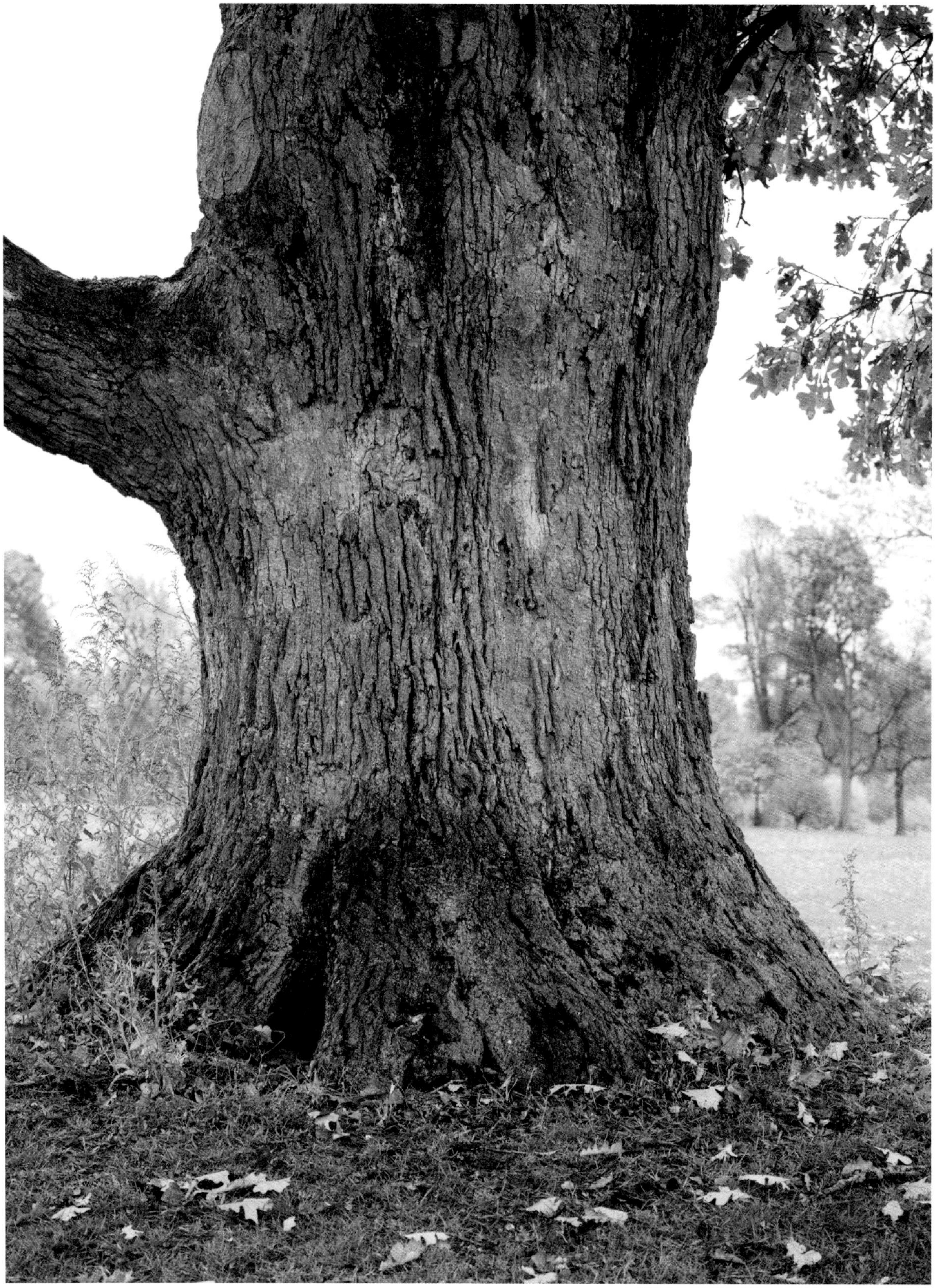

Quercus macrocarpa, Burr Oak, Bur-Eiche – Delaware Park, Buffalo, New York, 2020

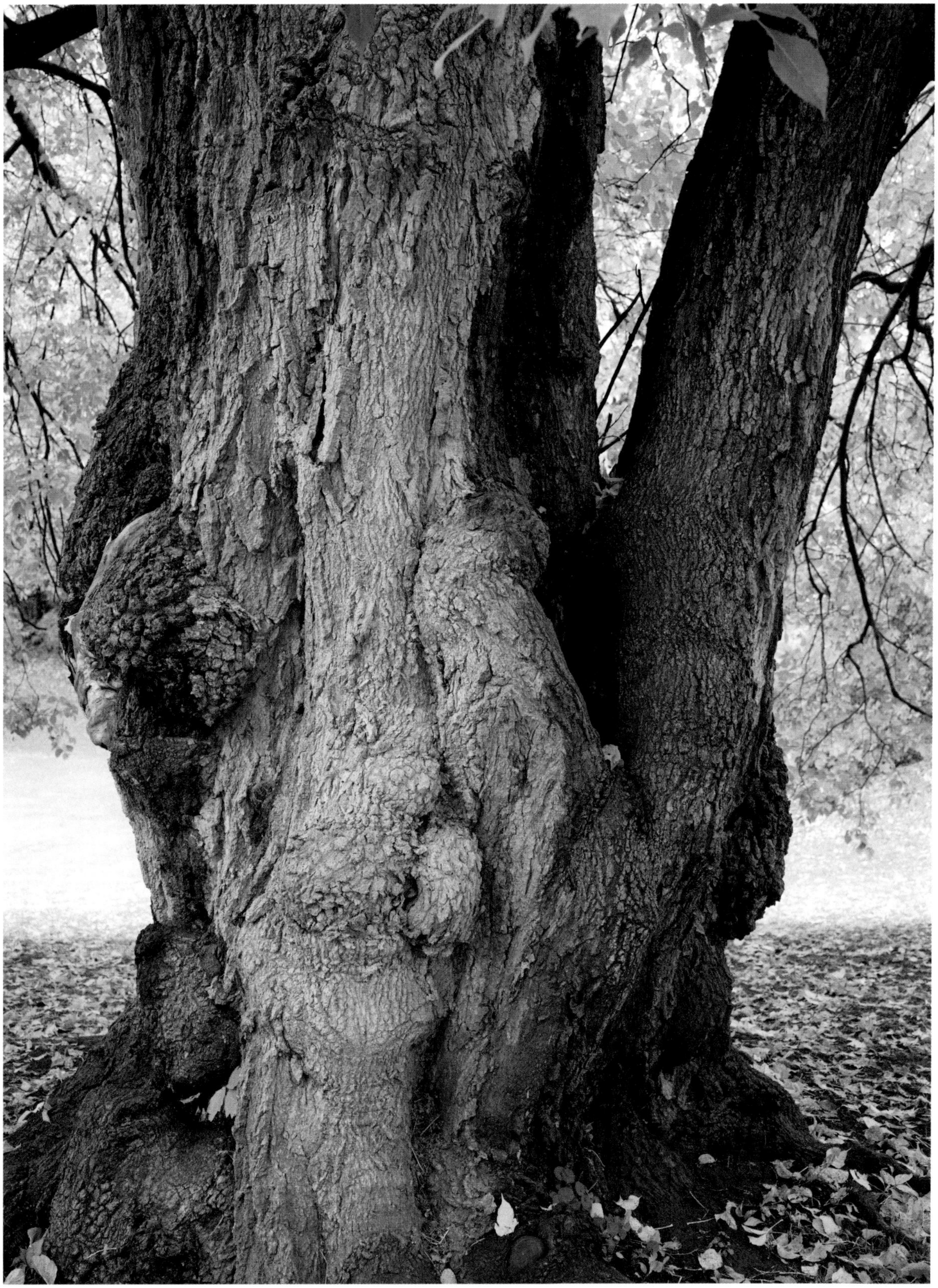

Acer negundo, Box Elder, Eschen-Ahorn – Highland Park, Rochester, New York 2020

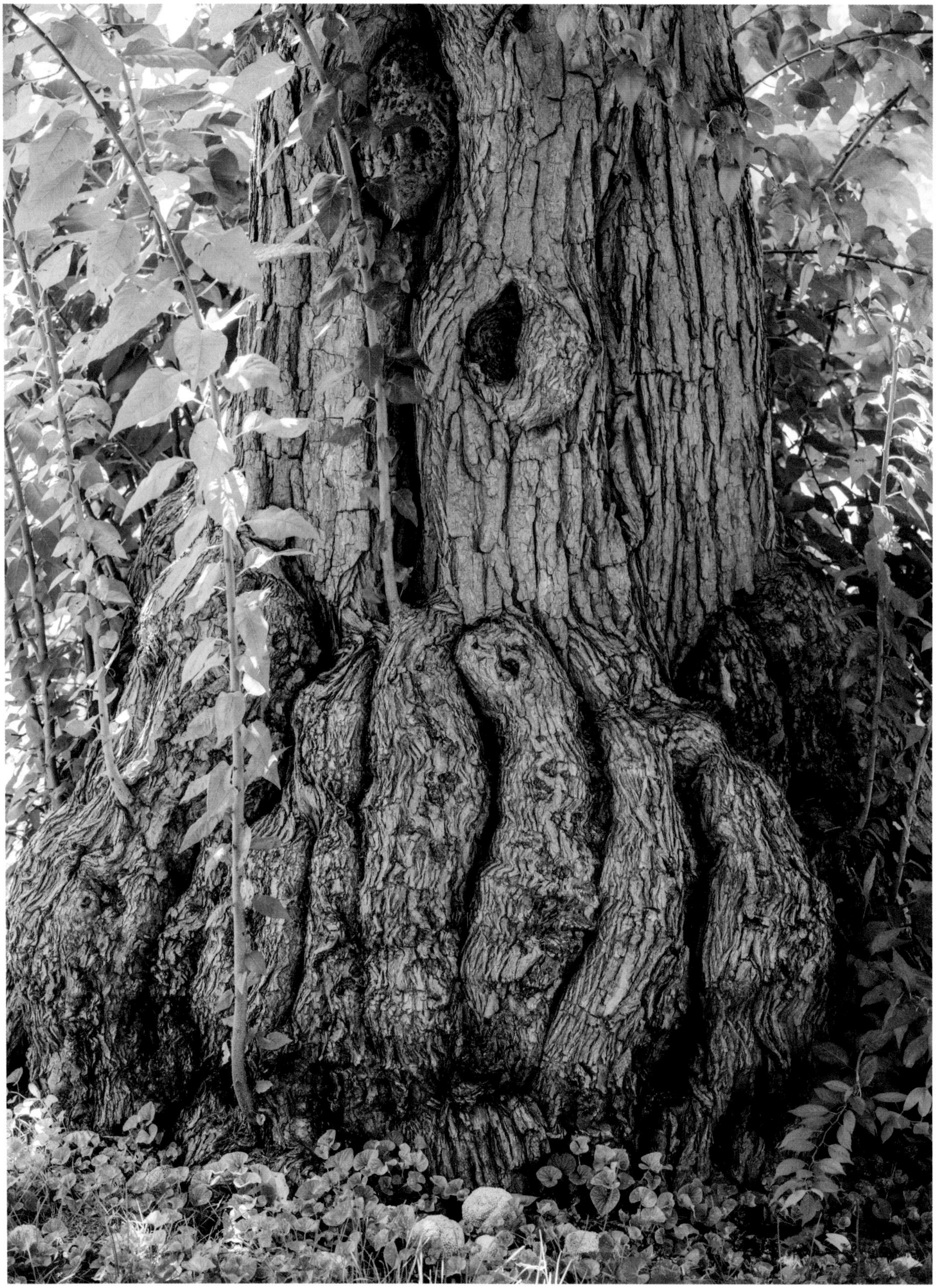

Maclura pomifera, Osage-Orange, Milchorangenbaum – US Capitol, Washington, DC, 2020

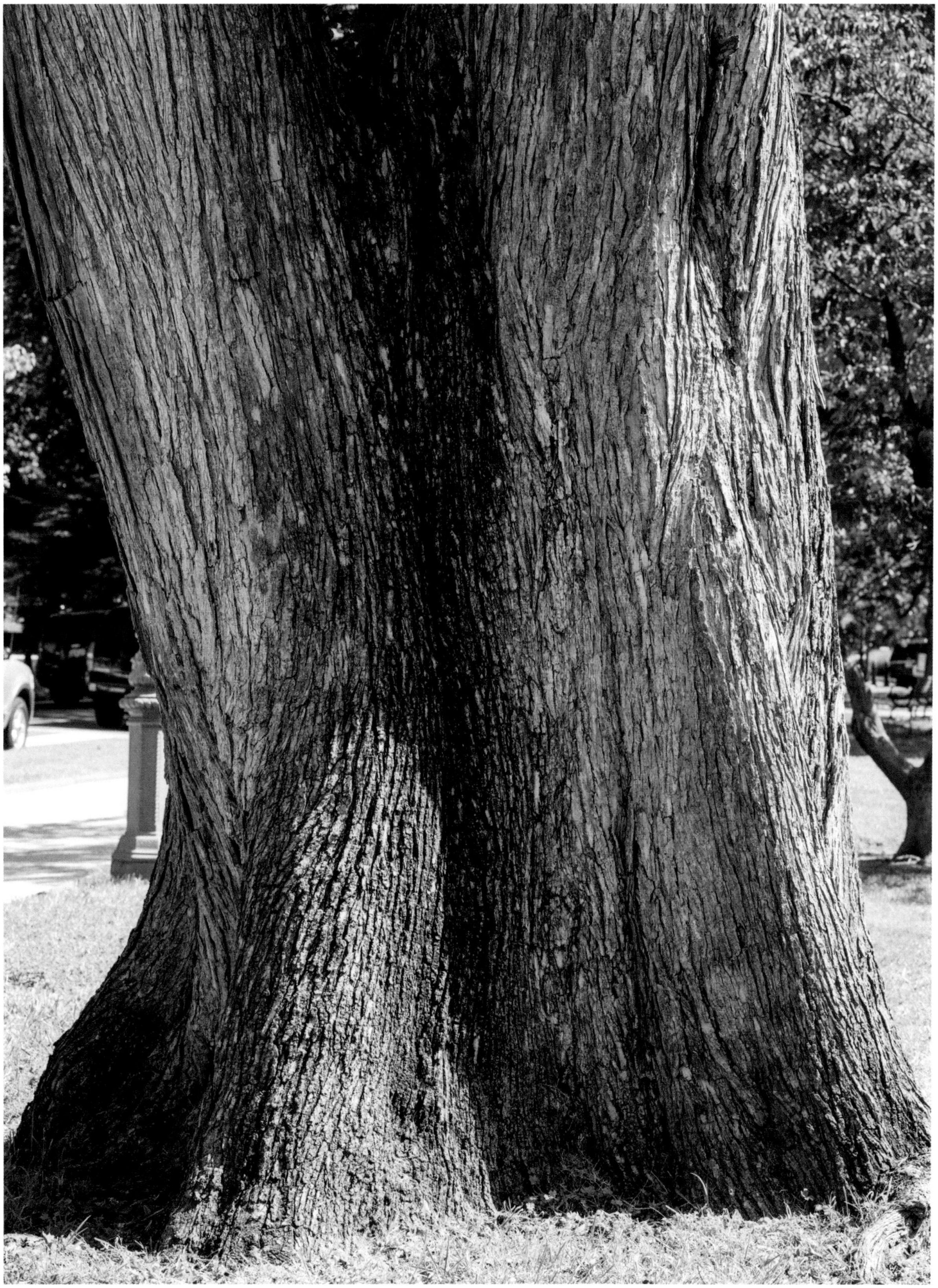

Ulmus × hollandica, Dutch Elm, Holländische Ulme – US Capitol, Washington, DC, 2020

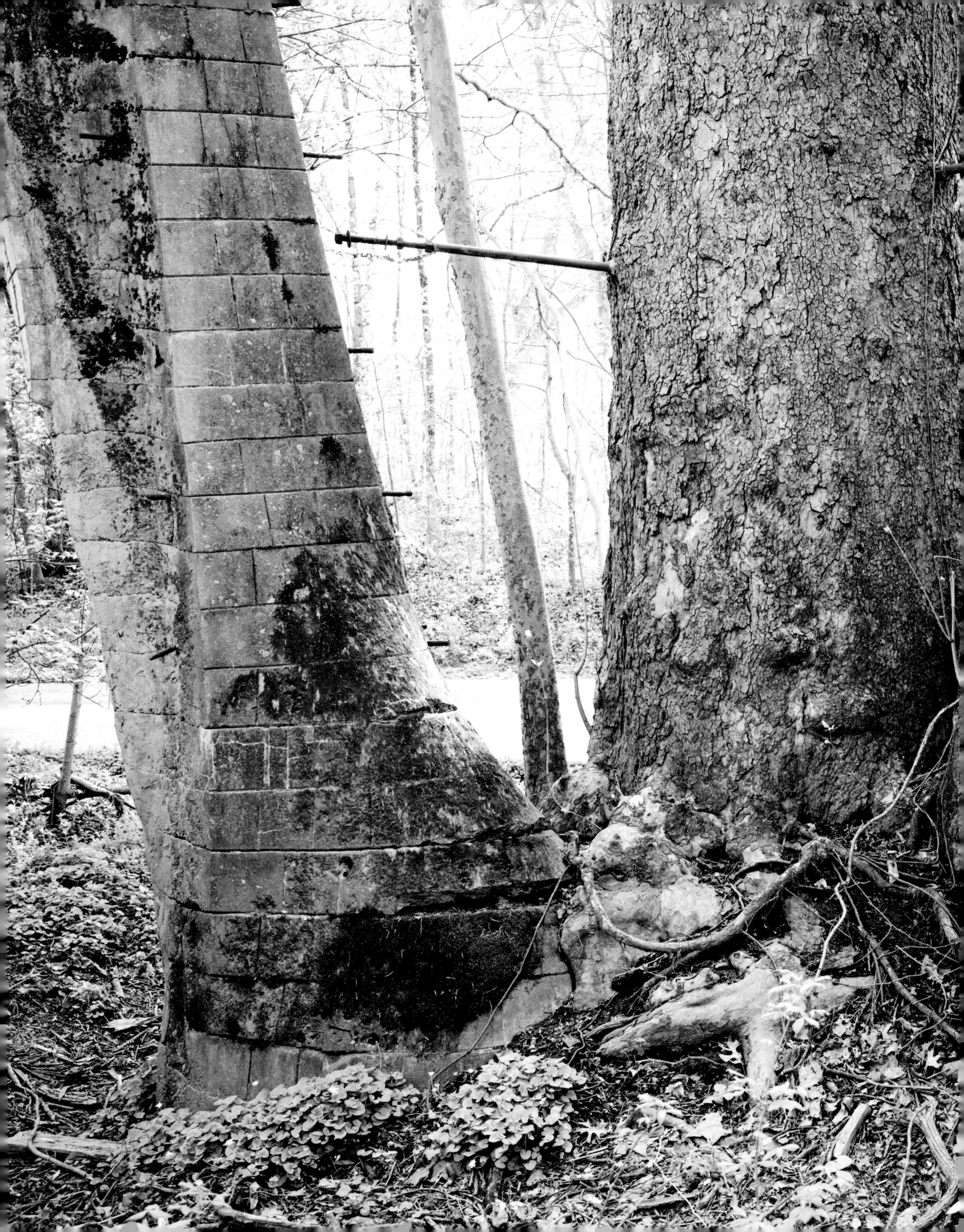

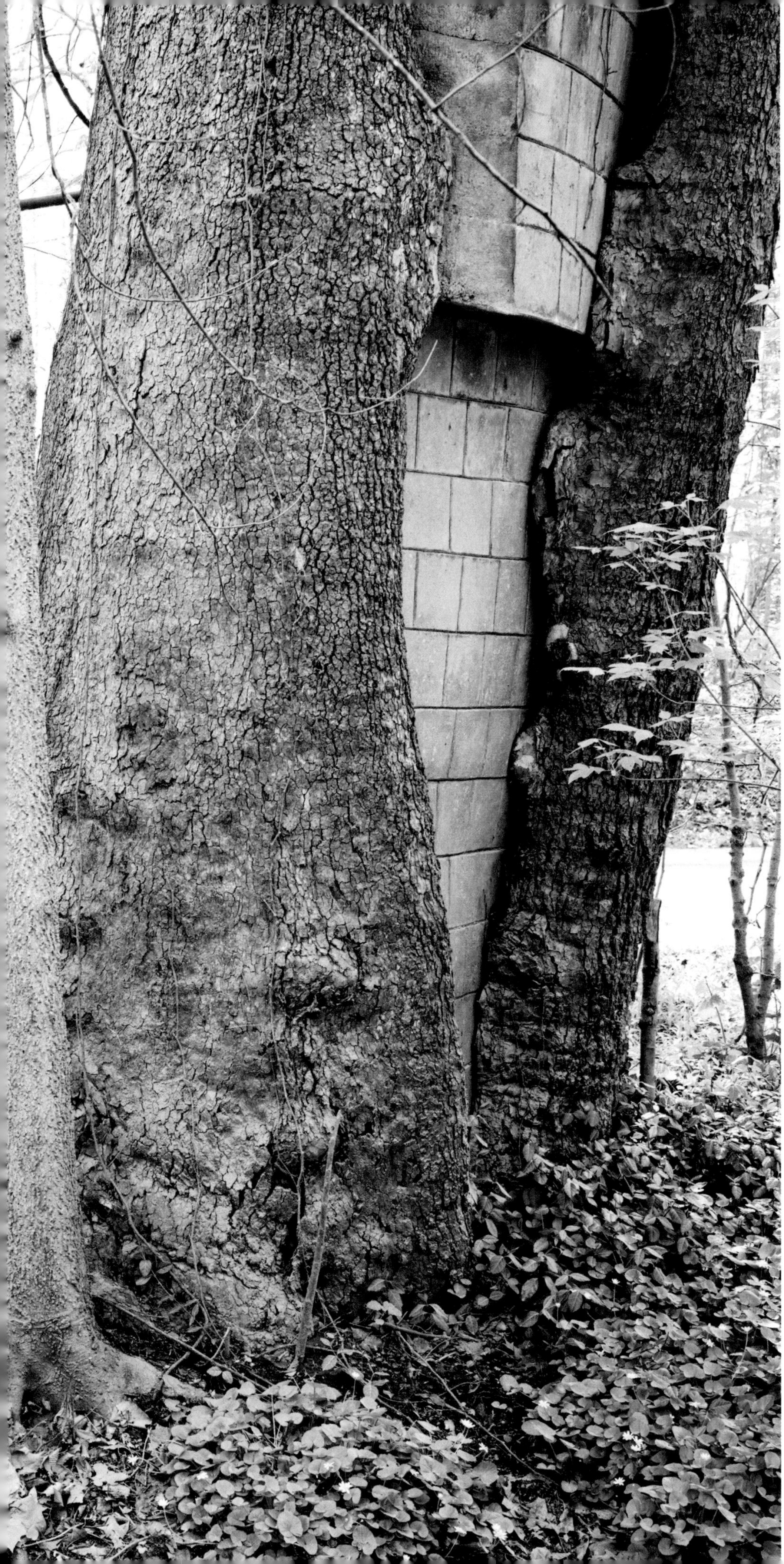

Platanus occidentalis, American Sycamore, Amerikanische Platane – Cherokee Park, Louisville, Kentucky, 2021

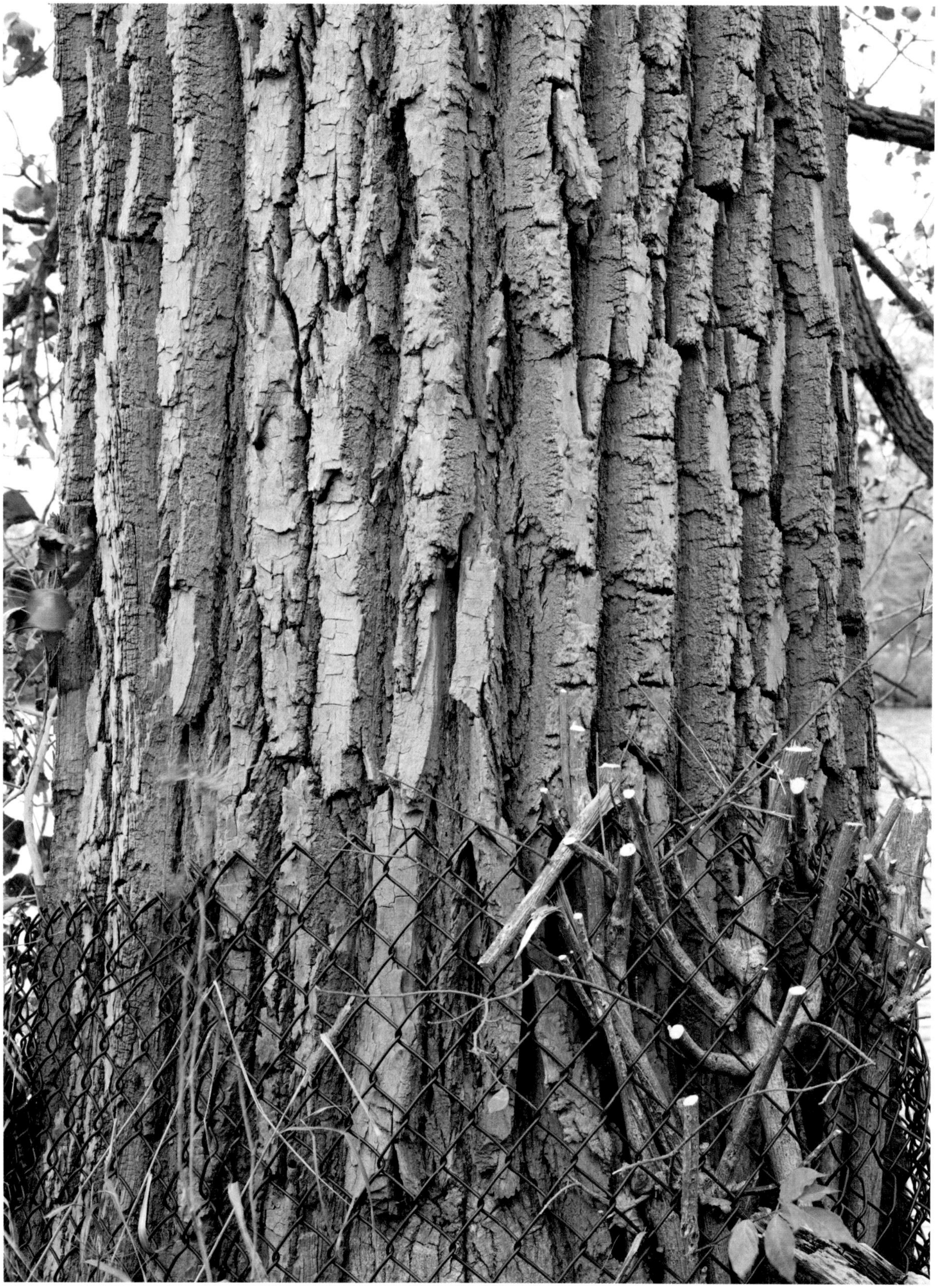

Populus deltoides, Eastern Cottonwood, Kanadische Schwarz-Pappel – Washington Park, Chicago, Illinois, 2019

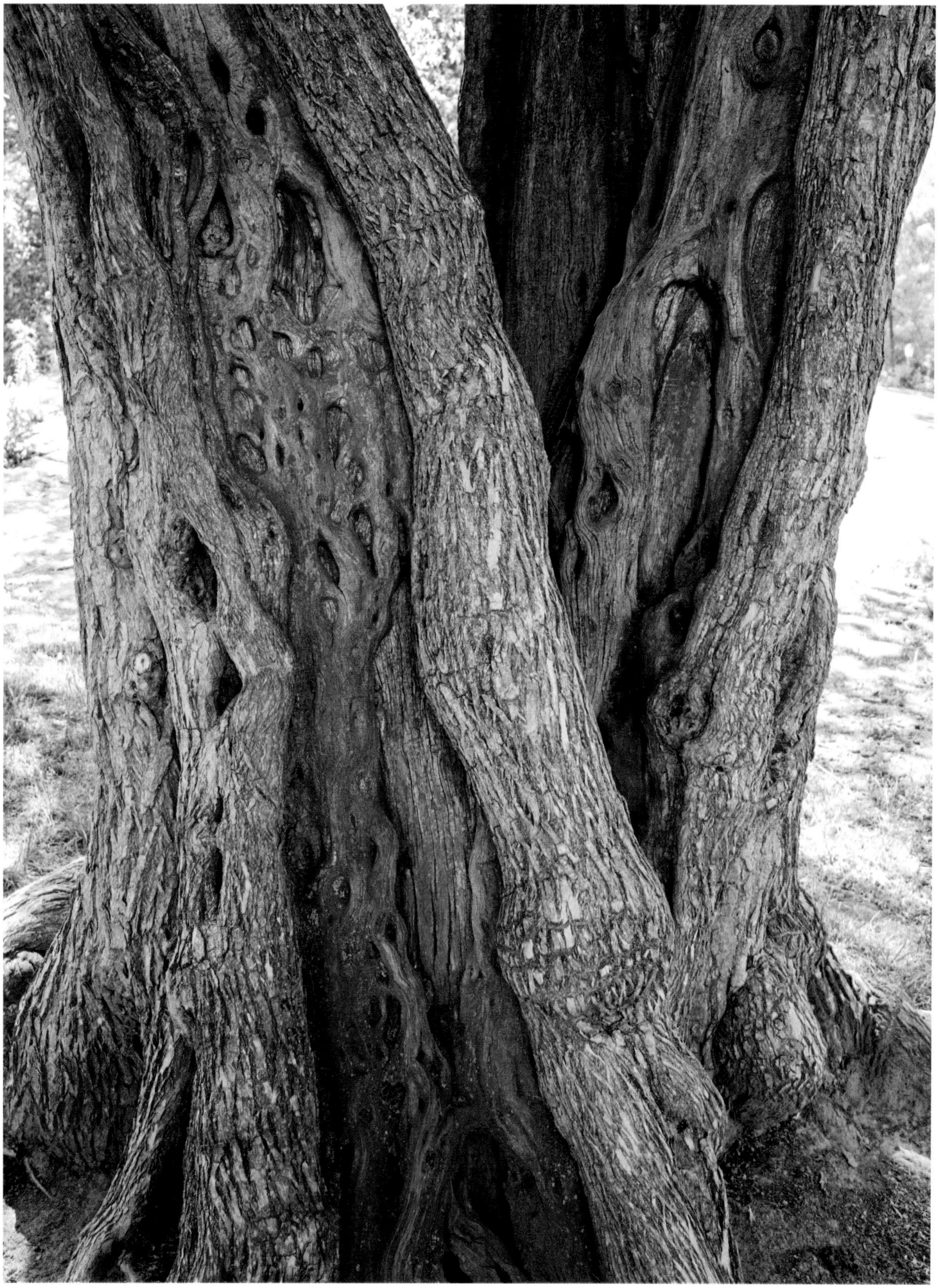

Maclura pomifera, Osage-Orange, Milchorangenbaum – Central Park, New York, New York, 2020

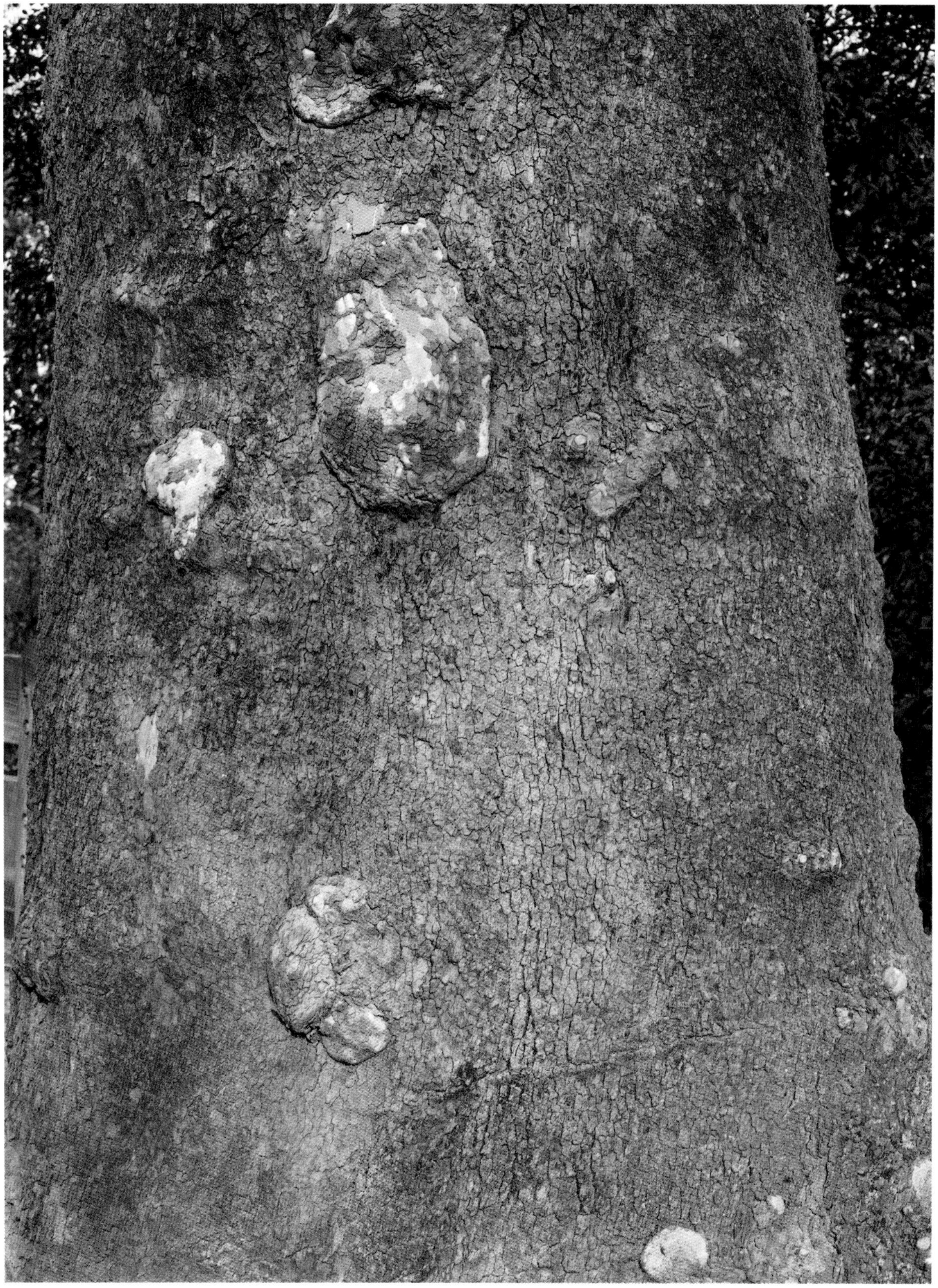

Platanus occidentalis, American Sycamore, Amerikanische Platane – Central Park, New York, New York, 2019

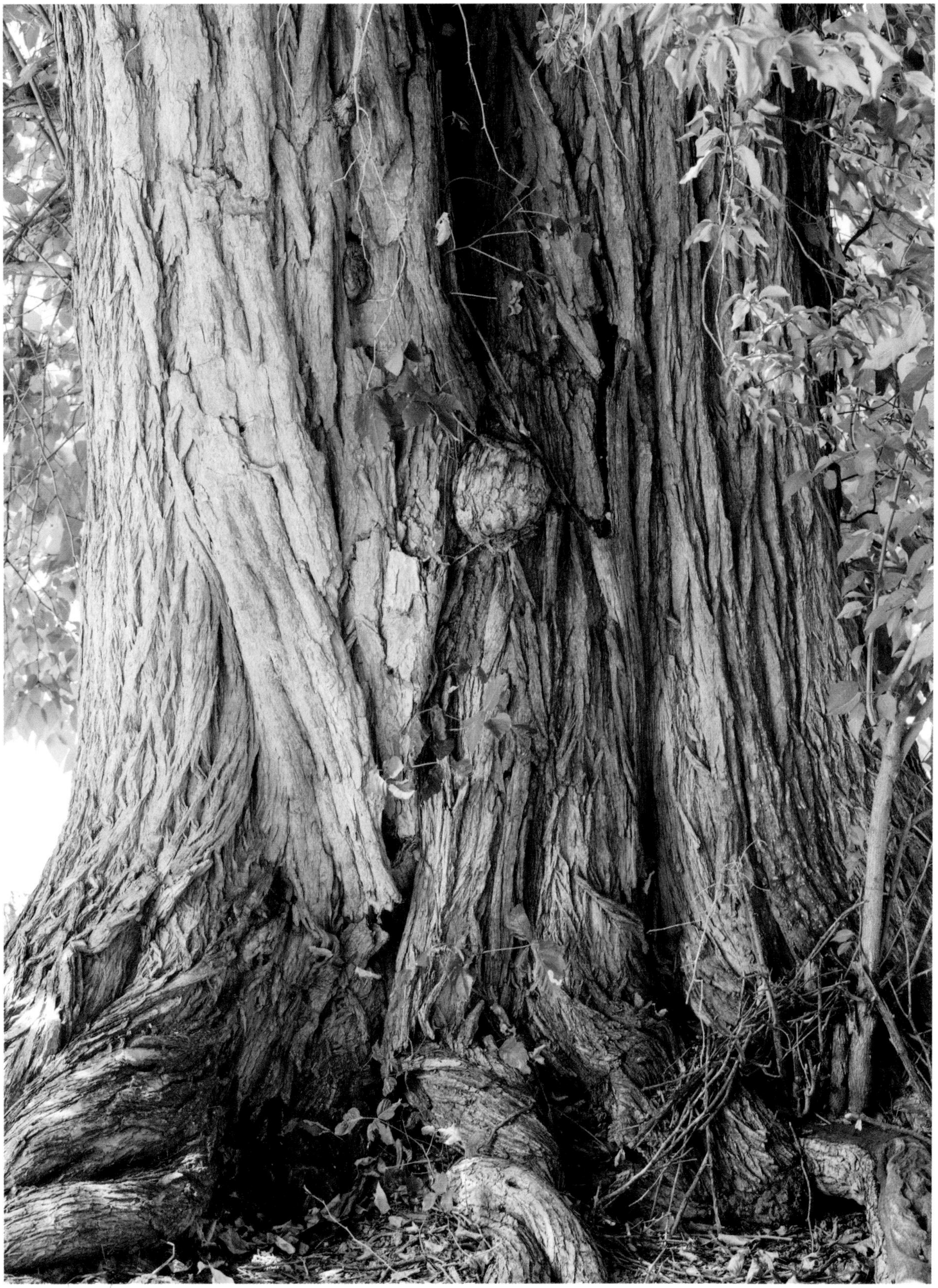

Maclura pomifera, Osage-Orange, Milchorangenbaum – Downing Park, Newburgh, New York, 2020

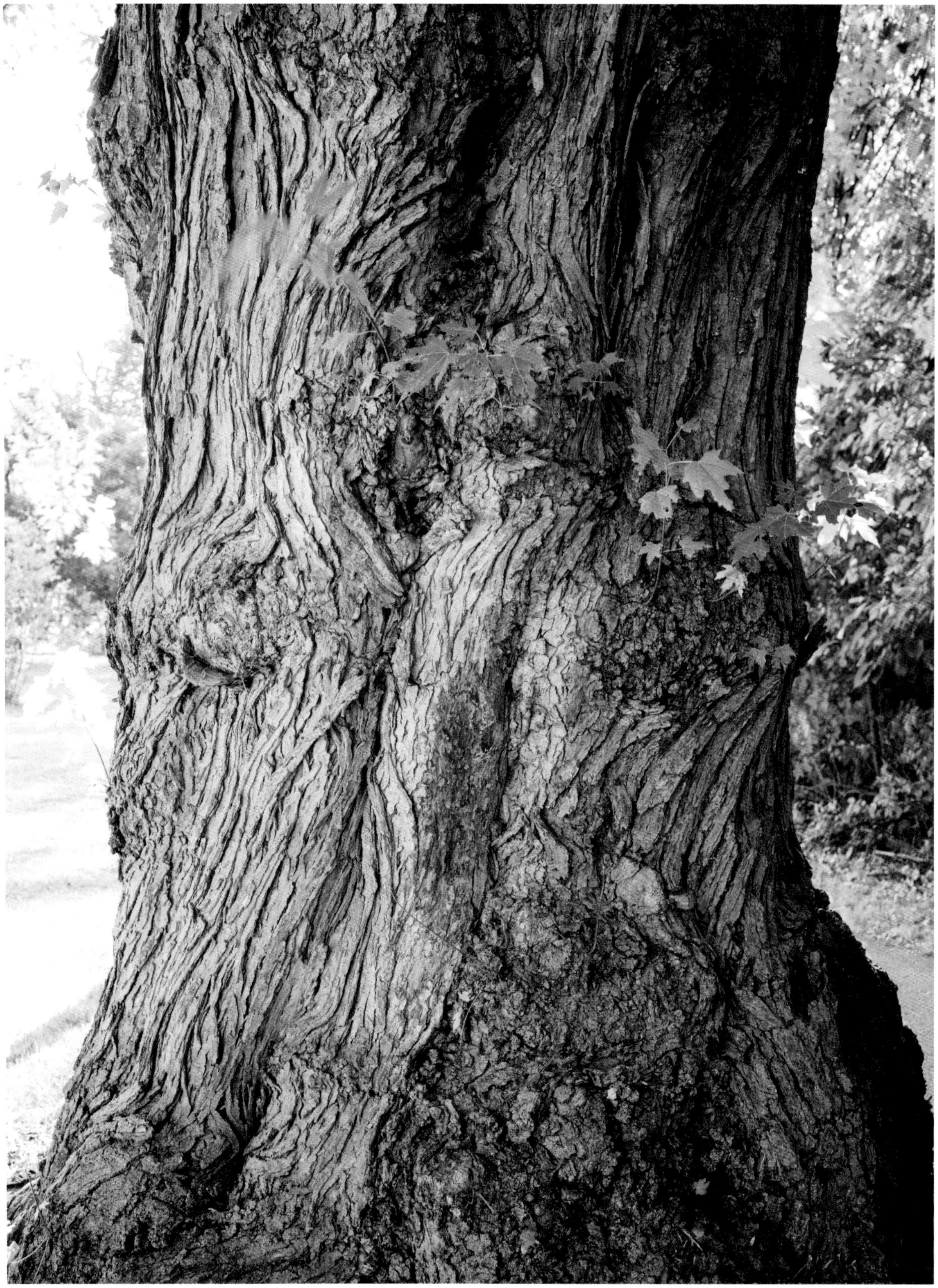

Acer saccharinum, Silver Maple, Silber-Ahorn – Lake Park, Milwaukee, Wisconsin, 2021

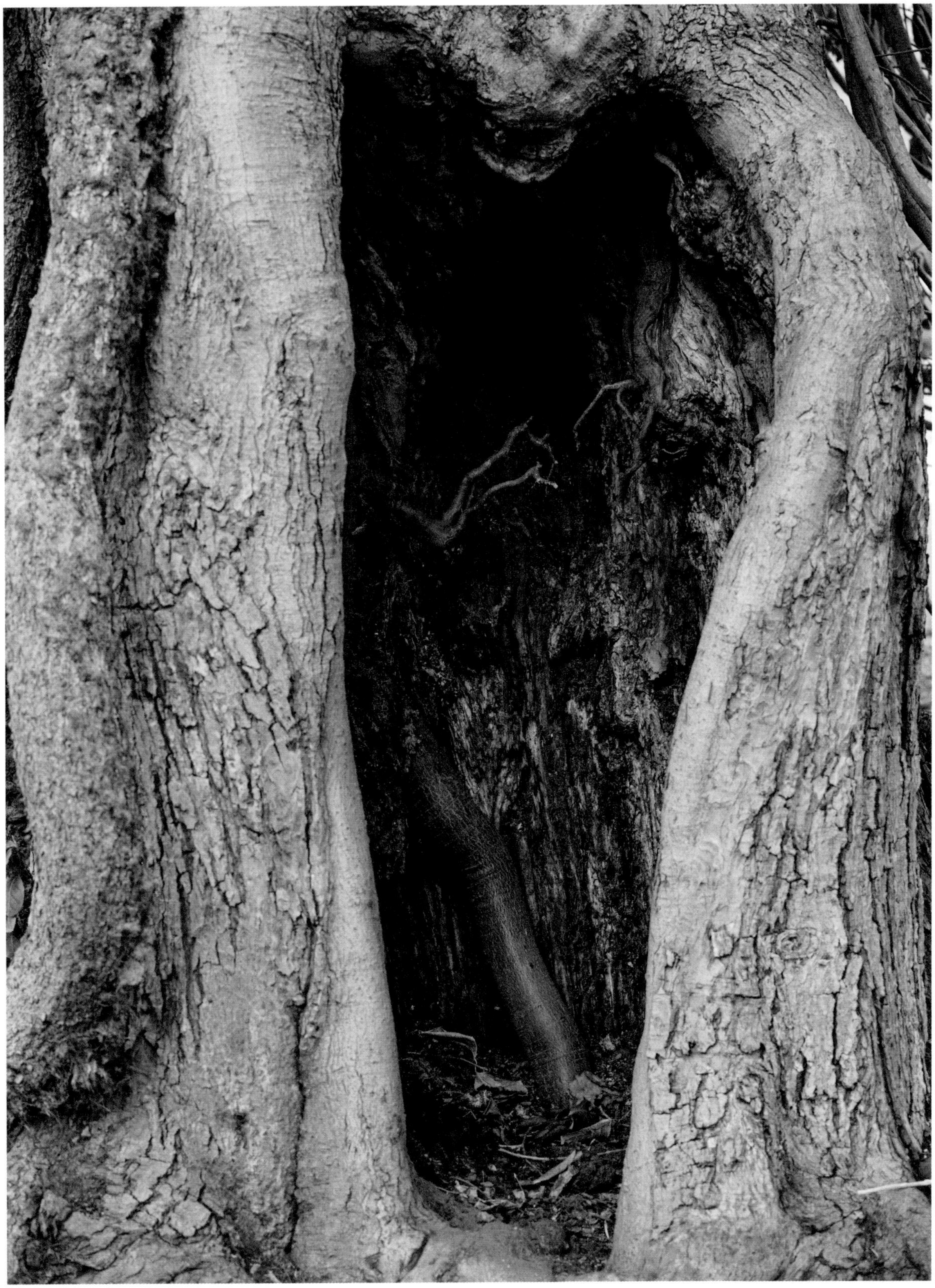

Acer rubrum, Red Maple, Rot-Ahorn – Arnold Arboretum, Boston, Massachusetts, 2020

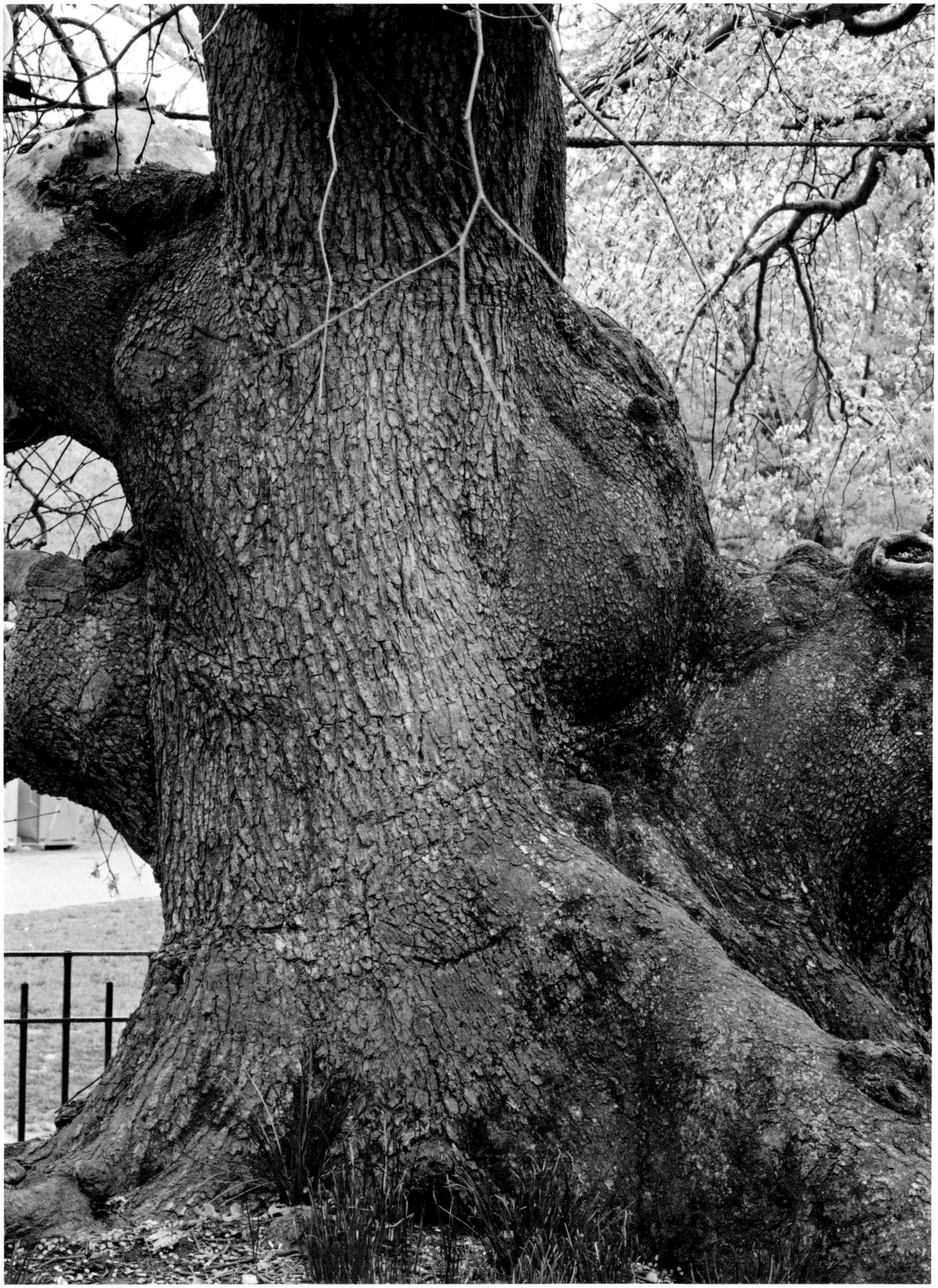

Ulmus glabra "Camperdownii," Camperdown Elm, Lauben-Ulme – Prospect Park, Brooklyn, New York, 2019

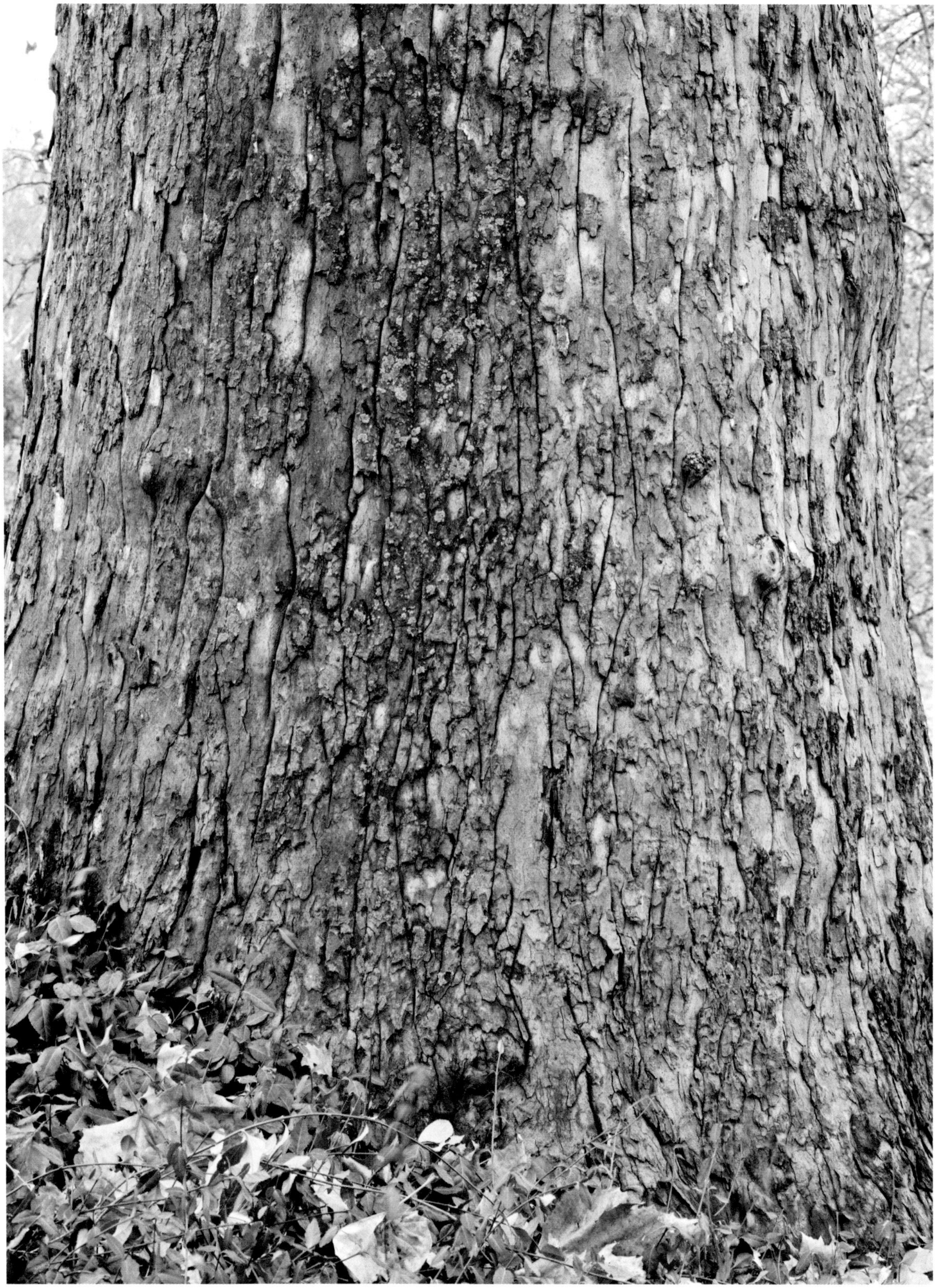

Platanus × acerifolia, London Plane, Ahornblättrige Platane – Arnold Arboretum, Boston, Massachusetts, 2019

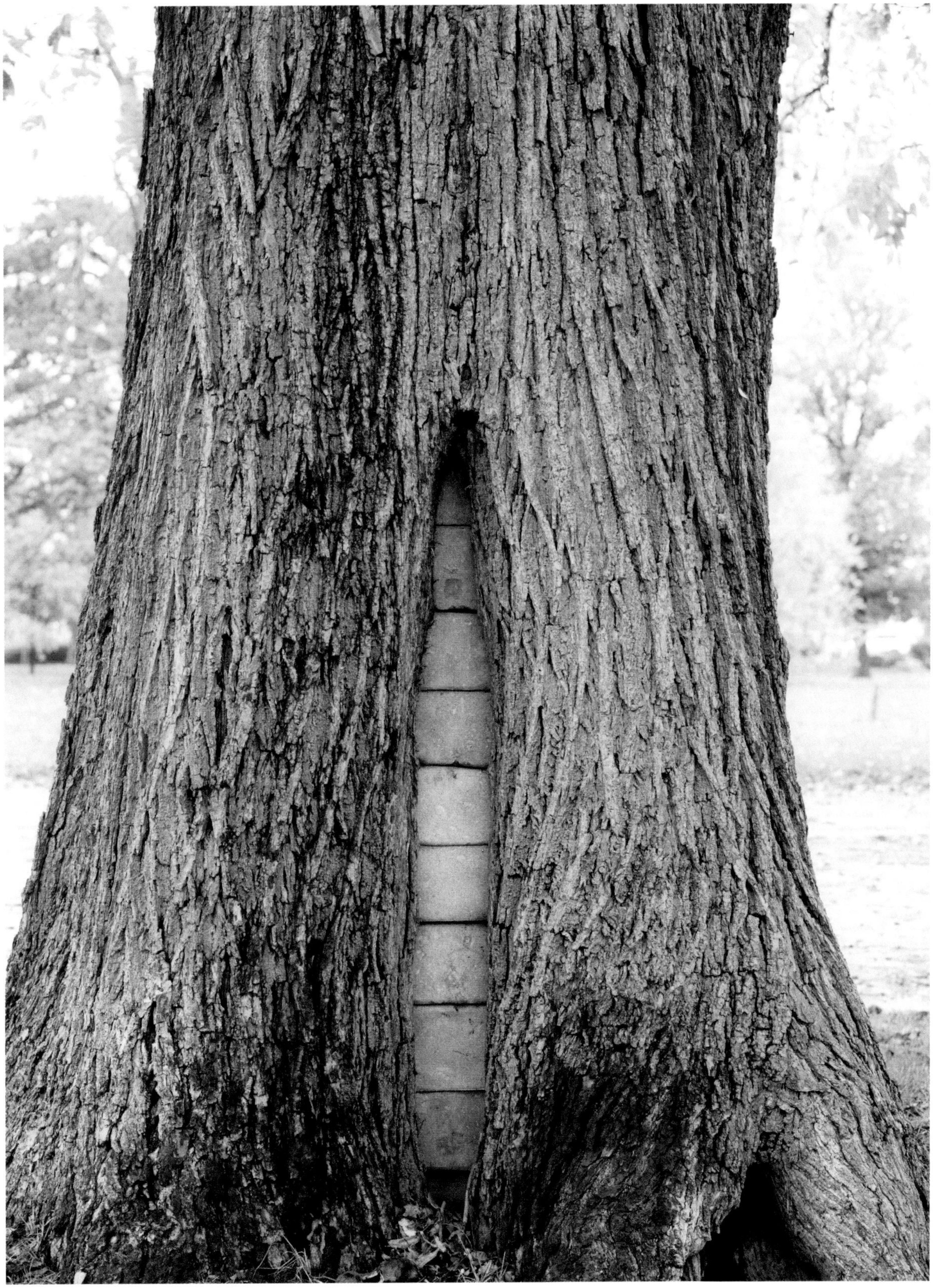

Juglans nigra, Black Walnut, Schwarznuss – Delaware Park, Buffalo, New York, 2020

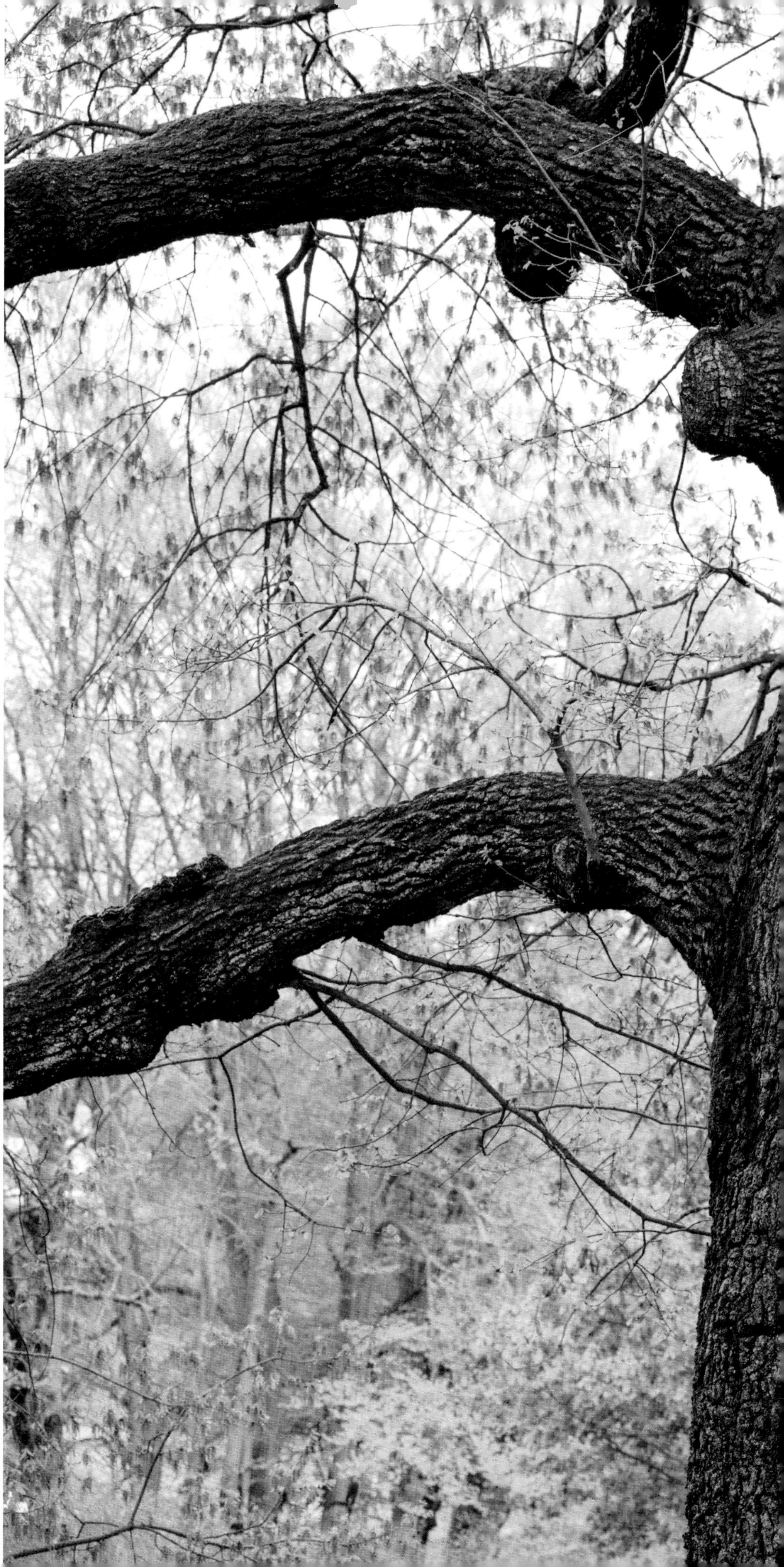

Quercus × sargentii,
Sargent Oak, Eiche (Hybridform)
– Arnold Arboretum, Boston,
Massachusetts, 2020

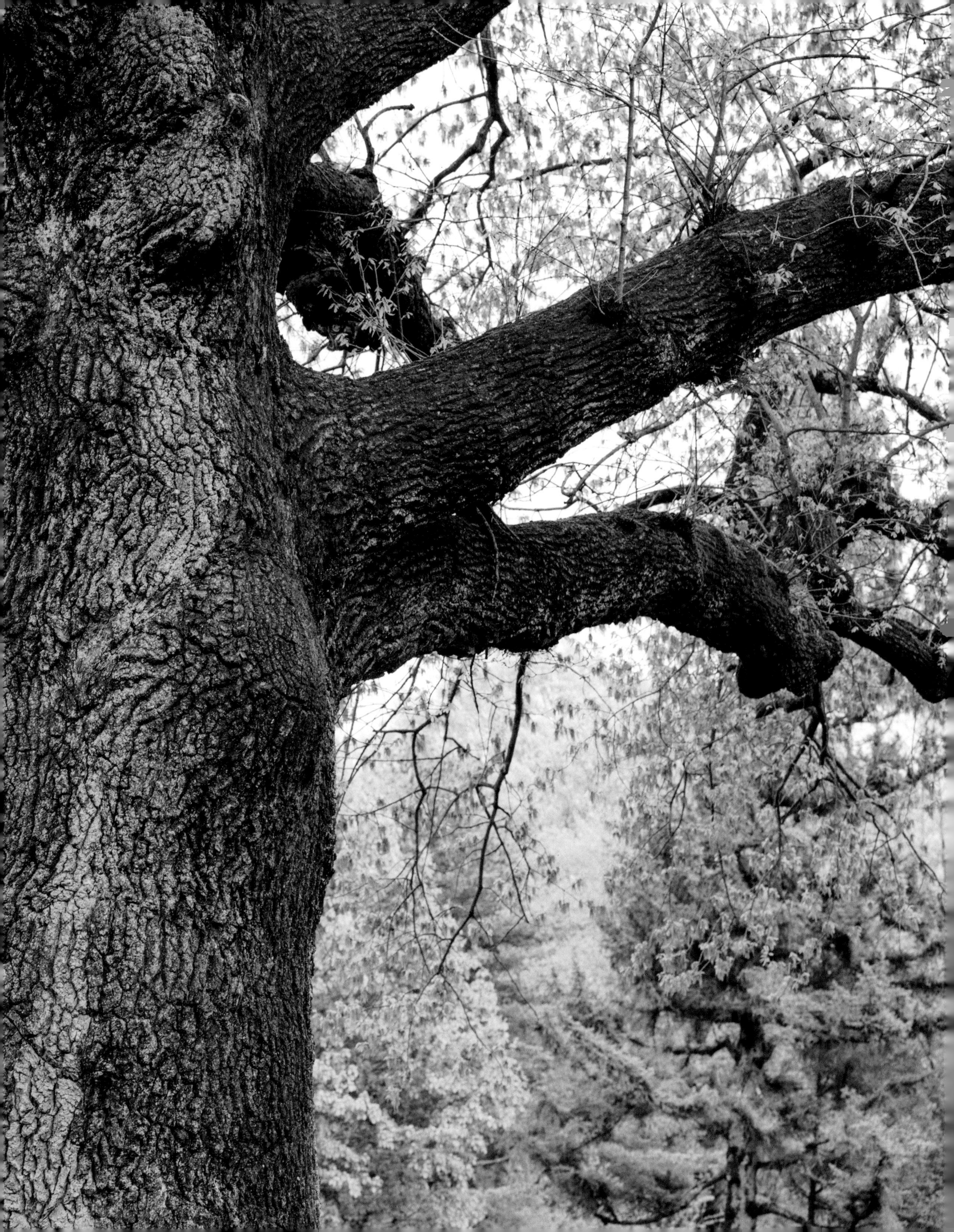

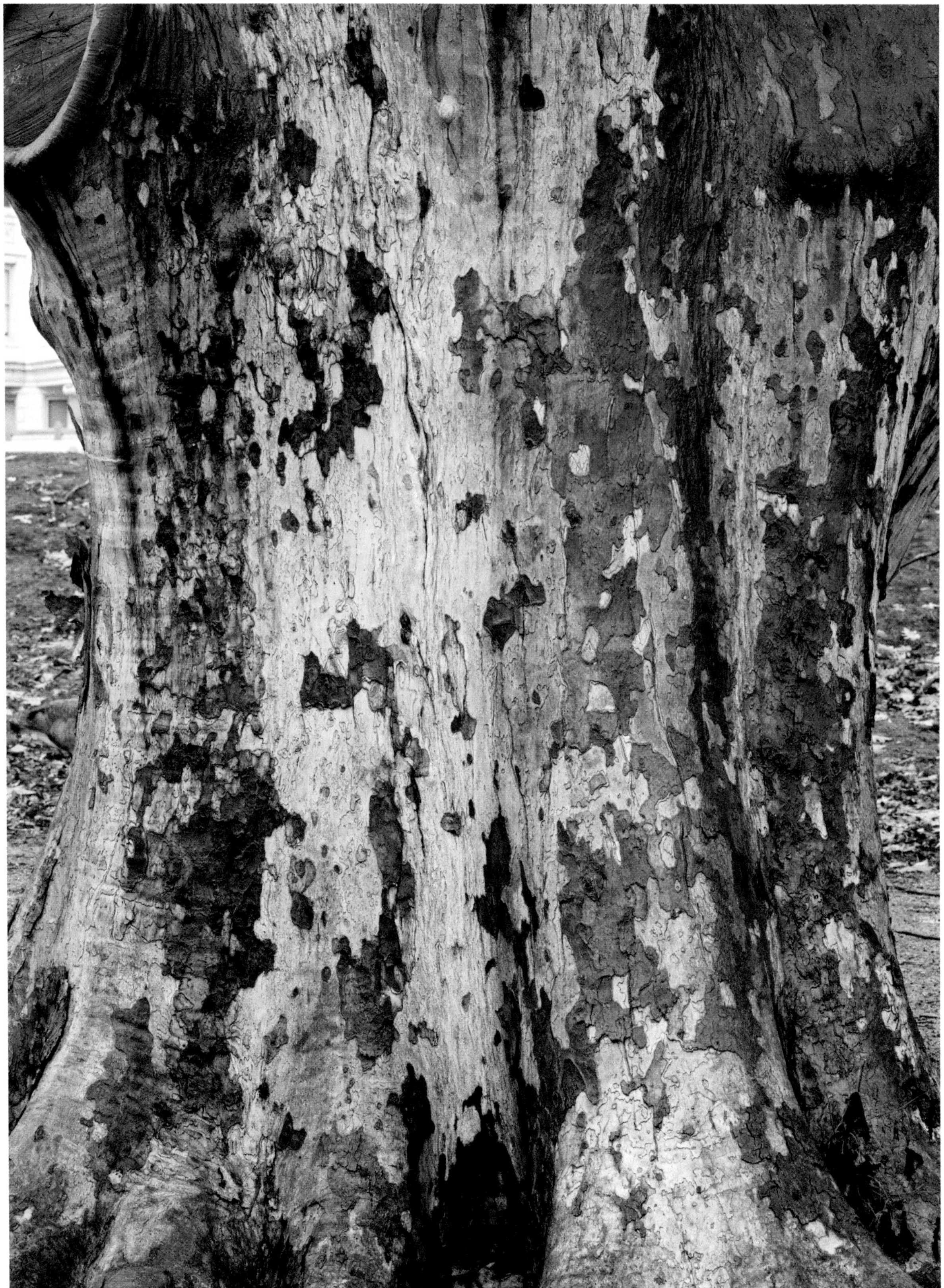

Platanus × acerifolia, London Plane, Ahornblättrige Platane – Backbay Fens, Boston, Massachusetts, 2019

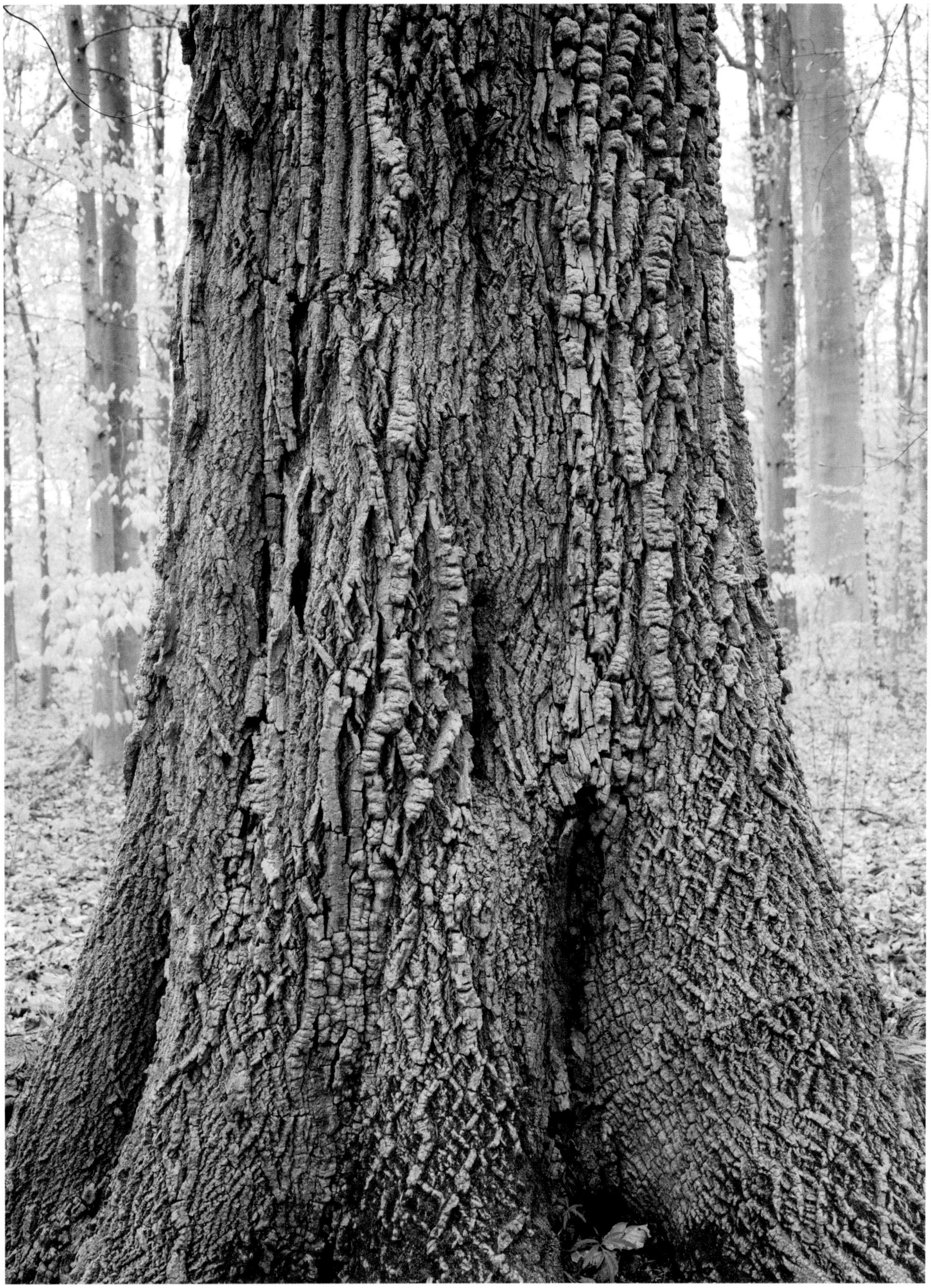

Liriodendron tulipfera, Tulip Tree, Tulpenbaum – Iroquois Park, Louisville, Kentucky, 2021

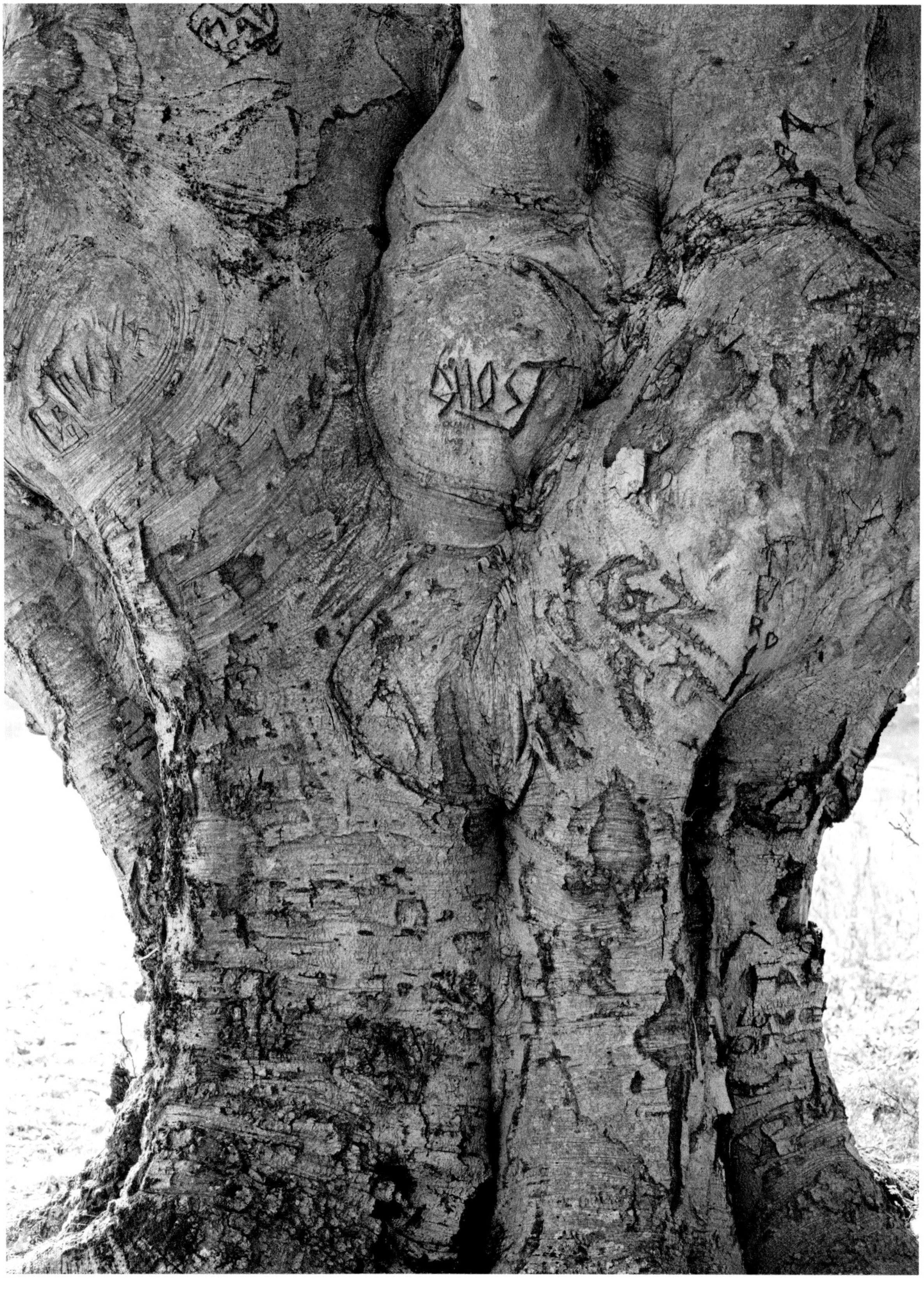

Fagus grandifolia, American Beech, Amerikanische Buche – Cadwalader Park, Trenton, New Jersey, 2019

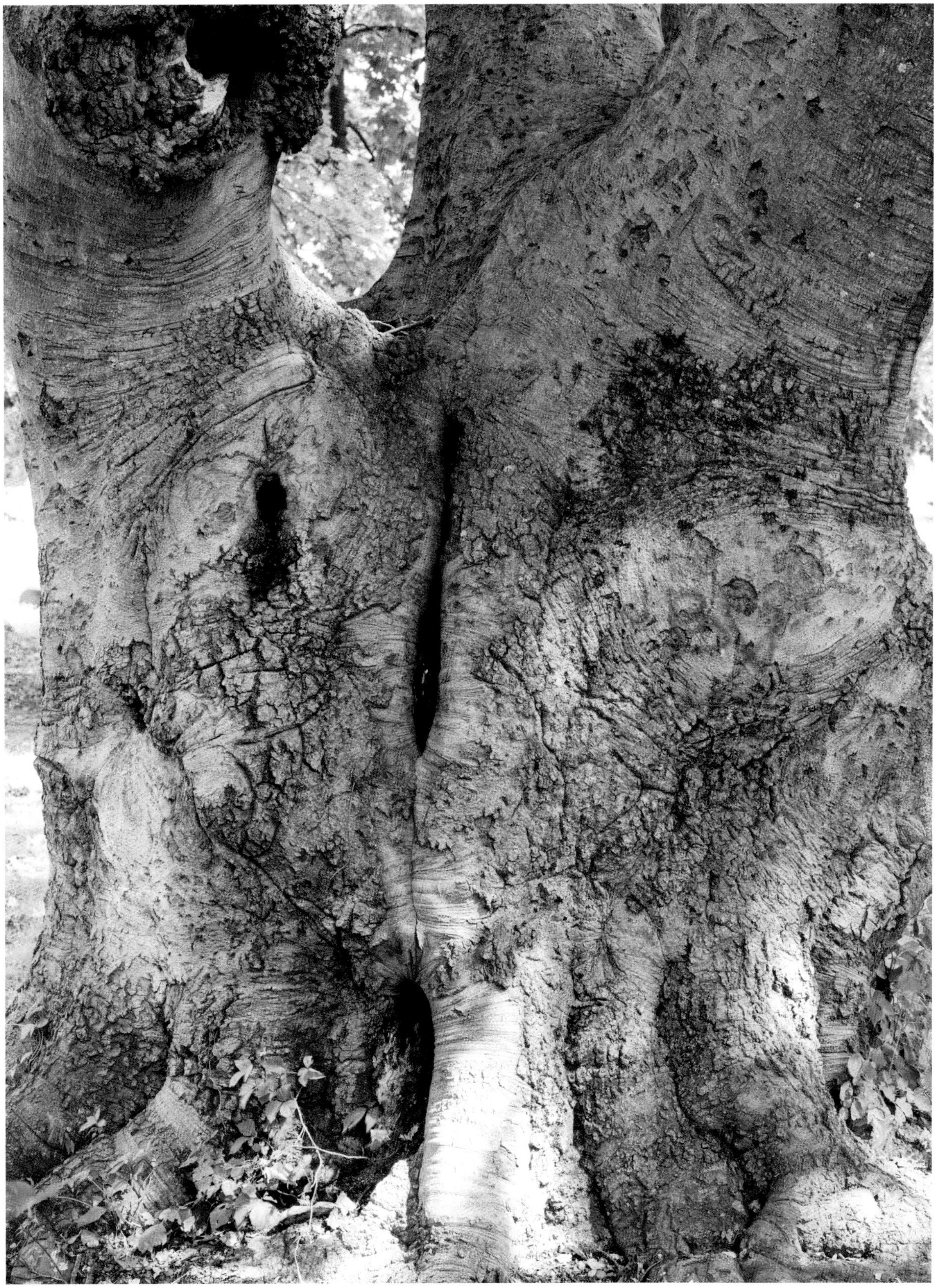

Fagus grandifolia, American Beech, Amerikanische Buche – Downing Park, Newburgh, New York, 2020

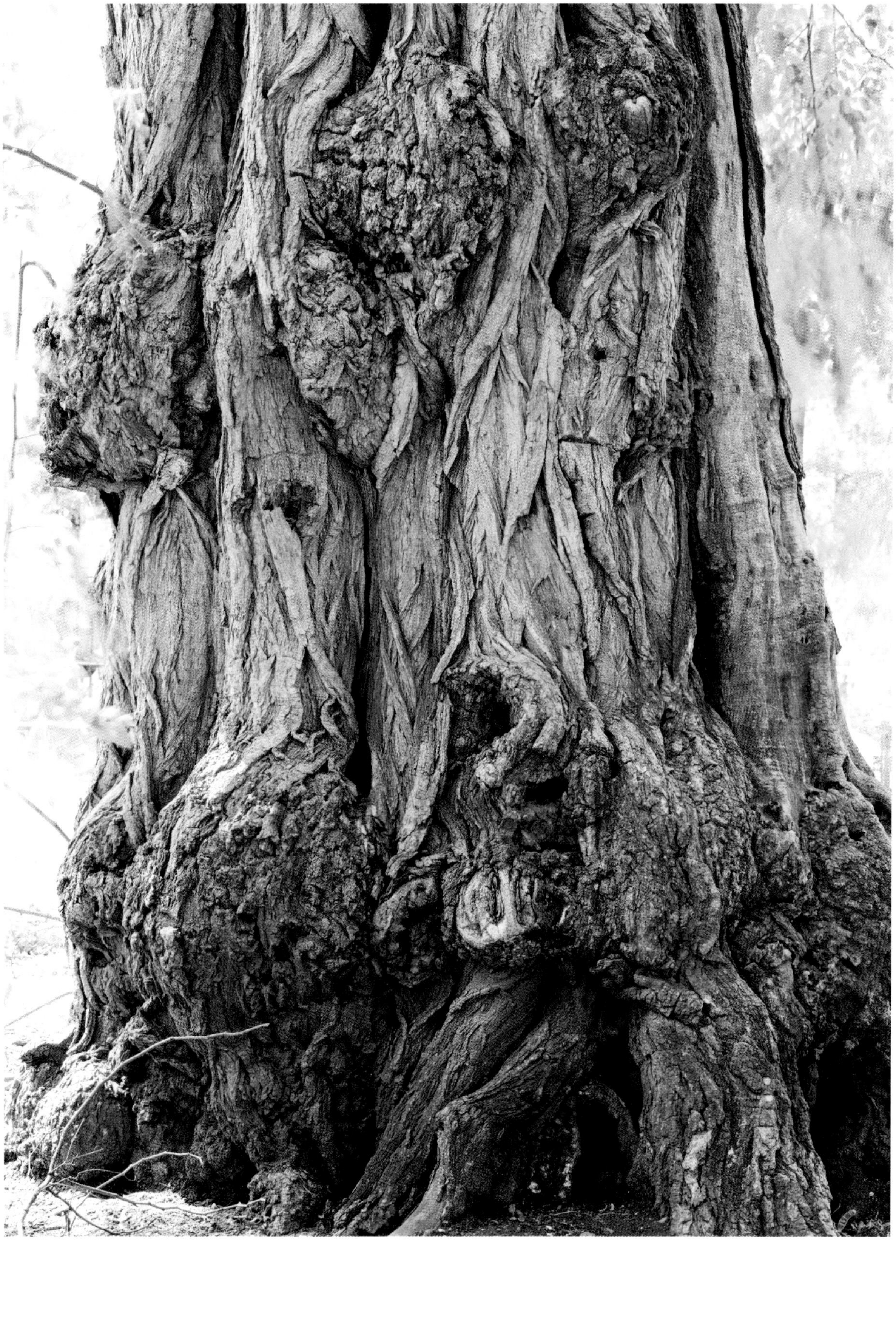

Robinia pseudoacacia, Black Locust, Scheinakazie (Robinie) – Tompkins Square Park, New York, New York, 2020

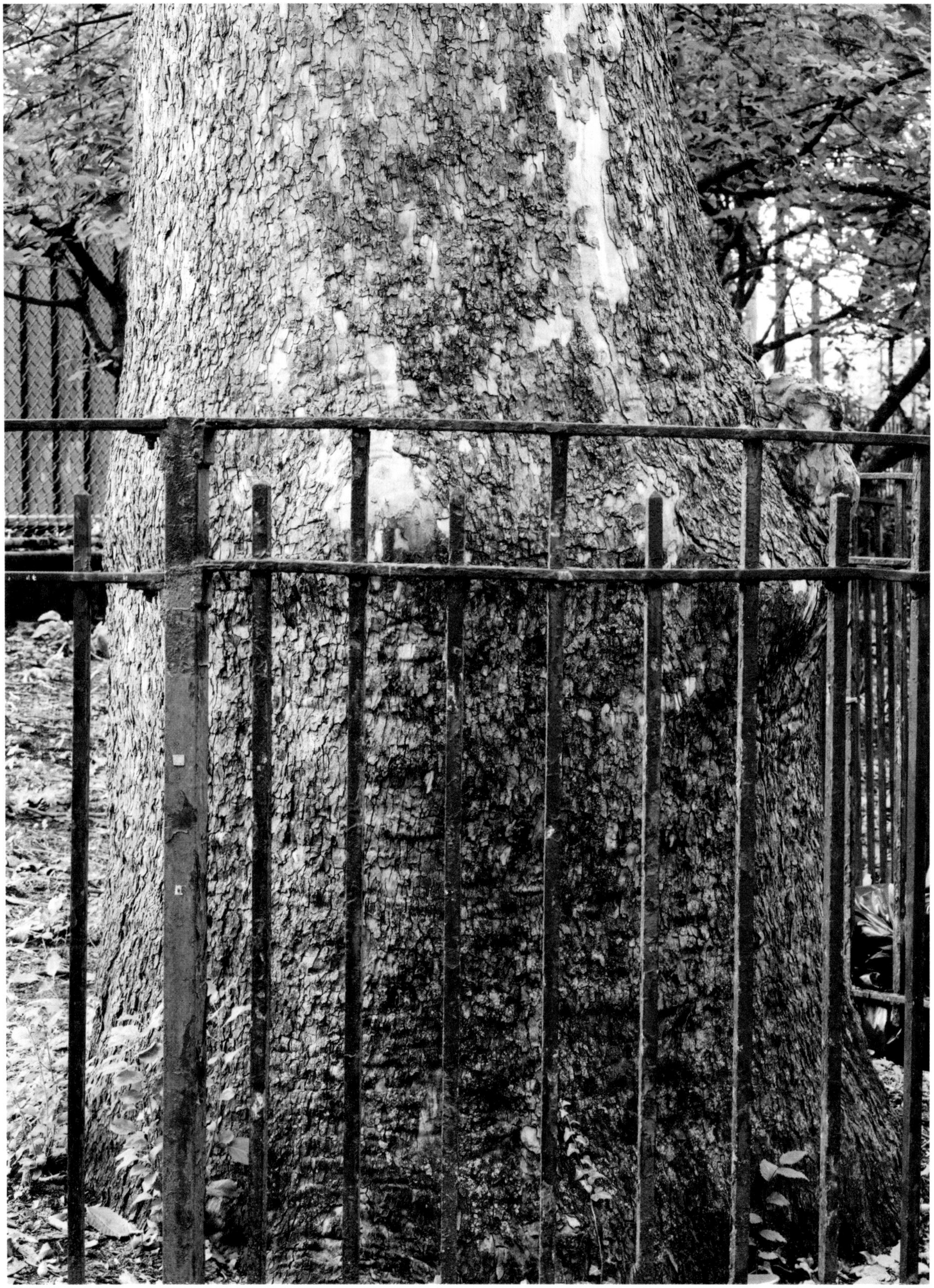

 Platanus occidentalis, American Sycamore, Amerikanische Platane – Tompkins Square Park, New York, New York, 2020

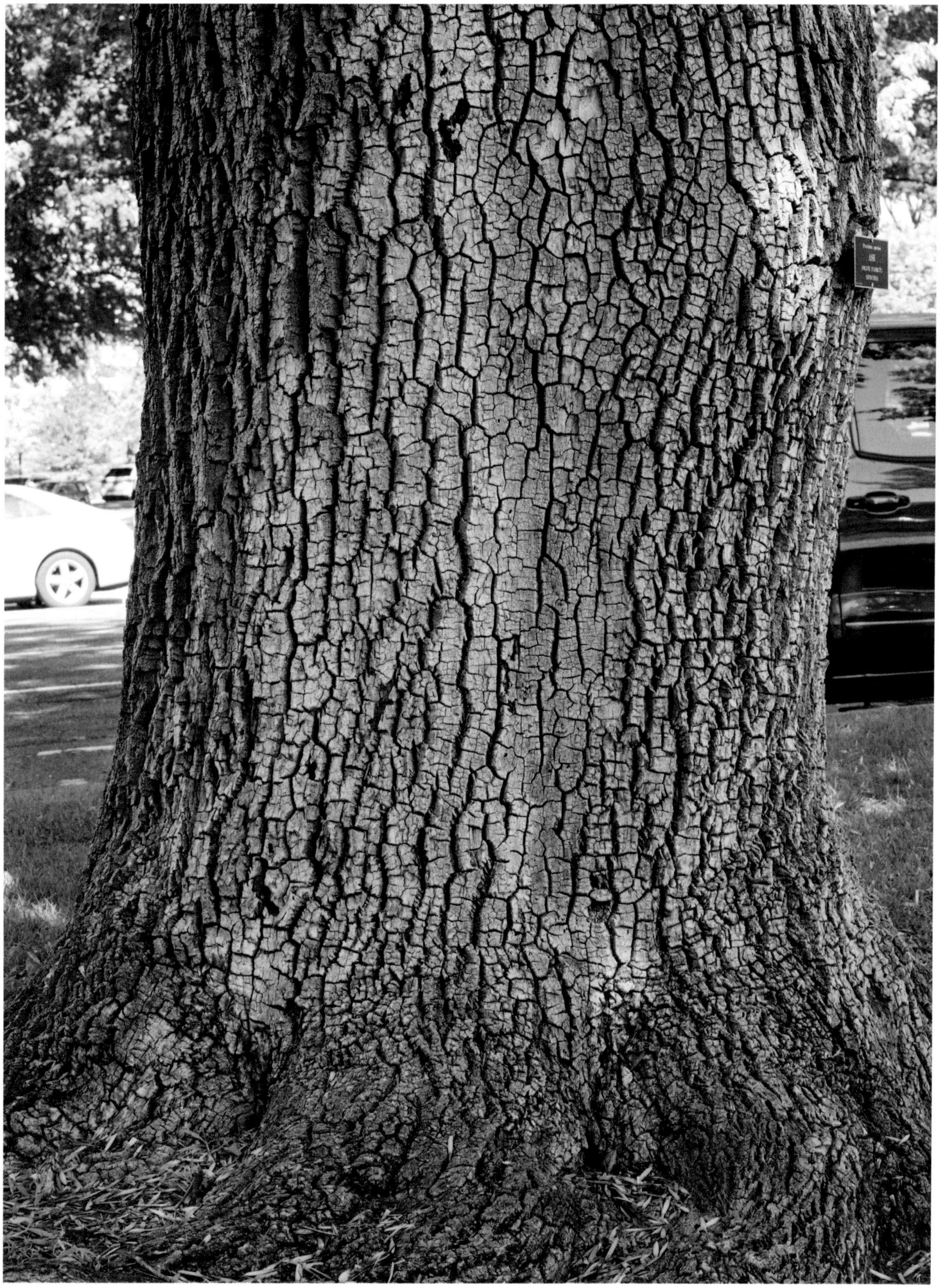

Fraxinus americana, White Ash, Weiß-Esche – US Capitol, Washington, DC, 2020

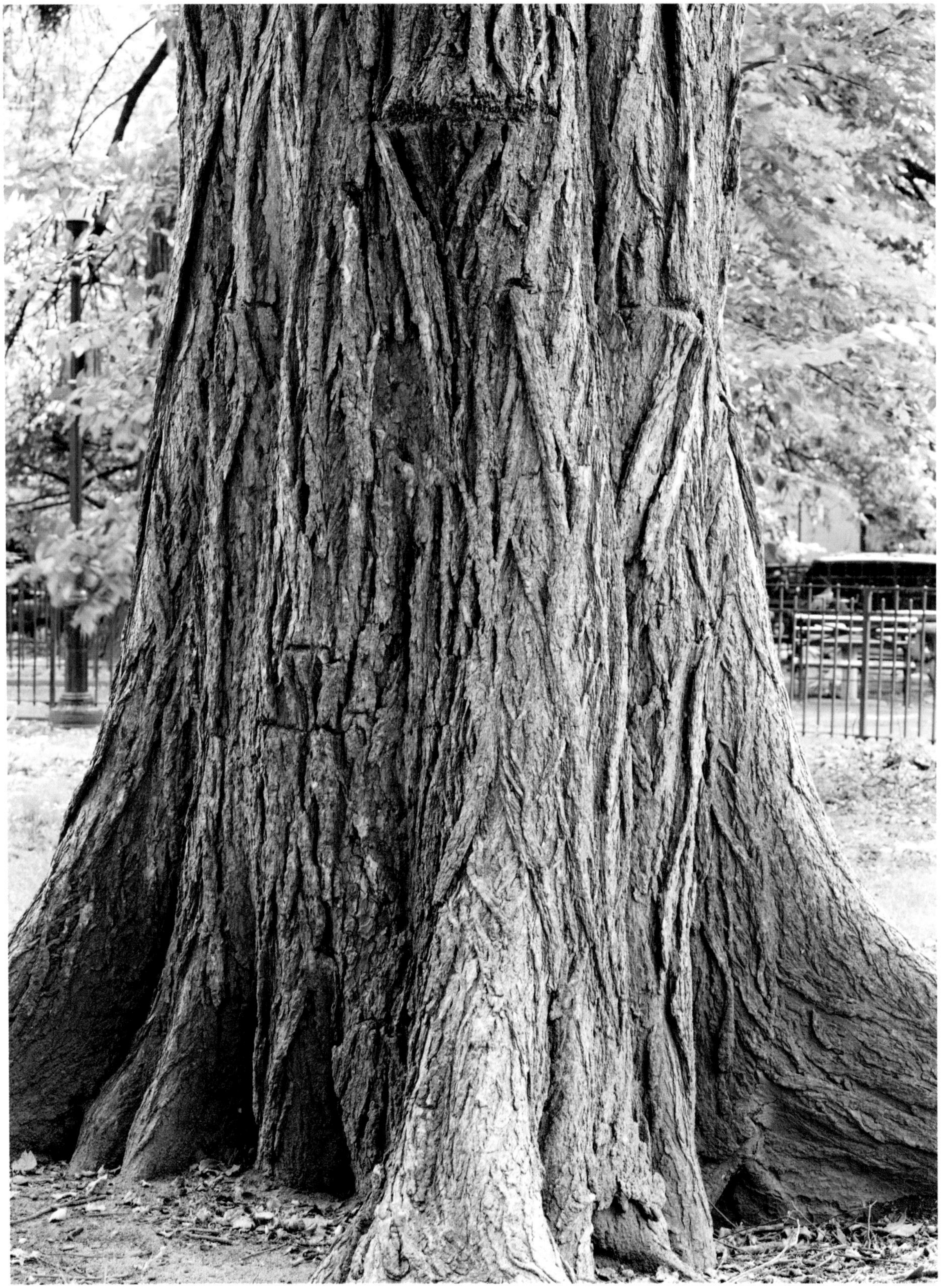

Ulmus americana, American Elm, Amerikanische Ulme – Tompkins Square Park, New York, New York, 2020

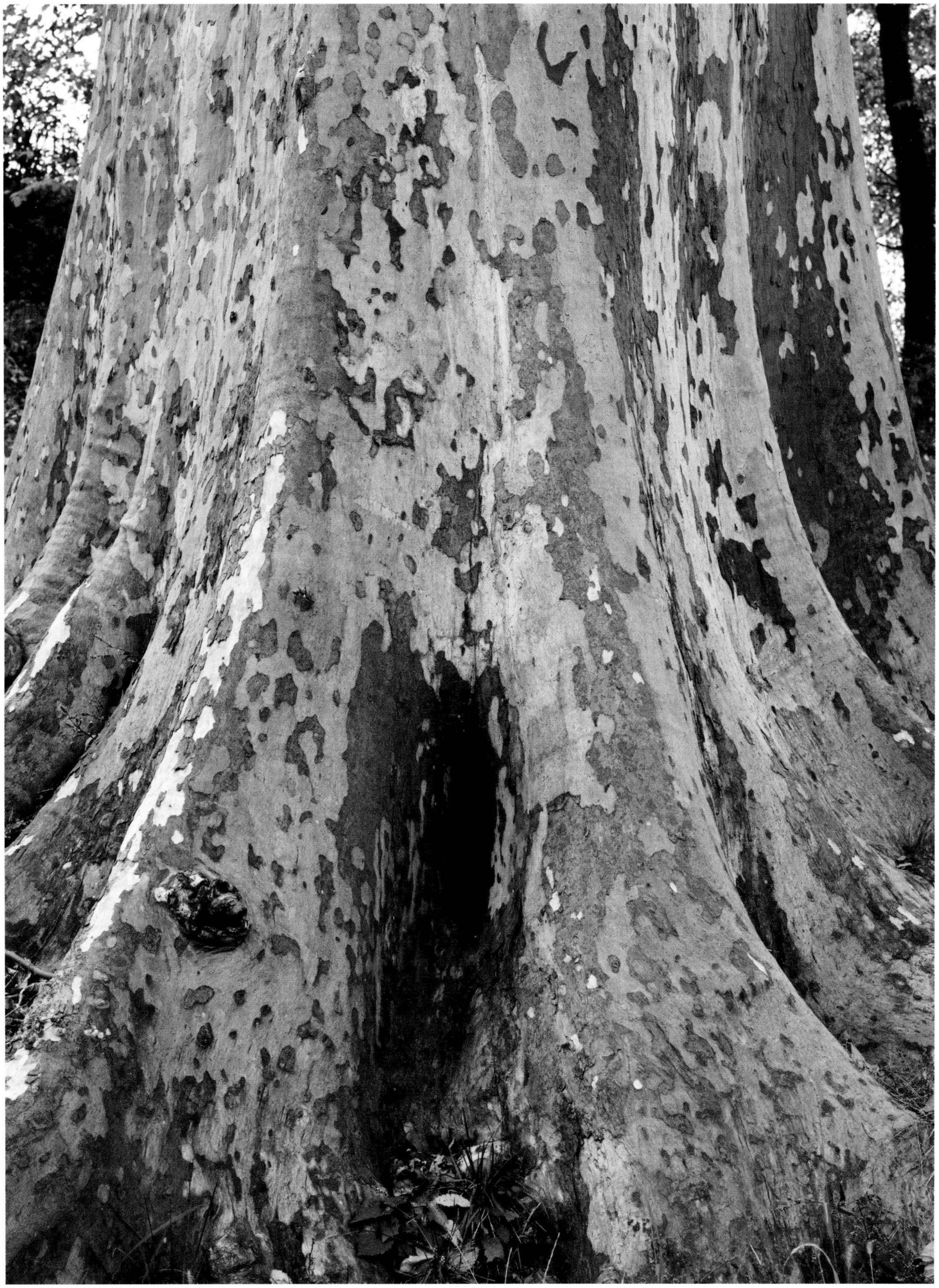

Platanus × acerifolia, London Plane, Ahornblättrige Platane – Central Park, New York, New York, 2019

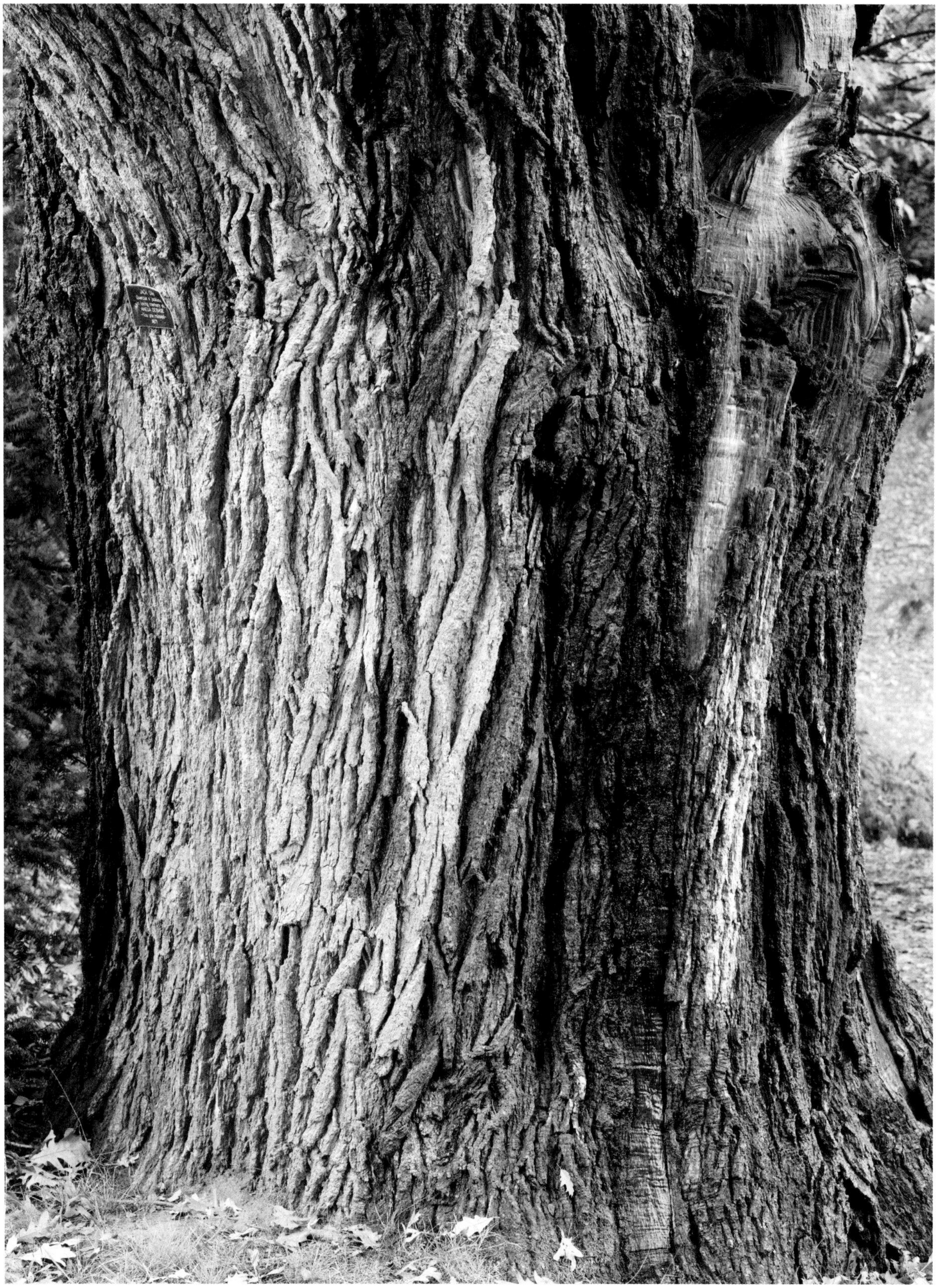

Quercus ellipsoidalis, Jack Oak, Nadel-Eiche – Highland Park, Rochester, New York, 2020

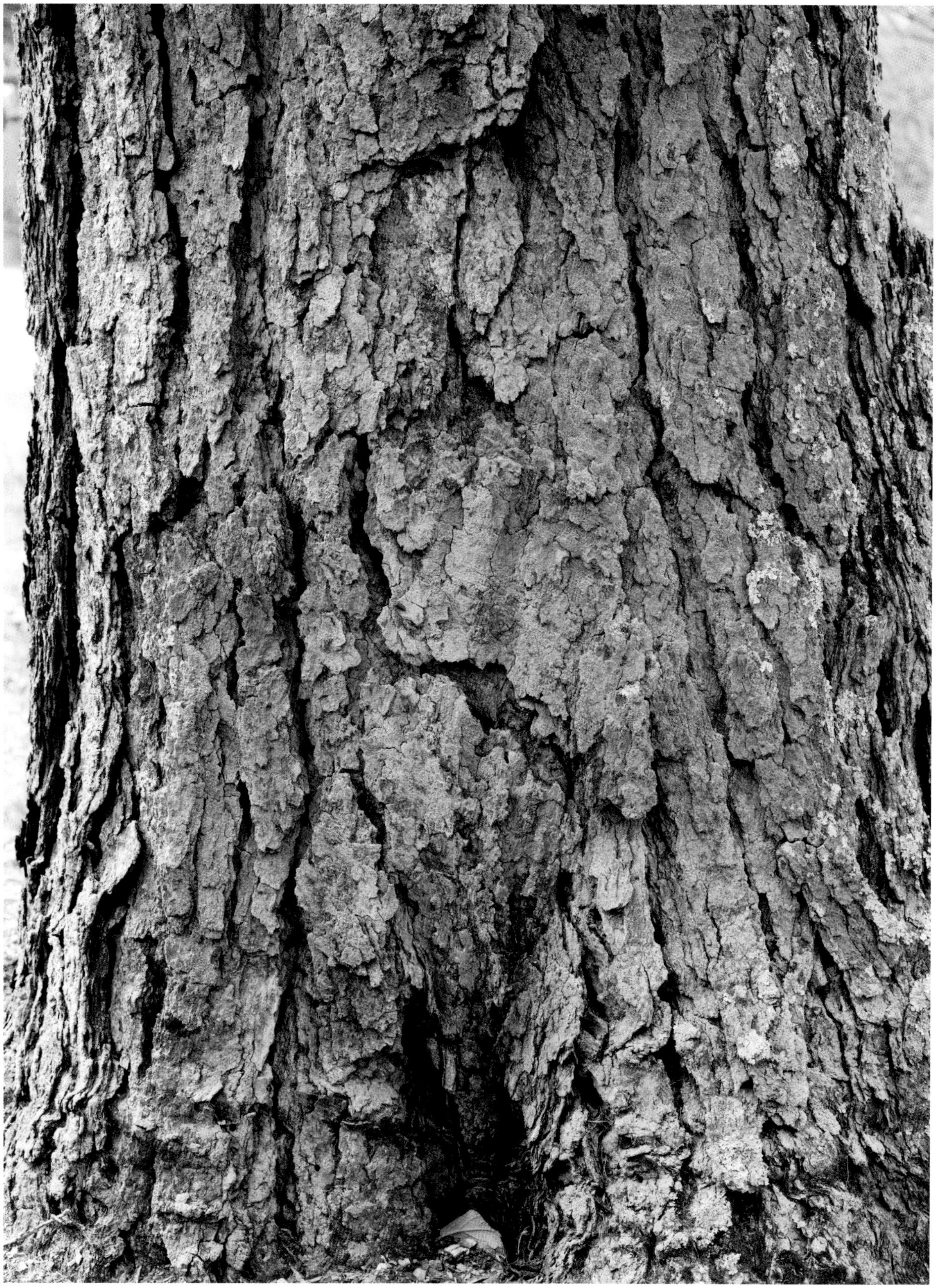

Betula nigra, River Birch, Schwarz-Birke – Arnold Arboretum, Boston, Massachusetts, 2020

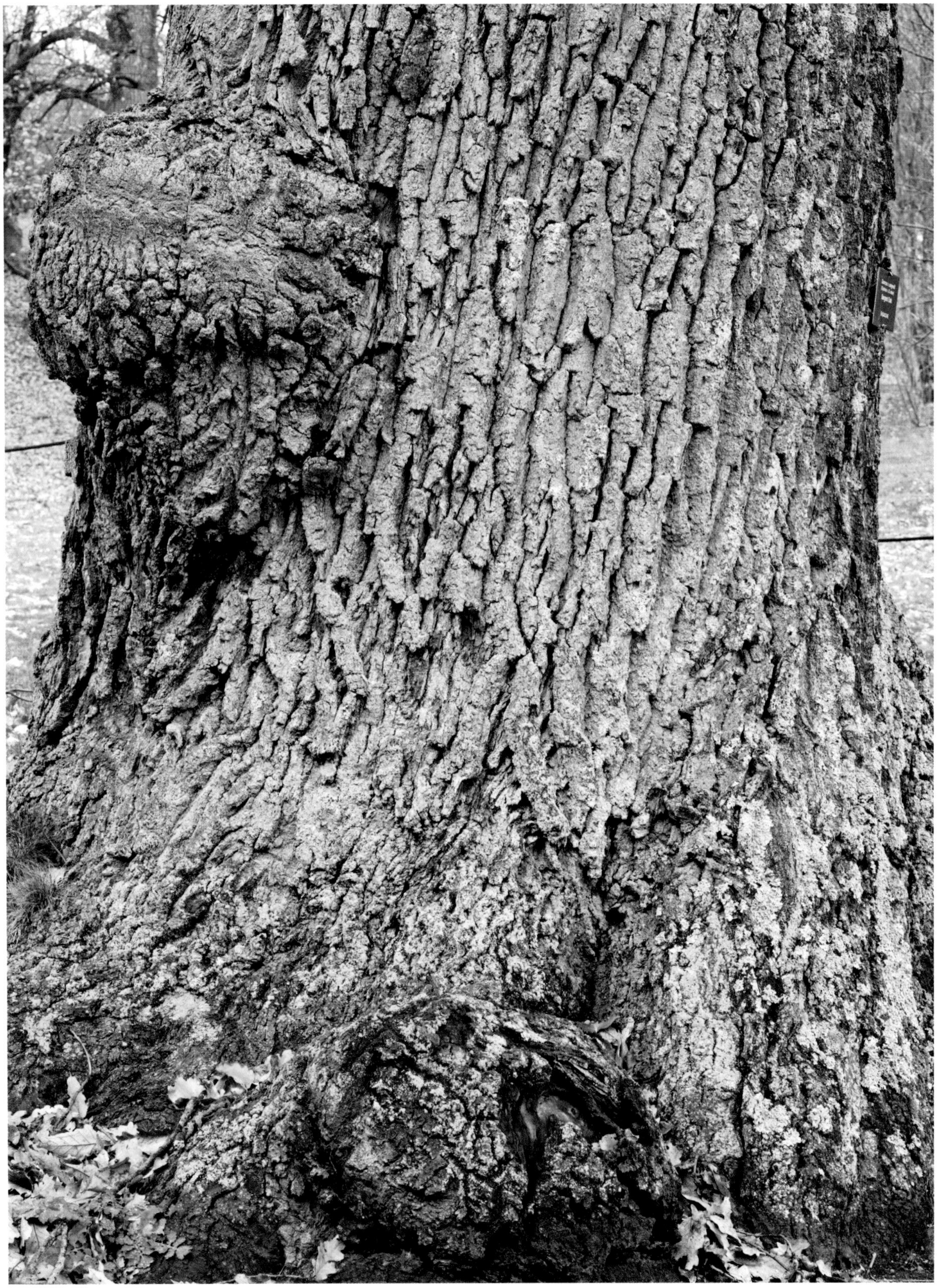

Quercus × sargentii, Sargent Oak, Eiche (Hybridform) – Arnold Arboretum, Boston, Massachusetts, 2019

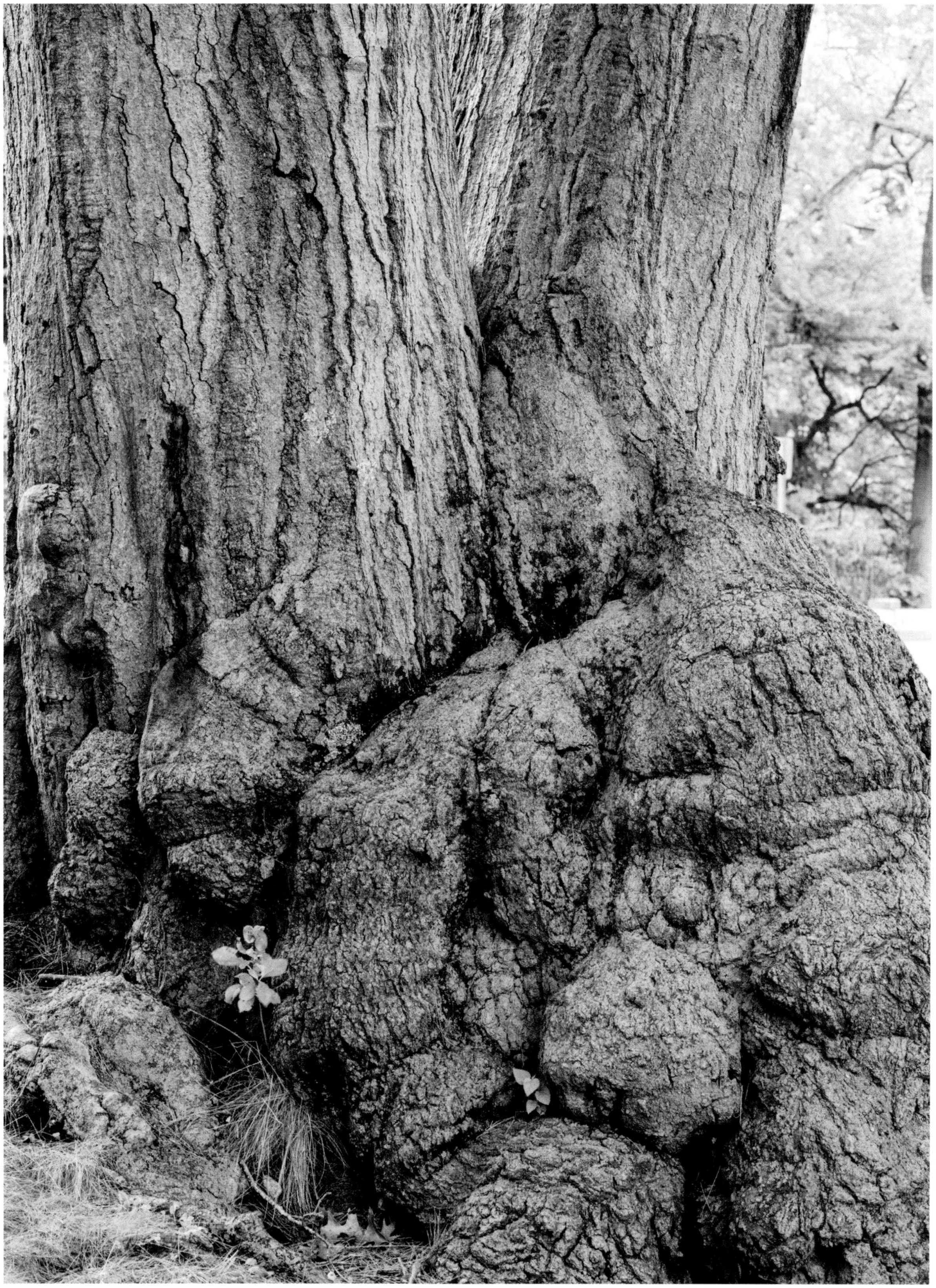

Quercus rubra, Northern Red Oak, Rot-Eiche – Beardsley Park, Bridgeport, Connecticut, 2020

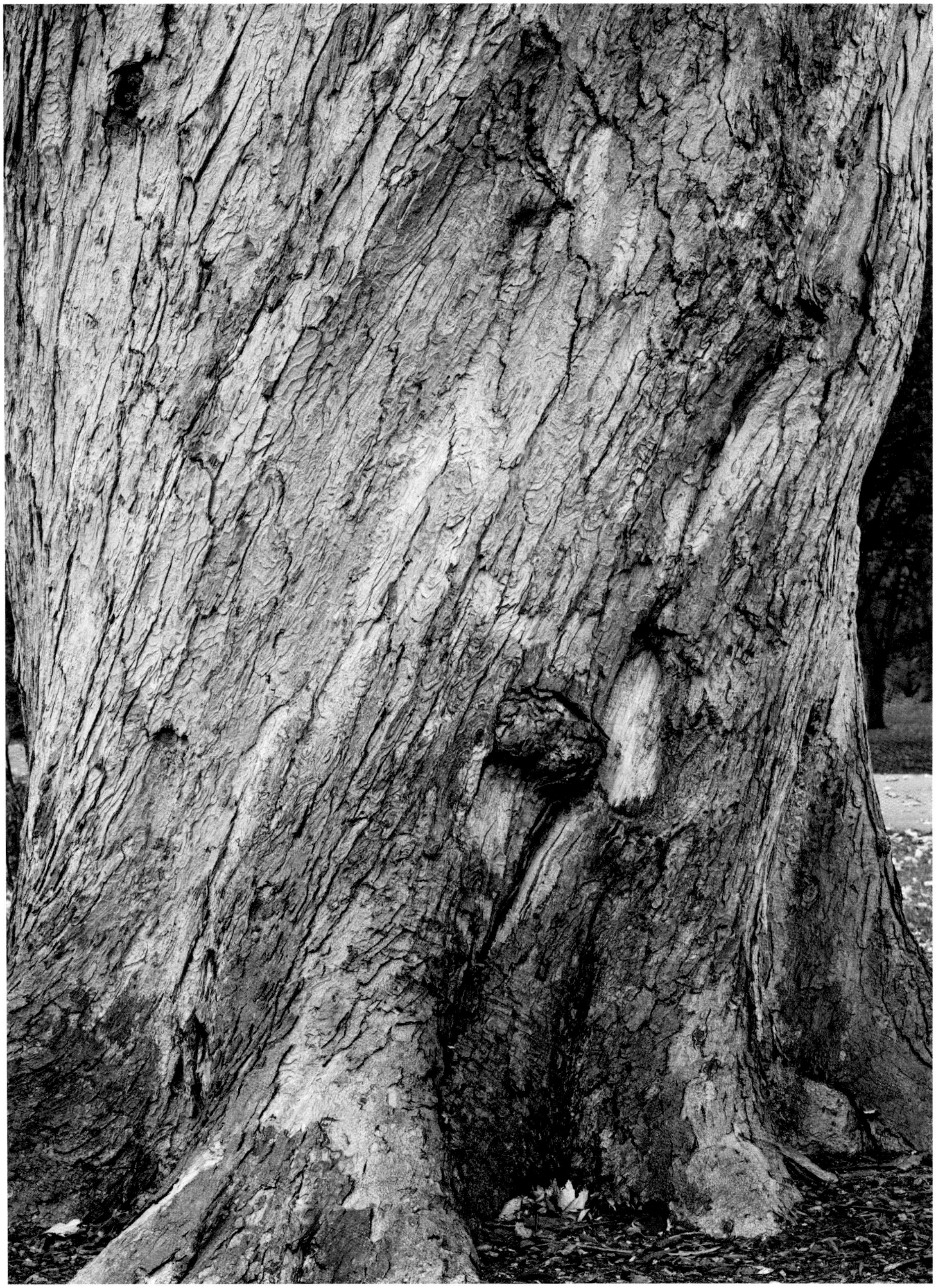

Acer saccharinum, Silver Maple, Silber-Ahorn – Arnold Arboretum, Boston, Massachusetts, 2019

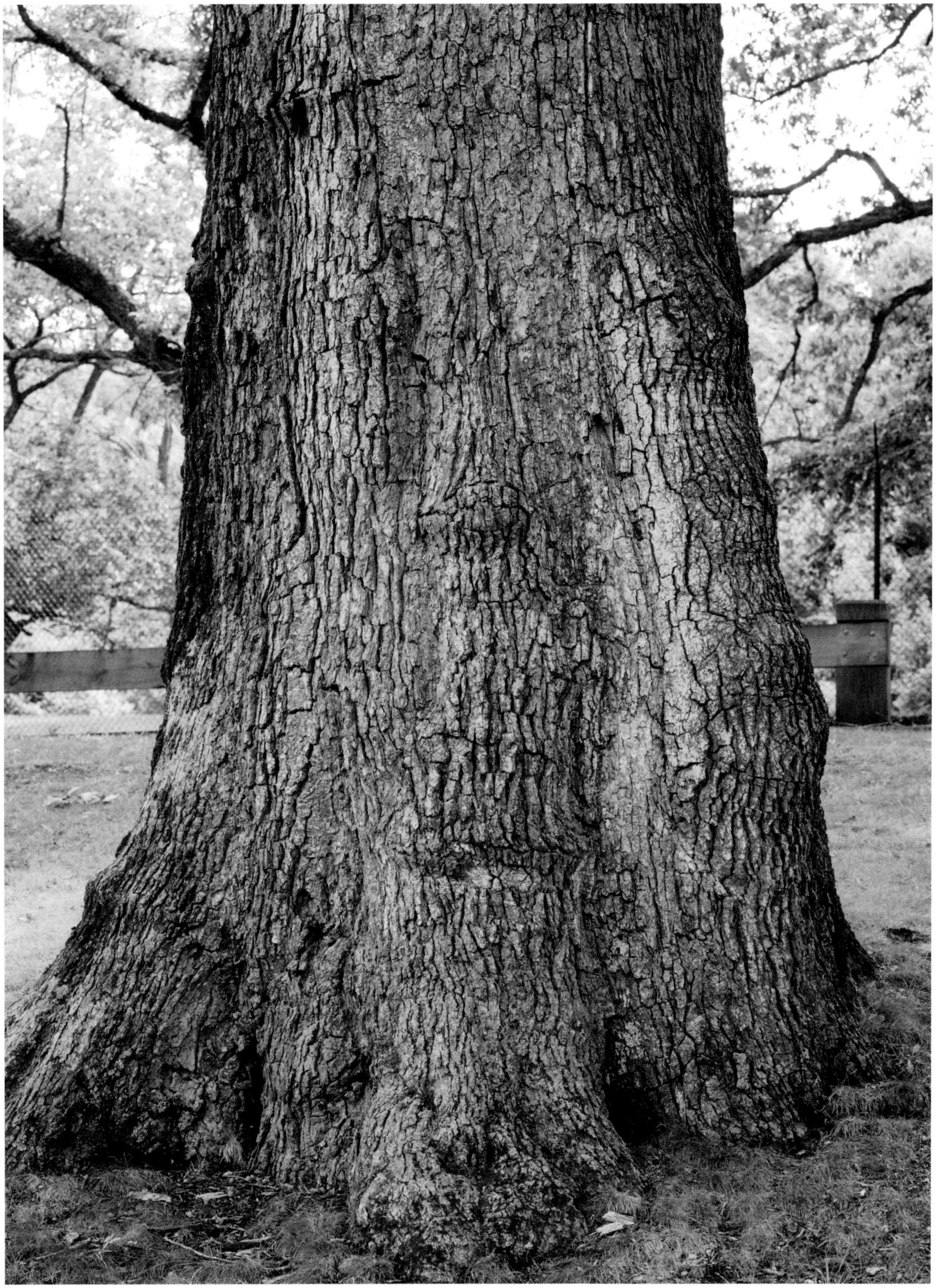

Quercus alba, White Oak, Amerikanische Weiß-Eiche – Beardsley Park, Bridgeport, Connecticut, 2020

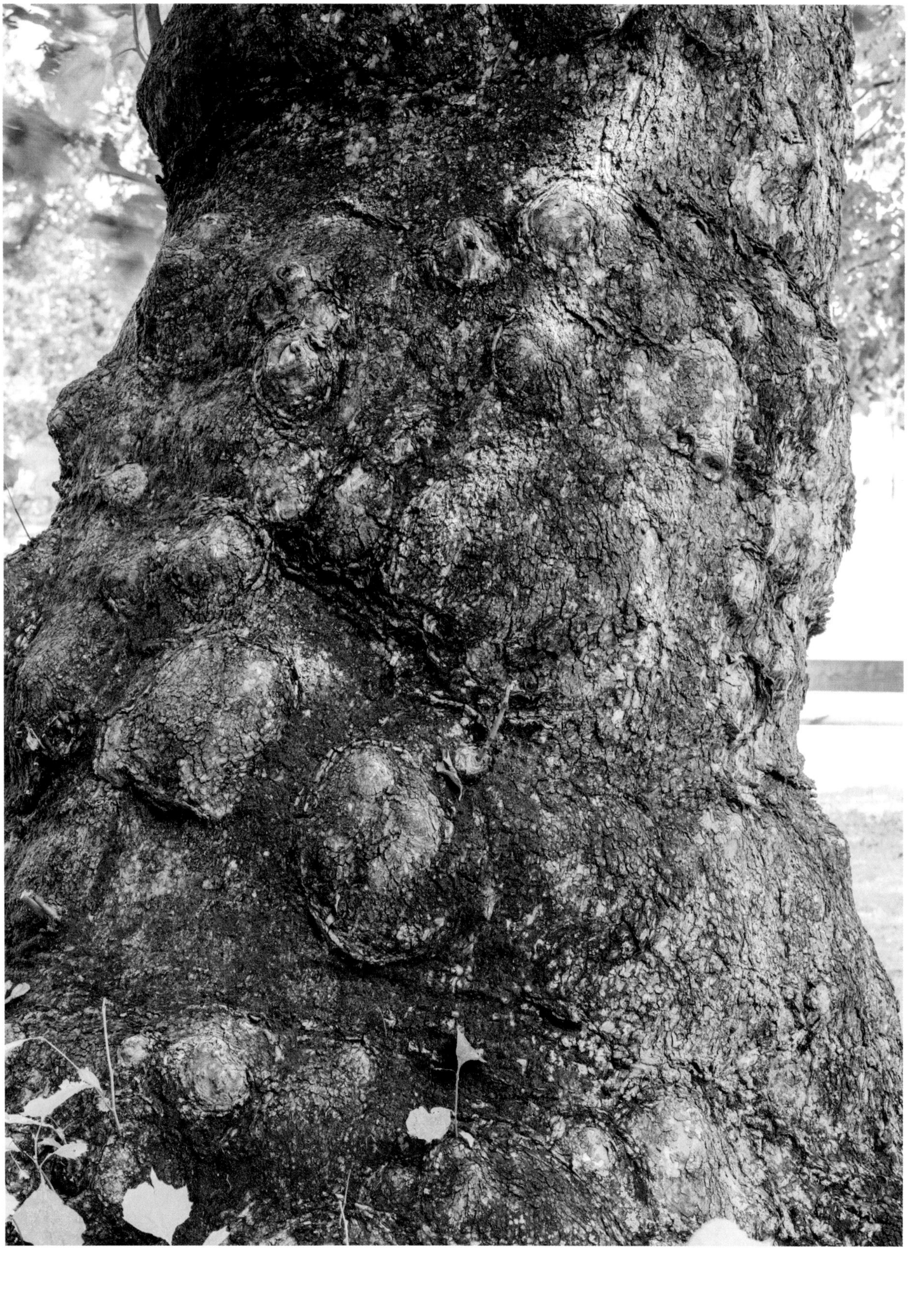

Platanus occidentalis, American Sycamore, Amerikanische Platane – Beardsley Park, Bridgeport, Connecticut, 2020

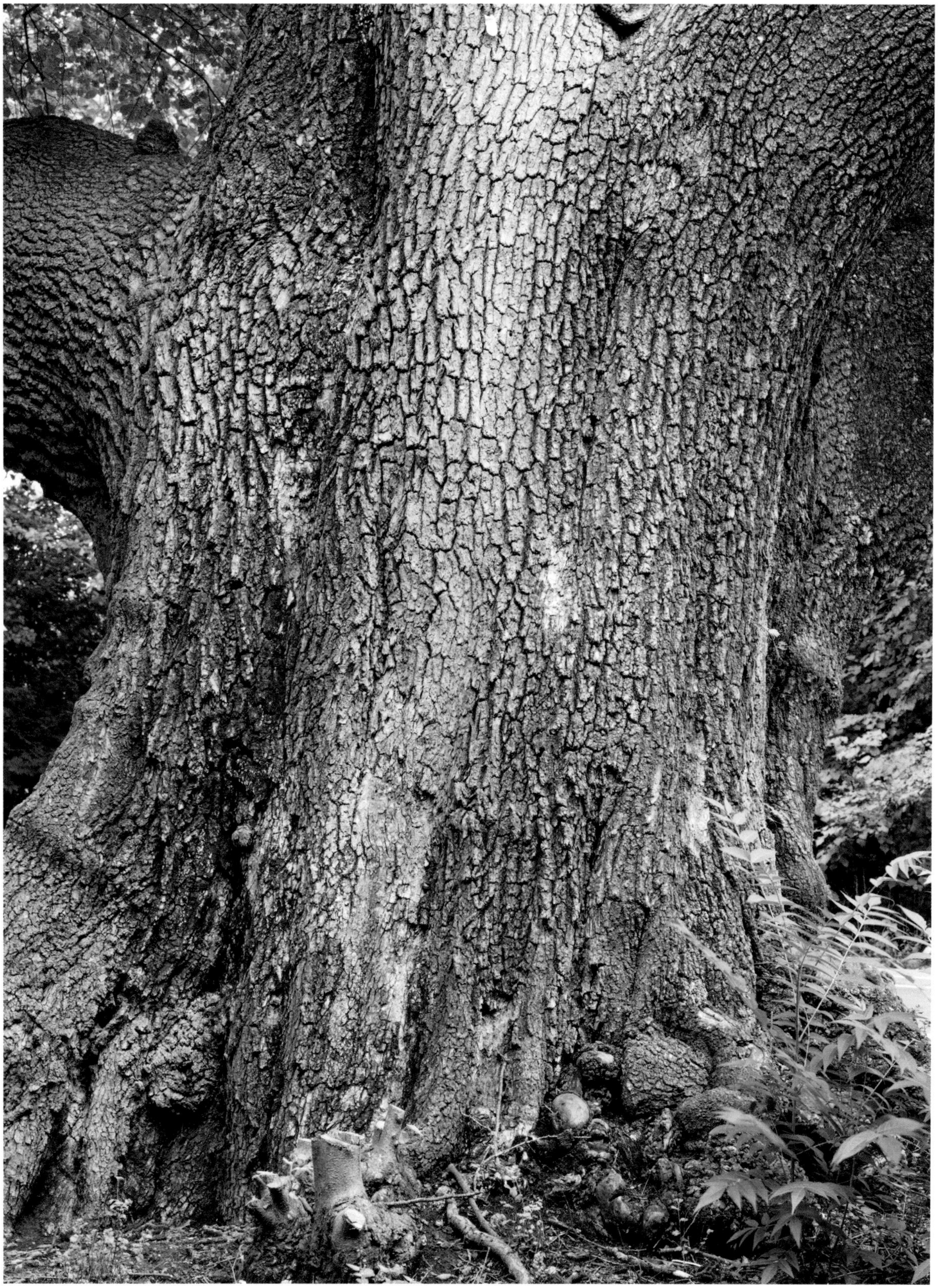

Ulmus rubra, Slippery Elm, Rot-Ulme – Prospect Park, Brooklyn, New York, 2019

Zivilisierte Wildnis: Die moderne amerikanische Stadt und die Landschaften von Frederick Law Olmsted

Tom Avermaete

> »Wir haben Grund zur Annahme, … dass es folglich bald größere Städte geben wird, als sie die Welt je gesehen hat, und dass der weitere Fortschritt der Zivilisation hauptsächlich davon abhängen wird, wodurch Geist und Charakter der Menschen beeinflusst werden, die in diesen großen Städten leben.«
> — Frederick Law Olmsted, 1870[1]

Der Beitrag von Frederick Law Olmsted zur Geschichte der modernen Stadtplanung kann gar nicht hoch genug eingeschätzt werden. Olmsted wirkte zu einer Zeit, in der Städte ein rasantes Wachstum erfuhren und sich ihr baulicher und sozialer Charakter stark veränderte. Olmsted sah sich in der Mitte des 19. Jahrhunderts in den USA mit Städten konfrontiert, die so dramatisch expandierten, dass sie nicht nur völlig neue Funktionen erfüllen mussten, sondern auch einen Großteil ihrer Lebensqualität einzubüßen drohten.

Während viele Stadtplaner versuchten, diese enormen Herausforderungen zu bewältigen, indem sie die öffentliche Infrastruktur durch neue Verkehrs- und Stromnetze oder Wasser- und Abwassersysteme erweiterten, lag für Olmsted die Lösung zur Gestaltung einer modernen Großstadt in der Anlage und Integration von Grünflächen. Er war überzeugt, dass »ein Park einen ganz anderen und viel größeren Einfluss auf den Fortschritt einer Stadt in ihrer allgemeinen Struktur ausübt als jede andere gewöhnliche öffentliche Einrichtung.«[2]

Inspiration für diesen Ansatz hatte er auf seinen Reisen durch England gewonnen, wo er um 1850 als Journalist gearbeitet hatte. Einen besonders starken Eindruck hatte der Birkenhead Park außerhalb von Liverpool bei ihm hinterlassen, entworfen von dem englischen Landschaftsarchitekten Joseph Paxton. Als Anhänger fortschrittlicher Weltanschauungen und Politik bewunderte Olmsted, dass »diese herrliche Parkanlage vollständig, vorbehaltlos und auf ewig dem Volk gehört. Der ärmste britische Bauer kann sich in all seinen Bereichen ebenso frei an diesen erfreuen wie die britische Königin.«[3]

1 Frederick Law Olmsted, Public Parks and the Enlargement of Towns, in: Journal of Social Science, Containing the Proceedings of the American Association (1869–1909), 3/1871, S. 10. Vortrag, gehalten vor der American Social Science Association im Lowell Institute, Boston, MA, 25.2.1870.

2 Witold Rybczynski, A Clearing in the Distance: Frederick Law Olmsted and America in the Nineteenth Century, New York 2003, S. 296.

3 Frederick Law Olmsted, Walks and Talks of an American Farmer in England, New York 1854, S. 54.

Civilized Wilderness: The Modern American City and the Landscapes of Frederick Law Olmsted

Tom Avermaete

> "We have reason to believe … that there will in consequence soon be larger towns than any the world has yet known, and that the further progress of civilization is to depend mainly upon the influences by which men's minds and characters will be affected while living in large towns."
> — Frederick Law Olmsted, 1870[1]

The contribution of Frederick Law Olmsted to the history of modern urban design can hardly be overestimated. Olmsted worked at a time when cities were growing rapidly, causing their physical and social character to be heavily transformed. Active in the middle of the nineteenth century in the United States, Olmsted was confronted with towns that were expanding in such a drastic fashion that they not only had to incorporate new urban functions but also saw much of their everyday quality of life threatened.

While many urban designers were trying to engage with these vast challenges by designing new public infrastructure such as transportation networks, electrical grids, or water and sewer systems, for Olmsted the solution for the large modern city was to include green spaces within them. He believed that "a park exercises a very different and much greater influence upon the progress of a city in its general structure than any other ordinary public work."[2]

The inspiration for this approach was sparked during his travels in England, where he had worked as a journalist around 1850. Birkenhead Park outside of Liverpool, designed by the English landscape architect Joseph Paxton, made an especially strong impression. As a supporter of progressive ideologies and politics, Olmsted admired how "this magnificent pleasure-ground is entirely, unreservedly, and forever, the People's own. The poorest British peasant is as free to enjoy it in all its parts as the British queen."[3]

For Olmsted, this inclusive "democratic" quality of Birkenhead Park was not only due to its offering free access to all people but also depended on the very design of the park, intended to appeal to various groups of citizens. The range of places that Paxton had

1 Frederick Law Olmsted, "Public Parks and the Enlargement of Towns," *Journal of Social Science, Containing the Proceedings of the American Association (1869–1909)*, no. 3 (1871), 10. Paper read before the American Social Science Association, at the Lowell Institute (Boston, MA, February 25, 1870).

2 Witold Rybczynski, *A Clearing in the Distance: Frederick Law Olmsted and America in the Nineteenth Century* (New York: Scribner, 2003), 296.

3 Frederick Law Olmsted, *Walks and Talks of an American Farmer in England* (New York: Riker, Thorne and Co, 1854), 54.

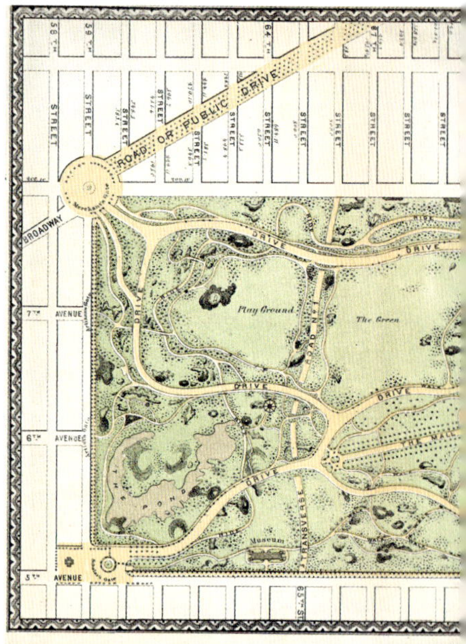

Für Olmsted erschöpfte sich diese integrative, »demokratische« Qualität des Birkenhead Park jedoch nicht darin, dass er allen Menschen frei zugänglich war, sie ergab sich vielmehr auch aus der Gestaltung des Parks selbst, die unterschiedliche bürgerliche Gruppen ansprechen wollte. Die von Paxton sorgfältig gestalteten Anlagen des Parks – Teiche und Steingärten, Cricketfelder und verschlungene Wege – machten Birkenhead zu einem radikalen sozialen Experiment, in dem sich einfache Bürgerinnen und Bürger sowie Mitglieder der Oberschicht gleichermaßen vergnügen und begegnen konnten.

Der Central Park: Begegnungsstätte für eine moderne Stadt

Als 1857 ein Wettbewerb für die Gestaltung des Central Park in New York City ausgschrieben wurde, war für Olmsted das zentrale Anliegen selbstverständlich, »ein tatsächlich öffentlich zugängliches Gelände [als] eine Notwendigkeit für zivilisiertes städtisches Leben«[4] zu schaffen. Das Areal des Central Park war bereits ab 1811 im sogenannten Commissioners' Plan festgeschrieben, der eine kontrollierte Raumplanung der rasch voranschreitenden Stadtentwicklung auf der Insel Manhattan vorsah. Als Olmsted 1857 das Gelände erstmals besichtigte, war dies noch ein weitgehend baumloses, felsiges Terrain, wenn auch stellenweise bewohnt. Um Land für die Anlage des Parks zu gewinnen, machte die Stadt von ihrem Enteignungsrecht Gebrauch. Es kam zu einer etwa 1600 Menschen betreffenden Zwangsräumung, wobei deren Häuser abgerissen wurden.[5] Unter ihnen waren auch die Bewohner von Seneca Village, einer größeren Siedlung afroamerikanischer Eigentümer auf der Westseite des Parks.

Olmsted reichte zusammen mit seinem Kollegen Calvert Vaux den Siegerentwurf des Wettbewerbs ein, den sogenannten Greensward Plan. Er unterschied sich von den anderen Beiträgen durch die Vielfalt und den Reiz seiner Landschaftselemente.

Um das vielfältige Spektrum an Parklandschaften, die sie erschaffen wollten, zu veranschaulichen, entwarfen Olmsted und Vaux zwölf Vorher-Nachher-Bildtafeln. Ausgehend von der aktuellen Situation mit dem künftigen Park im Blick erläuterten diese Tafeln nicht nur, wie durch sorgfältige Modellierung des Geländes und die Anpflanzung von Baumgruppen der bestehende kahle Boden in eine urbane Grünfläche verwandelt werden sollte, sondern auch, wie sich darin eine Vielzahl von atmosphärischen Orten und Nutzungsmöglichkeiten unterbringen ließ. Die Bildtafeln von Olmsted und Vaux zeigten ein bis dahin unbekanntes Nebeneinander von Landschaftsräumen und den in ihnen erzeugten Stimmungen, das die Komplexität einer modernen Großstadt widerspiegelte.

Diese Tafeln wiesen einigen Orten im Park sehr repräsentative Funktionen zu, so der Bethesda Terrace, die als offizieller Empfangssaal der Stadt unter freiem Himmel gedacht war. Olmsted und Vaux stellten sich vor, dass die Bürgerinnen und Bürger den Park über die Mall betraten, eine lange, von Bäumen und Bänken gesäumte Promenade im Südosten des Parks. Dem strengen Rhythmus von Bäumen und Parkbänken folgend, sollten die

4 Laura W. Roper, F.L.O.: A Biography of Frederick Law Olmsted, Baltimore 1973, S. 71.

5 Brent Staples, The Death of a Black Utopia, in: New York Times, 28.11.2019, URL: <https://www.nytimes.com/2019/11/28/opinion/seneca-central-park-nyc.html> [gelesen am 9.3.2022].

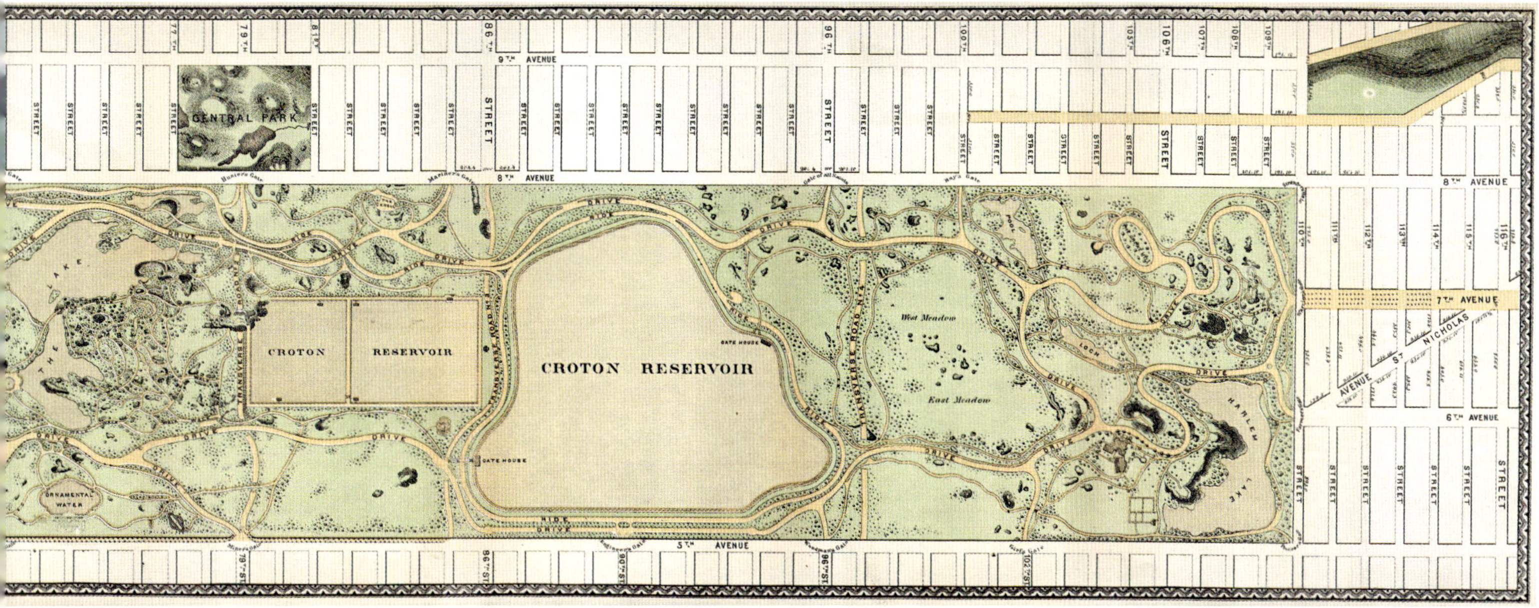

New York, Central Park, Greensward Plan, Frederick Law Olmsted und Calvert Vaux, 1858 – Plan mit Abbildung des New Yorker Straßennetzes | New York, Central Park, Greensward Plan, Frederick Law Olmsted and Calvert Vaux, 1858 — plan with indication of the Manhattan grid

carefully designed—including ponds and rock gardens, cricket fields and winding paths—turned Birkenhead into a radical civic experiment, where commoners and aristocrats could enjoy themselves and rub elbows.

Central Park: A Nexus for a Modern City

It should come as no surprise that when a competition was organized for the design of Central Park in New York City in 1857, creating truly "public grounds [as] a necessity to civilized urban living"[4] was a central concern for Olmsted. The site of Central Park had been reserved since 1811 in the so-called Commissioners' Plan, which proposed a system of controlled planning for Manhattan Island's rapidly expanding urban development. When Olmsted encountered the site in 1857, it was primarily a treeless and rocky terrain, though certain areas were inhabited. To clear land for the park's construction, the power of eminent domain was invoked, and approximately 1,600 people were evicted and their homes torn down.[5] Among them were the residents of Seneca Village, a major settlement of Black property owners located on the site's west side.

Olmsted designed the winning competition entry, called the Greensward plan, with his colleague Calvert Vaux. The Greensward design distinguished itself from other submissions through the sheer diversity and allure of its landscape features. To illustrate the multiplicity of environments that they wanted to generate, Olmsted and Vaux drafted twelve before-and-after panels for their submission. Composed of perspectives of the current condition and imagined future park, these panels not only illustrated how, by carefully modeling the terrain and planting groups of trees, the existing bare ground could be transformed into an urban green space, but also how a variety of atmospheres and uses could be accommodated. Olmsted and Vaux's panels illustrated an unprecedented juxtaposition of environments and ambiences that echoed the complexity of a large modern city.

4 Laura W. Roper, *F.L.O.: A Biography of Frederick Law Olmsted* (Baltimore: Johns Hopkins University Press, 1973), 71.

5 Brent Staples, "The Death of a Black Utopia," *New York Times* (Nov. 28, 2019), https://www.nytimes.com/2019/11/28/opinion/seneca-central-park-nyc.html (accessed Mar. 6, 2022).

New Yorker so zur Arkade geführt werden, einem langgestreckten, unter dem Parkniveau liegenden Raum, für dessen Decke eine Verzierung mit englischen Keramikfliesen vorgesehen war. Am Ende dieser Folge gelangte man auf die Bethesda Terrace, ein streng formal gestalteter Ort mit symmetrisch angelegten Treppen, die eine obere und eine untere Ebene miteinander verbinden sollten, und der Bethesda Fountain in ihrem Mittelpunkt.

Das Gegenstück zur förmlichen Atmosphäre der Mall, der Arkade und der Terrasse, die sich eindeutig an die wohlhabende New Yorker Bevölkerungsschicht richteten, bildete die Sheep Meadow, die Schafwiese, im Südwesten des Parks. Diese riesige Fläche von 61 000 Quadratmetern, die grasenden Schafen vorbehalten sein sollte, führt ein anderes Verständnis von Landschaft in die Parkgestaltung ein. Während einige Parkareale als Orte der Repräsentation oder zum optischen Genuss gestaltet wurden, verweist die Sheep Meadow auf eine ganz und gar praktische Nutzung des Geländes, nämlich auf die Haltung von Vieh.

Vorstellungen von einer ungezähmten Landschaft boten Olmsted und Vaux ebenso mit dem Ramble, einem »landschaftlichen Streifzug«, und dem Ravine, einer »Schlucht«, im Süden des Parks. Der Ramble besteht aus einer Reihe kleiner, gewundener Pfade entlang felsiger Aufschlüsse des örtlichen Schiefergesteins, während die Schlucht einen kleinen Bach und Wasserfälle umfasst und durch Bögen aus massiven, rauen Steinen führt. Während die Wettbewerbsausschreibung verlangte, dass der Central Park zumindest teilweise

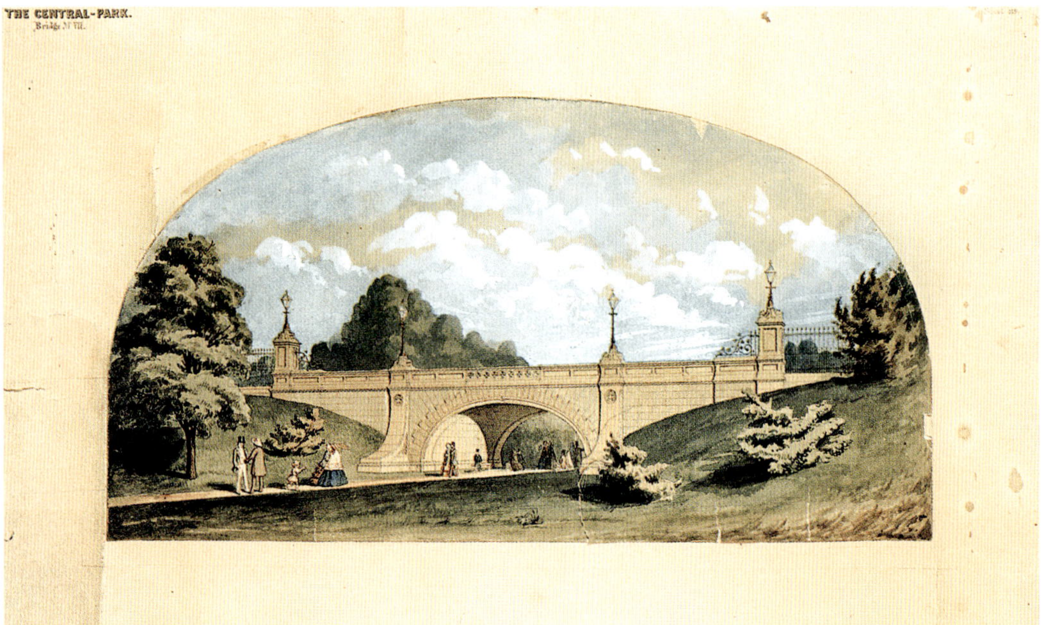

New York, Torbogen für einen Fußweg unter einer Querstraße südöstlich der Mall, Annual Report of the Board of Commissioners of the Central Park, Calvert Vaux, 1858 | New York, “Archway under traffic road, for footpath, southeast of the mall,” Annual Report of the Board of Commissioners of the Central Park, Calvert Vaux, 1858

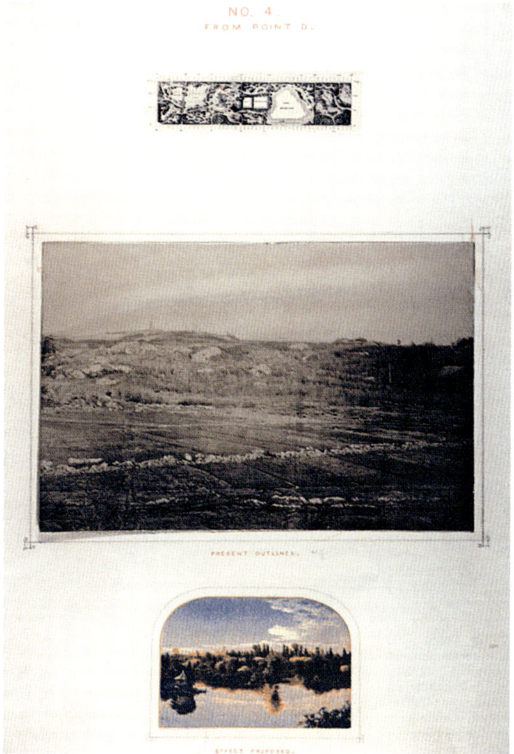

New York, Central Park, Greensward Study, Nr. 4 (»Blick über den See zum Vista Rock«), Frederick Law Olmsted und Calvert Vaux, 1858 | New York, Central Park, Greensward Study, No. 4 ("Across the Lake toward Vista Rock"), Frederick Law Olmsted and Calvert Vaux, 1858

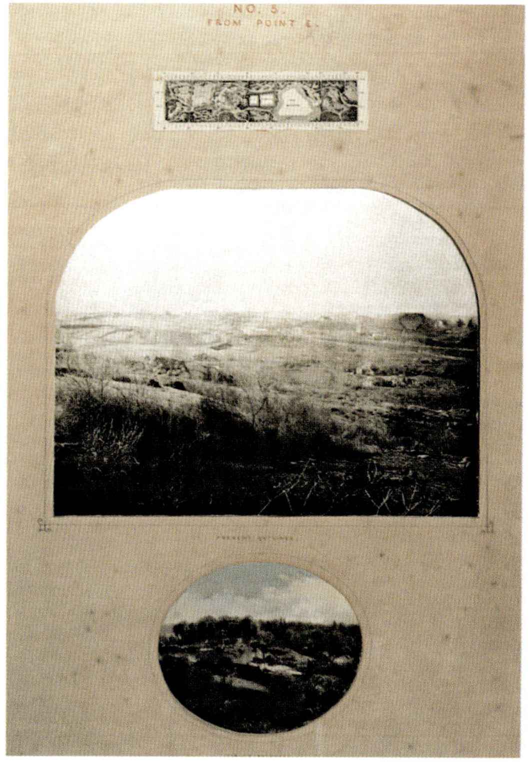

New York, Central Park, Greensward Study, Nr. 5 (»Blick über den See vom Vista Rock«), Frederick Law Olmsted und Calvert Vaux, 1858 | New York, Central Park, Greensward Study, No. 5 ("Across the Lake from Vista Rock"), Frederick Law Olmsted and Calvert Vaux, 1858

Proposed on their panels were some very formal places in the park, such as the Terrace, which was conceived of as a formal outdoor reception hall for the city. They imagined that citizens would enter the park through the Mall, a long tree- and bench-lined promenade in the southeast of the park. Following this strict rhythm of trees and benches, the New Yorkers would be led to the Arcade, an elongated subterranean space with a ceiling decorated with English ceramic tiles. At the end of this sequence they would land on the Terrace, a formal environment of symmetrical stairs connecting an upper and lower terrace, with the Bethesda Fountain at its center.

The formal atmosphere of the Mall, the Arcade, and the Terrace, which clearly addressed New York's gentry, is complemented by the Sheep Meadow in the southwest of the park. This vast area of fifteen acres (61,000 square meters), which was reserved for the grazing of sheep, introduces a different understanding of landscape into the park. While other park areas were designed as sites of formal representation or visual enjoyment, the Sheep Meadow relates to a more practical use of the terrain, that of accommodating livestock.

Conceptions of an untamed landscape are also offered by Olmsted and Vaux with the Ramble and the Ravine in the south of the park. The Ramble consists of a series of small, twisting paths along rocky outcroppings of the local schist, while the Ravine includes a small brook and waterfalls and passes through arches made from massive rough-faced stones. While the original competition brief had required that Central Park be conceived, at least partially, as a "parade ground," Olmsted and Vaux aimed to create "a great open common," a place where a variety of citizens could feel at ease.[6]

6 *Documents of the Board of Commissioners of the Central Park for the Year Ending April 30, 1858* (New York: Bryant & Co, 1858).

auch als »Paradeplatz« genutzt werden konnte, zielten Olmsted und Vaux auf die Schaffung »eines großen, offenen Gemeinschaftsbereiches« ab, auf einen Ort, an dem eine Vielzahl unterschiedlichster Gesellschaftsmitglieder Erholung finden könnte.[6]

Ein moderner Park war für Olmsted nicht nur ein Ort, den man auf demokratische Weise betreten und genießen konnte, sondern auch ein Areal, das unterschiedliche Formen moderner urbaner Mobilität integrierte. Die Wettbewerbsvorgaben für den Central Park sahen vier Straßen vor, die die Ost- und Westseite Manhattans durch den Park hindurch verbinden sollten. Zu diesem Zweck entwickelten Olmsted und Vaux eine ausgeklügelte Trennung von Fußgänger- und den Park kreuzendem Kutschenverkehr: Sie legten die geforderten Querstraßen tiefer, was die Möglichkeit bot, auf Parkebene ein dichtes System von verschlungenen Kutsch- und Reitpfaden sowie Gehwegen zu schaffen, die durch verschiedene Baumgruppen optisch voneinander getrennt und alle in eine sorgfältig gestaltete Topografie eingebunden waren.

An den Kreuzungen dieser verschiedenen Wegenetze errichteten Olmsted und Vaux eine Reihe eigens entworfener Brücken. Diese dienten nicht nur der Überquerung von Straßen und Wegen, sondern wurden durch ihre besonderen architektonischen Merkmale auch zu Orientierungspunkten im weitläufigen Gelände des Central Park. Olmsted übernahm persönlich die Leitung für die Anlage des Parks und arbeitete mit Bauingenieuren, Gärtnern und Architekten in kleinen Teams an der Fertigstellung einzelner Bereiche. Das Ergebnis erscheint als eine *contradictio in terminis*: eine ländlich-idyllische pastorale Landschaft, die den Bürgerinnen und Bürgern eine kurze Flucht – physisch, optisch und mental – aus der Enge des modernen städtischen Lebens ermöglicht, und zugleich Teil von ihr ist.

Boston: Eine Kette von Parks und Parkways

Während es beim Central Park darum ging, einen völlig neuen Stadtpark zu erschaffen, zeigte Olmsted in Boston, wie eine urbane Grünfläche aus dem Nebeneinander und der Verbindung bestehender Elemente erwachsen kann. Als Olmsted 1870 in Cambridge, Massachusetts, seinen Vortrag »Public Parks and the Enlargement of Towns« (»Öffentliche Parks und die Erweiterung von Städten«) hielt, war Boston eine aus allen Nähten platzende, laute und schmutzige Metropole. Kein Wunder, dass sich die Stadtverwaltung von Boston von seinen Ansichten inspirieren ließ und ihn beauftragte, nicht nur einen großen Park, sondern ein ganzes Parksystem zu entwerfen.

Olmsted entwickelte ein lineares System von etwa elf Kilometern Länge, das sogenannte Emerald Necklace (»Smaragdkollier«), wo die Bürgerinnen und Bürger von Boston »nach getaner Arbeit einfach hingehen konnten, um dort eine Stunde lang zu spazieren, ohne etwas von der Hektik und dem Lärm der Straßen ringsum zu sehen, zu hören und zu spüren.«[7] Er sah darin einen Weg, die moderne Metropole neu zu strukturieren und ihrem Zentrum ein Stück alltägliche Lebensqualität zurückzugeben. Sein Projekt für ein »grünes

6 Documents of the Board of Commissioners of the Central Park for the Year Ending April 30, 1858, New York 1858.

7 Olmsted 1871 (wie Anm. 1), S. 10.

A modern park was for Olmsted not only a place that could be democratically accessed and enjoyed, but also a site that integrated various forms of modern urban movement. The competition brief for Central Park called for four roadways to connect the east and west sides of Manhattan through the park. To this end, Olmsted and Vaux developed an ingenious separation of pedestrian and cross-park carriage traffic: these transverse roads were situated below ground level, giving the opportunity to create, above ground, a dense system of winding carriage paths, equestrian trails, and footpaths that were visually separated by various groups of trees and were all incorporated in a carefully designed topography.

Olmsted and Vaux situated a series of specially designed bridges at the crossings of these various movement networks. These bridges not only deal with the crossing of roads and pathways, their specific architectural features also turn them into orientation points in the vast terrain of Central Park. Olmsted would himself become the superintendent for the construction of Central Park and worked with civil engineers, horticulturalists, and architects in small teams to complete specific parts of the park. The result would seem to be a *contradictio in terminis*: a pastoral oasis that allows the citizens a brief escape—physically, visually, and mentally—from the density of modern urban life, while still being fully part of it.

Boston: A Necklace of Parks and Parkways

While Central Park was an exercise in creating an entirely new city park, Olmsted would show in the city of Boston that an urban green space could emerge from the juxtaposition and connection of existing realities. When Olmsted delivered his lecture “Public Parks and the Enlargement of Towns” in Cambridge, Massachusetts, in 1870, Boston was an

New York, Bethesda Terrace, Annual Report of the Board of Commissioners of the Central Park, Calvert Vaux, 1858 |
New York, Bethesda Terrace, Annual Report of the Board of Commissioners of the Central Park, Calvert Vaux, 1858

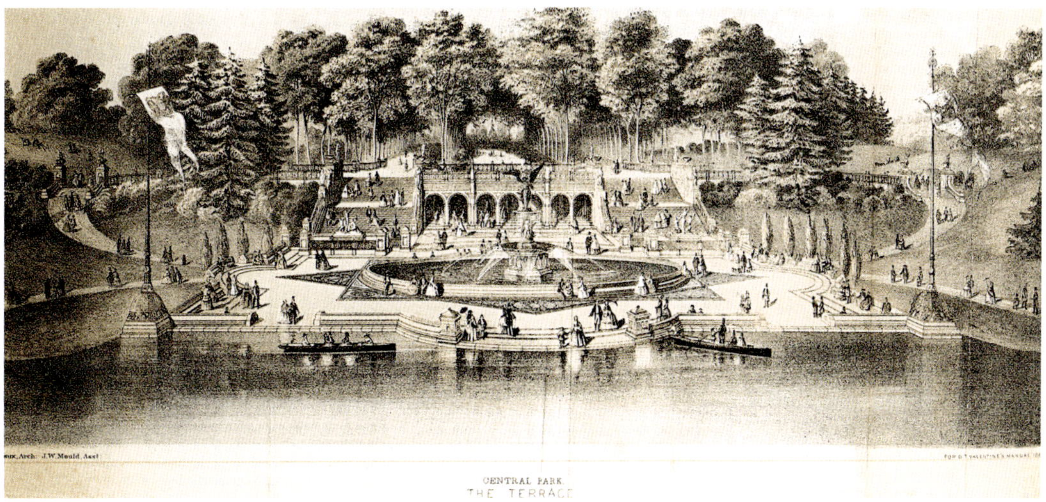

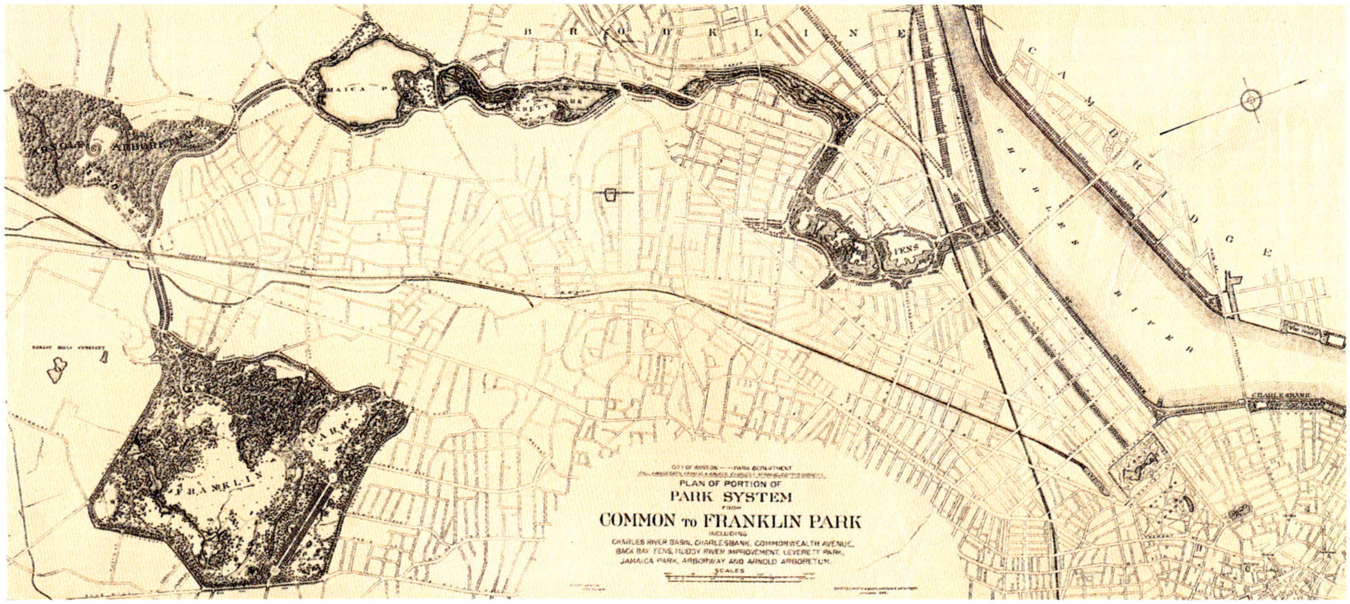

Boston, Emerald Necklace, Frederick Law Olmsted, 1878 — Übersichtsplan | Boston, Emerald Necklace, Frederick Law Olmsted, 1878 — general plan

Band«, wie er es nannte, begann am Boston Common, einer Wiese inmitten der Stadt, und verband mehrere bestehende Gelände.

Ähnlich dem Central Park für die New Yorker sollte das Emerald Necklace den Bostoner Bürgerinnen und Bürgern eine große Vielfalt an landschaftlichen Erlebnissen bieten. Olmsted begann mit dem problematischen Areal der Back Bay Fens, einem durch Abwässer belasteten Sumpfgebiet. Durch die Umleitung der Abwasserkanäle vom Muddy River in den Charles River verwandelte er es in eine Salzwiesen- und Parklandschaft. Dieser Ansatz wurde bei der Gestaltung des Riverway fortgesetzt. Durch die Umleitung des Flusses und die kunstvolle Gestaltung und Bepflanzung seiner Ufer gelang es Olmsted, den Eindruck einer abgeschiedenen Hirtenlandschaft zu kreieren, und dies trotz der geringen Fläche des Riverway. Was einst ein offener Abwasserkanal und öffentliches Ärgernis gewesen war, wurde so in ein wertvolles Gemeinschaftsgut verwandelt.

Die Wasserlandschaften der Back Bay Fens und des Riverway wurden durch die Umwandlung von Ackerland in das Arnold Arboretum ergänzt. Das Arboretum hat die Form einer weitläufigen Naturlandschaft mit einem gewundenen Wege- und Straßensystem, entlang dessen eine große Vielfalt von Bäumen und Pflanzen nach Familien und Gattungen arrangiert wurde. Als lebendes botanisches Museum sollte dieser Teil des Emerald Necklace nach Olmsteds Absicht eine pädagogische Funktion erfüllen, indem hier den Bürgerinnen und Bürgern die verschiedenen Pflanzenarten nähergebracht wurden, die im Raum Boston gedeihen konnten: »Ein Besucher, der durch das Arboretum fährt, wird in der Lage sein, sich einen Überblick über die Baumvegetation der nördlichen gemäßigten Zone zu verschaffen, ohne auch nur seine Kutsche zu verlassen. Es ist zu hoffen, dass eine solche Anordnung, die die strengen und formalen Achsen des konventionellen botanischen Gartens meidet, das umfassende Studium der Sammlungen sowohl unter wissenschaftlichen als auch unter malerischen Aspekten erleichtert.«[8]

Auch der Jamaica Pond, eine weitere bekannte Örtlichkeit Bostons, die von den Bürgerinnen und Bürgern schon lange zum spontanen Baden oder Schlittschuhlaufen genutzt

8 Charles Sprague Sargent, Direktor des Arnold Arboretum und enger Mitarbeiter von Olmsted bei der Parkgestaltung, zit. nach: URL: <https://arboretum.harvard.edu/about/our-history/> [gelesen am 14.1.2022].

overcrowded, noisy, and dirty city. Hence it came as no surprise that the Boston city government was inspired by his viewpoints and hired him to design not just one large park, but an entire park system.

Olmsted set out to design a linear system approximately seven miles (eleven kilometers) in length, the so-called Emerald Necklace, where the citizens of Boston could "easily go when the day's work is done, and where they may stroll for an hour, seeing, hearing, and feeling nothing of the bustle and jar of the streets."[7] He looked upon this system as a way to restructure the modern metropolis and to reintroduce some everyday quality of life at its very center. His project for what he called a "green ribbon" started at the Boston Common, a pasture in the middle of the city, and connected several other existing sites.

Just as Central Park did for New Yorkers, the Emerald Necklace was designed to offer Bostonians a wide variety of landscape experiences. Olmsted began with the problematic site of the Back Bay Fens, a sewage-clogged swamp which he redesigned into a salt marsh and parkland by rerouting the sewers from the Muddy River into the Charles River. This approach was continued in the design for the Riverway. By rerouting the river and artfully shaping and planting its banks, Olmsted created what seems to be a secluded pastoral landscape, despite the Riverway's narrow form. What once had been an open sewer and a public nuisance was turned into a community asset.

The water landscapes of the Back Bay Fens and the Riverway were complemented with the transformation of farmland into the Arnold Arboretum. The arboretum took the form of a vast natural area with a sinuous path and roadway system, along which a wide variety of trees and plants were organized by family and genus. As a living museum of horticulture, this part of the Emerald Necklace could, in Olmsted's view, fulfill a pedagogical function, teaching the citizens about the various plant species that were able to thrive in the Boston area: "a visitor driving through the Arboretum will be able to obtain a general idea of the arborescent vegetation of the north temperate zone without even leaving his carriage. It is hoped that such an arrangement, while avoiding the stiff and formal lines of the conventional botanic garden, will facilitate the comprehensive study of the collections, both in their scientific and picturesque aspects."[8]

The Jamaica Pond, another significant site in the Boston area that had always been informally used for swimming and skating, was also included in the park system. The place was already known for its natural beauty; hence, Olmsted's role was somewhat different than in the other Boston parks. The existing vegetation and topography were carefully mapped, and only little filling was done to provide room for a perimeter path and other pedestrian walkways that allowed for public use of the site. Special care was given to the preservation of existing trees, including specimen trees from the estates which previously occupied the area. With Jamaica Park, Olmsted added another type of water landscape to the Emerald Necklace.

Not only the character of the different parks but also the connection between them was a challenge. Very often the spaces in between the parks had already been urbanized

7 Olmsted, "Public Parks and the Enlargement of Towns," 10.

8 Charles Sprague Sargent, director of the Arnold Arboretum and close collaborator of Olmsted in the design of the park, as quoted in https://arboretum.harvard.edu/about/our-history/ (accessed Jan. 14, 2022).

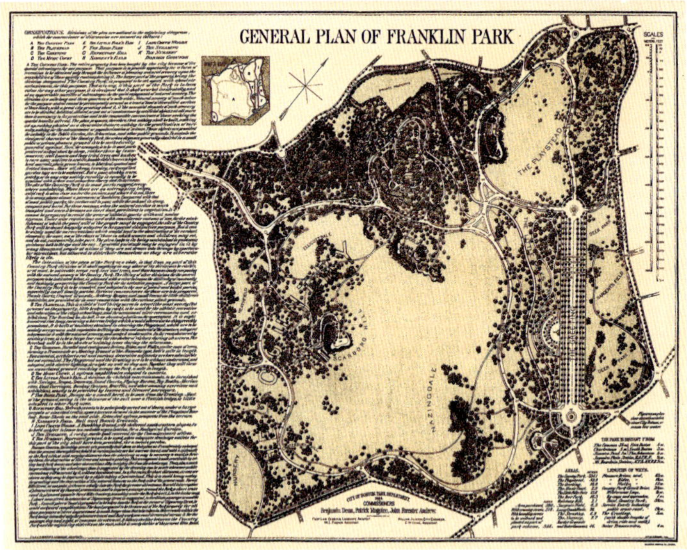

Boston, Emerald Necklace, Frederick Law Olmsted, 1878 — Plan des Franklin Park | Boston, Emerald Necklace, Frederick Law Olmsted, 1878 — plan of Franklin Park

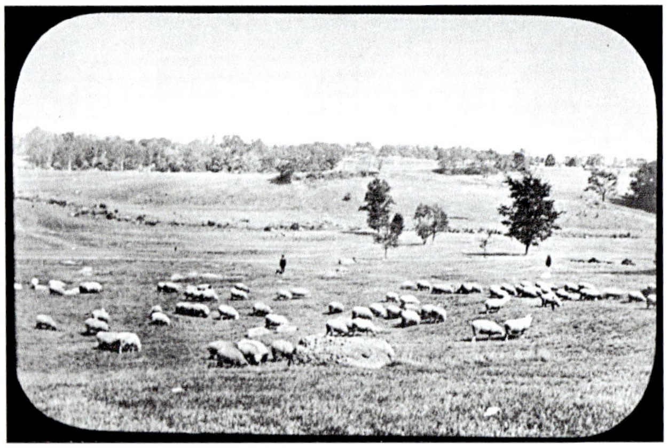

Boston, Emerald Necklace, Frederick Law Olmsted, 1878 — Ansicht der vorgefundenen landwirtschaftlichen Nutzfläche | Boston, Emerald Necklace, Frederick Law Olmsted, 1878 — view of the existing agricultural land

wurde, wurde in das Parksystem integriert. Dieser Teich wurde allein schon aufgrund seiner natürlichen Schönheit geschätzt, daher ging Olmsted hier anders vor als in den anderen Bostoner Parks. Die vorhandene Vegetation und die Topografie wurden sorgfältig kartiert, und es wurden nur geringfügige Aufschüttungen vorgenommen, um Platz für einen Rundweg und weitere Spazierwege zu bieten und das Gelände so für das Publikum zugänglich zu machen. Besonderes Augenmerk wurde auf den Erhalt der vorhandenen Bäume gelegt, darunter auch Solitärbäume von Anwesen, die sich einst auf dem Gelände befanden. Mit dem Jamaica Park fügte Olmsted dem Emerald Necklace einen weiteren Typus von Wasserlandschaft hinzu.

Nicht nur der Charakter der verschiedenen Parks, sondern auch deren Verbindung untereinander war eine herausfordernde Aufgabe. Oft waren die Areale zwischen den einzelnen Teilen bereits urbanisiert und die verfügbare Freifläche begrenzt. Aus diesem Grund ersann Olmsted ein völlig neues Konzept der Landschaftsgestaltung: den Parkway. Konzipiert als eine Straße oder ein Weg, der von engstehenden Bäumen gesäumt wird, erweckt ein Parkway den Eindruck, als bewege man sich durch dichte Parkanlagen, obwohl es sich nur um einen schmalen Landschaftsstreifen handelt. So verwandelte Olmsted ehemalige Kutschenwege in die von Bäumen gesäumten Parkwege Arborway, Riverway und Jamaicaway. Zusammen mit den verschiedenen Parks sollten diese Parkways das System des Emerald Necklace bilden und den Bürgerinnen und Bürgern von Boston den Anschein vermitteln, sich in einer zusammenhängenden natürlichen Landschaft zu bewegen.

Die Planung und Realisierung des Emerald Necklace war ein langfristiges Projekt, für das die Stadt Boston Land erwerben, Ackerland räumen, Häuser abreißen und Gewässer auffüllen musste. Der zwischen 1872 und 1892 entworfene und dann bis 1895 fertiggestellte Park ist ein hervorragendes Beispiel dafür, wie Olmsted versuchte, Parklandschaften zu schaffen, die den ursprünglichen Charakter des Geländes nutzten, indem er einheimische Pflanzen verwendete und auf gärtnerische Effekthascherei verzichtete. Zugleich erforderte

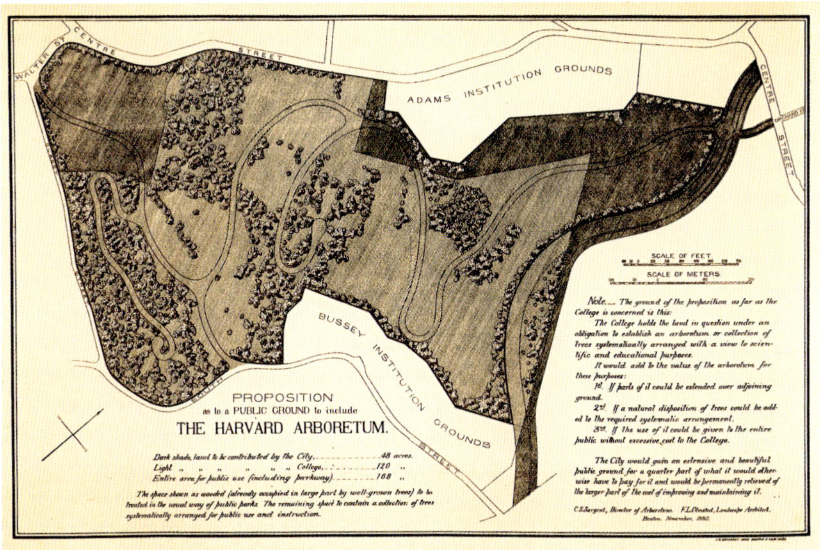

Boston, Emerald Necklace, Frederick Law Olmsted, 1878 — Plan des Harvard Arboretum | Boston, Emerald Necklace, Frederick Law Olmsted, 1878 — plan of Harvard Arboretum

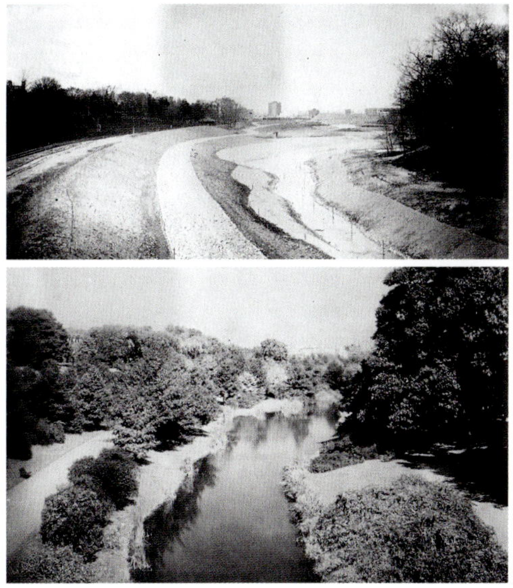

Boston, Emerald Necklace, Frederick Law Olmsted, 1878 — Ansicht des Riverway-Abschnitts | Boston, Emerald Necklace, Frederick Law Olmsted, 1878 — view of the Riverway

and the available open space was limited. To this purpose, Olmsted invented a new landscaping concept: the parkway. Conceived as a road or a path aligned with dense trees, a parkway creates the impression of moving through dense park areas while on narrow stretches of land. Olmsted converted former carriage paths into the tree-lined parkways of Arborway, Riverway, and Jamaicaway. Together with the various parks, these parkways would constitute the system of the Emerald Necklace and give the citizens of Boston the impression of being in a continuous natural landscape.

The design and realization of the Emerald Necklace was a long-term project that required the city of Boston to acquire land, clear farmlands, remove houses, and fill in bodies of water. Designed between 1872 and 1892 and under construction until 1895, it is a prime example of how Olmsted sought to create park environments that were consistent with the site's original character, using native plants and avoiding ostentatious gardening effects. At the same time, the Emerald Necklace came into existence because rivers were relocated and ponds created, the land was carefully sculpted, thousands of trees and shrubs were planted, and a circulation system was created to draw visitors into and through the park system. Even today Olmsted's design has the paradoxical quality of appearing as a remnant of natural New England scenery while being a wholly man-made landscape.

Civilized Wilderness

The main contribution of Frederick Law Olmsted to the history of urban design resides in his capacity to tackle the large issues that the nineteenth-century modern metropolis was facing with the creation of natural landscapes. With his park designs, Olmsted showed how green spaces could serve as complements to the commotion of the modern city. As the antithesis of the hard metropolitan environment, parks with trees, shrubs, and fields could "present an aspect of spaciousness and tranquility with variety and intricacy of arrangement, thereby affording the most agreeable contrast to the confinement, bustle,

die Realisierung des Emerald Necklace das Umlegen von Wasserläufen und das Anlegen von Teichen ebenso wie die Modellierung des Geländes, die Pflanzung Tausender Bäume und Sträucher und das Angebot eines Verkehrssystems, um Besuchende in und durch das Parksystem zu locken. Auch heute noch hat Olmsteds Entwurf die paradoxe Eigenschaft, wie ein Überbleibsel der natürlichen Landschaft Neuenglands zu wirken, während es sich doch um eine voll und ganz künstlich gestaltete Parkanlage handelt.

Zivilisierte Wildnis

Der wichtigste Beitrag von Frederick Law Olmsted zur Geschichte der Stadtplanung liegt in seiner Fähigkeit, den großen Problemen, mit denen die moderne Großstadt des 19. Jahrhunderts konfrontiert war, mit der Schaffung von naturnahen Landschaften zu begegnen. Mit seinen Parkentwürfen zeigte Olmsted, wie Grünflächen einen Kontrapunkt zum Trubel der modernen Stadt setzen konnten. Als Gegenpol zur harschen großstädtischen Umgebung konnten Parks mit Bäumen, Sträuchern und Feldern »einen Aspekt von Weitläufigkeit und Ruhe mit abwechslungsreichen und komplexen Anlagen verbinden und damit den angenehmsten Kontrast zur Enge, Hektik und monotonen Straßenaufteilung der Stadt bieten.«[9] Der Central Park und das Emerald Necklace geben den Bürgerinnen und Bürgern von New York und Boston bis heute die Möglichkeit, sich in die Natur zurückzuziehen – und dies mitten in der Stadt.

Olmsteds Entwürfe für New York und Boston sind jedoch mehr als nur eine Demonstration, wie die Natur die städtische Umgebung ergänzen und verbessern kann. Sie waren der Beginn einer sozialen und politischen Bewegung, die als Parks Movement bekannt wurde und den Kurs der Stadtplanung in Nordamerika und weit darüber hinaus veränderte. Olmsted sah in der modernen Stadtplanung einen demokratischen Prozess, an dem die Menschen teilhaben sollten. Seiner Ansicht nach boten Parks eine großartige Gelegenheit, bei allen Bürgerinnen und Bürgern ein Bewusstsein zu schaffen, für die grünen und weiteren Ressourcen ihrer Stadt kollektiv Verantwortung zu übernehmen.

Auf der Grundlage dieser Überzeugung entwarf Olmsted Parks, die explizit einen gleichberechtigten Zugang zur Natur ermöglichen. Sie sind ein Zusammenspiel aus atmosphärisch dichten Orten, die unterschiedlichste Stimmungen erzeugen und so möglichst eine Vielzahl von Menschen ansprechen sollen. Ein solcher demokratischer Sinn für den natürlichen Raum, so behauptete Olmsted, beeinflusst das Denken und den Charakter aller Bürgerinnen und Bürger und fördert zivilisiertes Verhalten. Es ist dieses politische Verständnis von städtischer Natur, diese Auffassung von zivilisierter Wildnis, die Olmsteds Parks bis heute ihre Bedeutung verleiht.

9 Frederick Law Olmsted, Creating Central Park: 1857–1861, hg. von Charles E. Beveridge und David Schuyler, Baltimore 1983, S. 212.

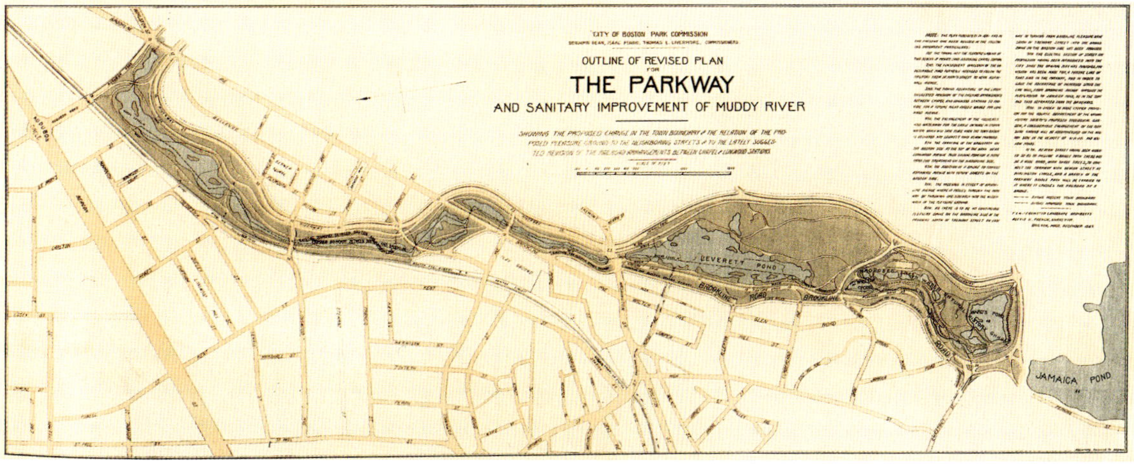

Boston, Emerald Necklace, Frederick Law Olmsted, 1878 — Plan für den Parkway und die Gewässersanierung des Muddy River | Boston, Emerald Necklace, Frederick Law Olmsted, 1878 — plan for the parkway and sanitary improvement of the Muddy River

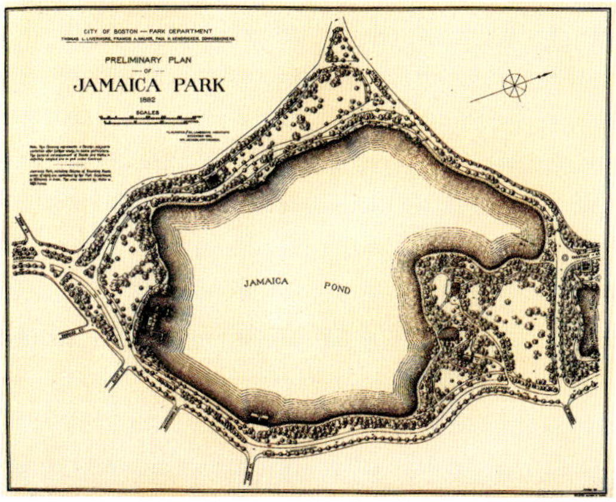

Boston, Emerald Necklace, Frederick Law Olmsted, 1878 — Plan des Jamaica Park | Boston, Emerald Necklace, Frederick Law Olmsted, 1878 — plan of Jamaica Park

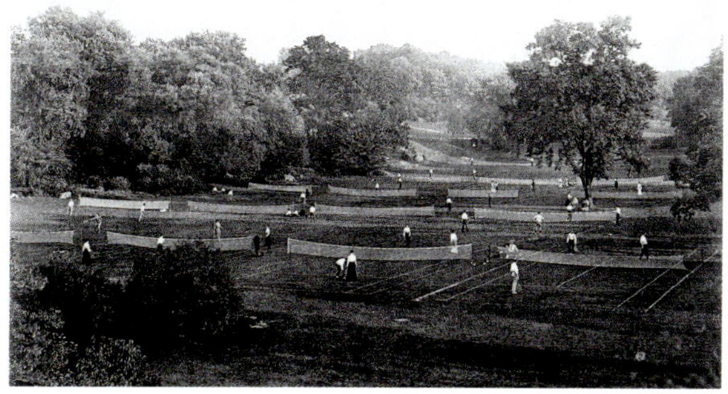

Boston, Emerald Necklace, Frederick Law Olmsted, 1878 — Rasentennis im Franklin Park | Boston, Emerald Necklace, Frederick Law Olmsted, 1878 — lawn tennis in Franklin Park

and monotonous street-division of the city."[9] Central Park and the Emerald Necklace continue to offer the citizens of New York and Boston opportunities for retreating from the city into nature, even in the city's very center.

Olmsted's designs for New York and Boston are, however, more than just a demonstration of how nature can complement and improve the urban environment. They represented the start of a social and political movement, known as the Parks Movement, which changed the course of urban design in North America and beyond. For Olmsted, modern urban planning was a democratic process in which people should participate. In his view, parks offered a great opportunity to raise awareness with all citizens about their collective responsibility to take care of the resources, green and otherwise, of the city.

Based on this view, Olmsted designed parks that explicitly provided equal access to nature. His parks are patchworks of diverse places and atmospheres that aim to appeal to a broad variety of people. Such a democratic sense of natural space, he claimed, would influence the minds and character of all citizens, promoting civilized behavior. It is this political understanding of urban nature, this conception of civilized wilderness, that gives Olmsted's parks their enduring relevance.

9 Frederick Law Olmsted, *Creating Central Park: 1857–1861*, eds. Charles E. Beveridge and David Schuyler (Baltimore: Johns Hopkins University Press, 1983), 212.

Die Parks von Frederick Law Olmsted in den USA | The Parks of Frederick Law Olmsted in the USA

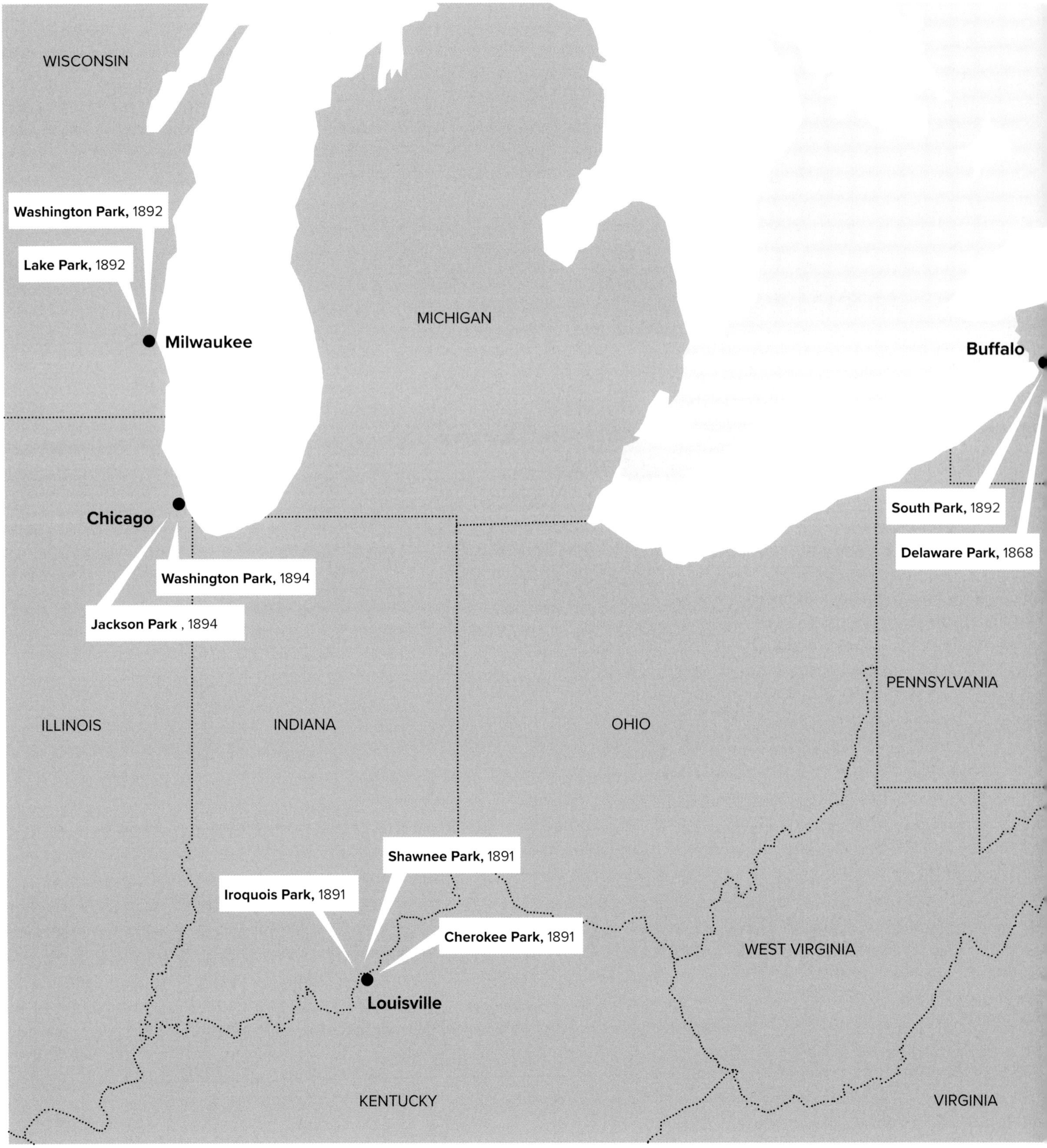

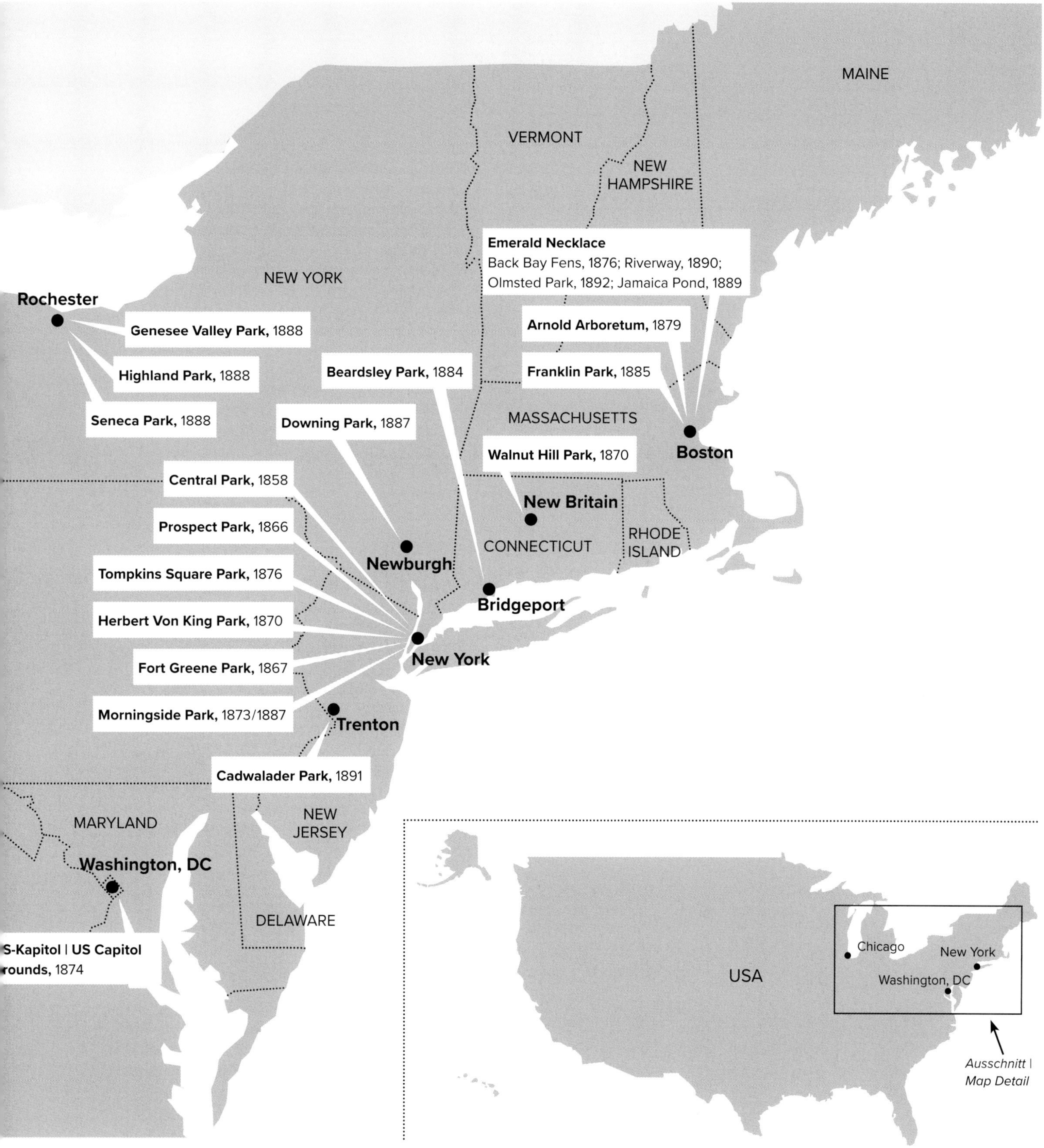
MAINE
VERMONT
NEW HAMPSHIRE
NEW YORK
Rochester
Genesee Valley Park, 1888
Highland Park, 1888
Seneca Park, 1888
Emerald Necklace
Back Bay Fens, 1876; Riverway, 1890; Olmsted Park, 1892; Jamaica Pond, 1889
Arnold Arboretum, 1879
Franklin Park, 1885
Beardsley Park, 1884
Downing Park, 1887
MASSACHUSETTS
Boston
Walnut Hill Park, 1870
Central Park, 1858
New Britain
Prospect Park, 1866
CONNECTICUT
RHODE ISLAND
Newburgh
Tompkins Square Park, 1876
Bridgeport
Herbert Von King Park, 1870
New York
Fort Greene Park, 1867
Morningside Park, 1873/1887
Trenton
Cadwalader Park, 1891
MARYLAND
NEW JERSEY
Washington, DC
DELAWARE
S-Kapitol | US Capitol
rounds, 1874
USA
Chicago
New York
Washington, DC
Ausschnitt | Map Detail

Die Parks von Frederick Law Olmsted: Datierung und Standorte

zusammengestellt von Stanley Greenberg

Die in diesem Band abgebildeten Bäume wurden in den im Folgenden aufgeführten Parks fotografiert. Aufgrund der Schwierigkeit einer eindeutigen Zuordnung von Entstehungsjahr und exakter Fläche der jeweiligen Parks handelt es sich hierbei lediglich um Orientierungswerte. Mit Entstehungsdatum kann sowohl der Zeitpunkt gemeint sein, an dem Olmsted erstmals bezüglich einer gewünschten Parkanlage kontaktiert wurde, oder aber der Zeitpunkt der Auftragserteilung bzw. jener, an dem er die ersten oder auch die endgültigen Pläne vorlegte, manchmal auch der Termin des Beginns der tatsächlichen Umsetzung. Für die Fertigstellung der Parks ist kein Datum angegeben, da sich diese in vielen Fällen über Jahrzehnte hinzog, etliche Anlagen aber bereits lange zuvor dem Publikum zugänglich waren. Was die Größe betrifft, so wurden einige Parks im Laufe der Zeit erweitert, andere verloren Terrain, und manche wurden entgegen Olmsteds Plänen durch einen Zoo und sonstige Einrichtungen ergänzt. Daher sind alle Daten und Größenangaben als Näherungswerte zu betrachten. Es gibt viele ausgezeichnete Bücher über Olmsted und seine Entwürfe, die der interessierte Leser konsultieren kann. Die National Association for Olmsted Parks (www.olmsted.org) bietet auf ihrer Website zusätzlich eine Zeitleiste. Aufgeführt sind im Folgenden auch die Namen der indigenen Völker, die ursprünglich auf dem Land lebten, auf dem die Parks entstanden. Soweit nicht anders angegeben, bezieht sich »Olmsted« auf Frederick Law Olmsted Sr.

CONNECTICUT
Bridgeport:
Beardsley Park, 1884 – Olmsted und John C. Olmsted, 50,6 Hektar. Nicht abgetretenes Land der Pequonnock.
New Britain:
Walnut Hill Park, 1870 – Olmsted und Vaux, 39,67 Hektar. Nicht abgetretenes Land der Tunxis.

ILLINOIS
Chicago:
Jackson Park (ehemals South Park), 1894 – Olmsted und John C. Olmsted, 223 Hektar. Nicht abgetretenes Land der Kickapoo.
Washington Park, 1894 – Olmsted, 150 Hektar. Nicht abgetretenes Land der Kickapoo.

KENTUCKY
Louisville:
Shawnee Park, 1891 – Olmsted, 115 Hektar. Nicht abgetretenes Land der Osage.
Cherokee Park, 1891 – Olmsted, 166 Hektar. Nicht abgetretenes Land der Osage.
Iroquois Park, 1891 – Olmsted, 293 Hektar. Nicht abgetretenes Land der Osage.

MASSACHUSETTS
Boston:
Arnold Arboretum, 1879 – Olmsted und Charles S. Sargent, 55 Hektar. Nicht abgetretenes Land der Massachusett.
Franklin Park, 1885 – Olmsted, 213 Hektar. Nicht abgetretenes Land der Massachusett.
Emerald Necklace, Olmsted: Back Bay Fens, 1876 – 33 Hektar; Riverway, 1890 – 12,9 Hektar; Olmsted Park (ehemals Leverett Park), 1892 – 5,2 Hektar; Jamaica Pond, 1889 – 41,6 Hektar. Nicht abgetretenes Land der Massachusett.

NEW JERSEY
Trenton:
Cadwalader Park, 1891 – Olmsted, 40,4 Hektar. Nicht abgetretenes Land der Lenni Lenape.

NEW YORK
Buffalo:
Delaware Park, 1868 – Olmsted und Vaux, 205 Hektar. Nicht abgetretenes Land der Haudenosaunee.
South Park, 1892 – Olmsted und Eliot, 63,1 Hektar. Nicht abgetretenes Land der Haudenosaunee.

New York City:
Central Park, 1858 – Olmsted und Vaux, 341 Hektar. Ehemaliges Areal von Seneca Village, einer überwiegend von Afroamerikanern bewohnten Gemeinde, die nach Enteignung abgerissen wurde. Nicht abgetretenes Land der Wappinger und Munsee Lenape.
Prospect Park, 1866 – Olmsted und Vaux, 237 Hektar. Nicht abgetretenes Land der Munsee-Lenape und Canarsie.
Fort Greene Park, 1867 – Olmsted und Vaux, 12 Hektar. Nicht abgetretenes Land der Munsee-Lenape und Canarsie.
Morningside Park, 1873 (erster Plan) und 1887 (zweiter Plan, mit Vaux) – 12 Hektar. Nicht abgetretenes Land der Wappinger.
Tompkins Square Park, 1876 – Olmsted, 4,25 Hektar. Nicht abgetretenes Land der Munsee-Lenape.
Herbert Von King Park (ehemals Tompkins Park), 1870 – Olmsted und Vaux, 3,24 Hektar. Nicht abgetretenes Land der Canarsie.

Newburgh:
Downing Park, 1887 – Olmsted und Vaux, mit John C. Olmsted und Downing Vaux, 14 Hektar. Nicht abgetretenes Land der Munsee-Lenape.

Rochester:
Genesee Valley Park, 1888 – Olmsted, 320 Hektar. Nicht abgetretenes Land der Haudenosaunee.
Highland Park, 1888 – Olmsted, 61 Hektar. Nicht abgetretenes Land der Haudenosaunee.
Seneca Park, 1888 – Olmsted, 72,9 Hektar. Nicht abgetretenes Land der Haudenosaunee.

WASHINGTON, DC
US-Kapitol, 1874 – Olmsted, 23,5 Hektar. Nicht abgetretenes Land der Nacotchtank.

WISCONSIN
Milwaukee:
Lake Park, 1892 – Olmsted, 56 Hektar. Nicht abgetretenes Land der Menominee.
Washington Park, 1892 – Olmsted, 52,6 Hektar. Nicht abgetretenes Land der Menominee.

The Parks of Frederick Law Olmsted: Dates and Locations

compiled by Stanley Greenberg

Trees were photographed in the parks listed below. It is difficult to assign consistent dates, and even sizes, for the parks, so this information should be viewed only as a general guide. Beginning dates might be when Olmsted was first contacted, or hired, or when he submitted his first plans, when he submitted final plans, or when construction began. I have not included end dates for the parks, since many took decades to complete, and were open to the public long before completion. As for sizes, some parks became larger over time, some smaller, and others had zoos or other structures added against Olmsted's wishes. So all dates and sizes are approximate. There are many excellent books about Olmsted and his designs, and they should be consulted if more specific information is needed. The National Association for Olmsted Parks (www.olmsted.org) maintains a timeline on its website. I have also included the names of the indigenous people who originally inhabited the parklands. Unless otherwise noted, "Olmsted" refers to Frederick Law Olmsted, Sr.

CONNECTICUT
Bridgeport:
Beardsley Park, 1884 – Olmsted and John C. Olmsted, 125 acres, 50.6 hectares. Unceded Pequonnock land.

New Britain:
Walnut Hill Park, 1870 – Olmsted and Vaux, 98 acres, 39.67 hectares. Unceded Tunxis land.

ILLINOIS
Chicago:
Jackson Park (formerly South Park), 1894 – Olmsted and John C. Olmsted, 551.5 acres, 223 hectares. Unceded Kickapoo land.
Washington Park, 1894 – Olmsted, 372 acres, 150 hectares. Unceded Kickapoo land.

KENTUCKY
Louisville:
Shawnee Park, 1891 – Olmsted 284 acres, 115 hectares. Unceded Osage land.
Cherokee Park, 1891 – Olmsted, 409 acres, 166 hectares. Unceded Osage land.
Iroquois Park, 1891 – Olmsted, 725 acres, 293 hectares. Unceded Osage land.

MASSACHUSETTS
Boston:
Arnold Arboretum, 1879 – Olmsted and Charles S. Sargent, 137 acres, 55 hectares. Unceded Massachusett land.
Franklin Park, 1885 – Olmsted, 527 acres, 213 hectares. Unceded Massachusett land.
Emerald Necklace, Olmsted: Back Bay Fens, 1876 – 82 acres, 33 hectares; Riverway, 1890 – 32 acres, 12.9 hectares; Olmsted Park (formerly Leverett Park), 1892 – 12.94 acres, 5.2 hectares; Jamaica Pond, 1889 – 103 acres, 41.6 hectares. Unceded Massachusett land.

NEW JERSEY
Trenton:
Cadwalader Park, 1891 – Olmsted, 100 acres, 40.4 hectares. Unceded Lenni Lenape land.

NEW YORK
Buffalo:
Delaware Park, 1868 – Olmsted and Vaux, 506 acres, 205 hectares. Unceded Haudenosaunee land.
South Park, 1892 – Olmsted and Eliot, 156 acres, 63.1 hectares. Unceded Haudenosaunee land.

New York City:
Central Park, 1858 – Olmsted and Vaux, 843 acres, 341 hectares. Former site of Seneca Village, a predominantly Black-owned community demolished through eminent domain. Unceded Wappinger and Munsee Lenape land.
Prospect Park, 1866 – Olmsted and Vaux, 586 acres, 237 hectares. Unceded Munsee Lenape and Canarsie land.
Fort Greene Park, 1867 – Olmsted and Vaux, 30 acres, 12 hectares. Unceded Munsee Lenape and Canarsie land.
Morningside Park, 1873 (first plan) and 1887 (second plan, with Vaux) – 30 acres, 12 hectares. Unceded Wappinger land.
Tompkins Square Park, 1876 – Olmsted, 10.5 acres, 4.25 hectares. Unceded Munsee Lenape land.
Herbert Von King Park (formerly Tompkins Park), 1870 – Olmsted and Vaux, 8 acres, 3.24 hectares. Unceded Canarsie land.

Newburgh:
Downing Park, 1887 – Olmsted and Vaux, with John C. Olmsted and Downing Vaux, 35 acres, 14 hectares. Unceded Munsee Lenape land.

Rochester:
Genesee Valley Park, 1888 – Olmsted, 800 acres, 320 hectares. Unceded Haudenosaunee land.
Highland Park, 1888 – Olmsted, 150 acres, 61 hectares. Unceded Haudenosaunee land.
Seneca Park, 1888 – Olmsted, 180 acres, 72.9 hectares. Unceded Haudenosaunee land.

WASHINGTON, DC
US Capitol Grounds, 1874 – Olmsted, 58 acres, 23.5 hectares. Unceded Nacotchtank land.

WISCONSIN
Milwaukee:
Lake Park, 1892 – Olmsted, 138 acres, 56 hectares. Unceded Menominee land.
Washington Park, 1892 – Olmsted, 130 acres, 52.6 hectares. Unceded Menominee land.

Autorenbiografien

Stanley Greenberg ist Autor mehrerer Bücher, darunter *Invisible New York*, *Waterworks* und *CODEX New York*. Seine Fotografien sind u. a. Bestandteil der Sammlungen des Metropolitan Museum of Art und des Whitney Museum of American Art, New York, sowie der New York Public Library. Sie wurden in Einzelausstellungen im Art Institute of Chicago sowie im MIT Museum in Cambridge, Massachusetts, gezeigt. Greenberg erhielt Stipendien und Förderungen der John Simon Guggenheim Foundation, der Alfred P. Sloan Foundation, des New York State Council on the Arts und der New York Foundation for the Arts. Er lebt in Brooklyn, New York.
stanleygreenberg.org

Tom Avermaete ist Professor für Geschichte und Theorie des Städtebaus an der ETH Zürich. Seine Forschung konzentriert sich auf Stadtarchitektur und die sich aus interkultureller Perspektive verändernden Rollen, Ansätze und Möglichkeiten von Architekten und Stadtplanern. Zu seinen jüngsten Buchveröffentlichungen gehören *Casablanca – Chandigarh* (mit Maristella Casciato), *Shopping Towns Europe* (mit Janina Gosseye), *The New Urban Condition* (mit Leandro Medrano und Luiz Recamán) sowie *Urban Design in the 20th Century: A History* (mit Janina Gosseye).

Kevin Baker ist Romanautor, Historiker und Journalist. Zu seinen Romanen gehören *Dreamland, Die Straße zum Paradies, Strivers Row* und *The Big Crowd*. Nach der Veröffentlichung einer Geschichte des Baseballs in New York arbeitet er derzeit, gefördert durch ein Guggenheim-Stipendium, an einer Geschichte der Vereinigten Staaten zwischen den Weltkriegen. Er schreibt für zahlreiche bedeutende Zeitschriften und ist Redakteur des *Harper's Magazine*. Mit seiner Frau, der Dramatikerin Ellen Abrams, lebt er in New York.
kevinbaker.info

Mindy Thompson Fullilove, Life Fellow der American Psychiatric Association (APA) und Ehrenmitglied des American Institute of Architects (AIA), ist Sozialpsychiaterin sowie Professorin für Stadtpolitik und Gesundheit an der New School. Sie absolvierte ihren Bachelor am Bryn Mawr College, Pennsylvania, und ihren Master an der Columbia University, wo sie anschließend in Medizin promovierte. Sie ist staatlich geprüfte Psychiaterin, ihre Facharztausbildung durchlief sie am New York Hospital – Westchester Division und am Montefiore Medical Center. Sie hat über 100 wissenschaftliche Arbeiten und acht Bücher veröffentlicht, darunter die viel beachtete Trilogie über Stadtsanierung *Root Shock*, *Urban Alchemy* und *Main Street*.
mindyfullilove.com

Author Biographies

Stanley Greenberg is the author of several books, including *Invisible New York*, *Waterworks*, and *CODEX New York*. His photographs are in the collections of the Metropolitan Museum of Art, the Whitney Museum of American Art, and The New York Public Library, among others. He has had one-person exhibitions at the Art Institute of Chicago and the MIT Museum in Cambridge, Massachusetts. Greenberg has received fellowships and grants from the John Simon Guggenheim Foundation, the Alfred P. Sloan Foundation, the New York State Council on the Arts, and the New York Foundation for the Arts. Greenberg lives in Brooklyn, New York.
stanleygreenberg.org

Tom Avermaete is professor for the History and Theory of Urban Design at ETH Zurich. His research focuses on the architecture of the city and the changing roles, approaches, and tools of architects and urban designers from a cross-cultural perspective. Recent book publications include *Casablanca – Chandigarh* (with Maristella Casciato), *Shopping Towns Europe* (with Janina Gosseye), *The New Urban Condition* (with Leandro Medrano and Luiz Recamán), and *Urban Design in the 20th Century: A History* (with Janina Gosseye).

Kevin Baker is a novelist, historian, and journalist, whose novels include *Dreamland*, *Paradise Alley*, *Strivers Row*, and *The Big Crowd*. He recently completed a history of New York City baseball and is currently at work on a history of the United States between the world wars, for which he was awarded a Guggenheim Fellowship. He has written for many major periodicals, and is a contributing editor for *Harper's Magazine*. He lives in New York with his wife, the playwright Ellen Abrams.
kevinbaker.info

Mindy Thompson Fullilove, MD, LFAPA, Hon AIA, is a social psychiatrist and professor of urban policy and health at The New School. She completed her AB at Bryn Mawr College, Pennsylvania and MS and MD at Columbia University. She is board-certified in psychiatry, having completed residency in psychiatry at New York Hospital–Westchester Division and Montefiore Medical Center. She has published over 100 scientific papers and eight books, including her highly regarded urban restoration trilogy, *Root Shock*, *Urban Alchemy*, and *Main Street*.
mindyfullilove.com

Danksagung

Im Jahr 2019 begann ich mich auf die Suche nach den ältesten Bäumen in den Parks von Olmsted zu machen. Trotz der Corona-Pandemie, die Anfang 2020 ausbrach und vielerlei Reisebeschränkungen mit sich brachte, gelang es mir, das Projekt abzuschließen. Glücklicherweise liegen die meisten Parks in und um New York, einer gleich auf der anderen Straßenseite meiner Wohnung. Viele Leute halfen mir, die Bäume auszumachen, um die es mir ging. Die Meinungen darüber, welche tatsächlich noch von Olmsted selbst gepflanzt, welche vielleicht aus einem noch älteren Bestand stammen und welche später hinzukamen, gingen teilweise auseinander. Daher ist anzunehmen, dass einige der von mir fotografierten Exemplare doch erst nach Olmsteds Anlage hinzukamen, so gut ich auch beraten wurde. Andererseits hatte ich das Glück, einige Bäume zu identifizieren, die Olmsted bereits vorfand und die er in seine Entwürfe einbezog.

Mein Dank geht an Christian Zimmerman von der Prospect Park Alliance, John Dillon und Sara Cedar Miller von der Central Park Conservancy, Michael Sawyer, Andrew Rabb und Martha Neri von der Buffalo Olmsted Parks Conservancy, David Eylers von der Stadtverwaltung von Newburgh, Matt Spalding von der Louisville Olmsted Parks Conservancy, Ellen Arnstein, Evan Bradley und Jen Mergel von der Emerald Necklace Conservancy und Michael Dosmann, Kathryn Richardson und Larissa Glasser vom Arnold Arboretum. Gleichfalls dankbar bin ich dem Arnold Arboretum der Harvard University, das mir den Zugang zu den Bäumen ermöglicht hat.

Danken möchte ich auch Virginia Small, Susan Bence und Annemarie Sawkins in Milwaukee, Melissa Westbrook vom Office of the Architect of the Capitol und Anthony Reed von der Frederick Law Olmsted National Historic Site. Georgia Silvera Seamans und Ken Chaya scheuten weder Zeit noch Mühe, mir bei der Identifizierung einiger der Bäume zu helfen. Auch Dede Petrie von Olmsted 200 stand mir stets mit Rat und Tat zur Seite.

Meine Freunde Riva Blumenfeld, Heather Cristol, Greg Conniff, Jon Gold, Mark Hellerman, Dennis Hrehowsik, John Shapiro, John Trotter und Lisa Wilde unterstützten das Buchprojekt ebenfalls nach Kräften. Lynn Yellen und Lena Greenberg waren unermüdlich bereit, mit mir über die Bäume zu sprechen oder hinauszufahren, um sie zu betrachten – ihnen beiden ist das Buch gewidmet.

Thomas Zuhr vom Hirmer Verlag nahm sich des Buchprojekts nach mehr Ablehnungen, als ich überhaupt zählen kann, mit Begeisterung an. Cordula Gielen und Sabine Frohmader, beide ebenfalls vom Hirmer Verlag, arbeiteten mit mir unter den erschwerenden Bedingungen der Pandemie daran, den Band nach meinen Vorstellungen möglich zu machen. Auch für ihre Hilfe bin ich sehr dankbar.

— Stanley Greenberg

Acknowledgements

Beginning in 2019 I went in search of the oldest trees in Olmsted's parks. When the Coronavirus pandemic arrived in early 2020, with all the travel restrictions that entailed, the project was still in its early stages. Thankfully, many of the parks were in or around New York City, and one was across the street from where I live. Through it all, many people helped me find the trees I was looking for. They all had opinions about which trees were planted by Olmsted, which predated him, and which were later. I'm sure some of the trees I photographed came after Olmsted, despite the best advice of others. I was lucky to find a few trees that predated Olmsted, which he included in his designs.

I'd like to thank Christian Zimmerman of the Prospect Park Alliance; John Dillon and Sara Cedar Miller of the Central Park Conservancy; Michael Sawyer, Andrew Rabb, and Martha Neri of the Buffalo Olmsted Parks Conservancy; David Eylers of the City of Newburgh; Matt Spalding of the Louisville Olmsted Parks Conservancy; Ellen Arnstein, Evan Bradley, and Jen Mergel of the Emerald Necklace Conservancy; and Michael Dosmann, Kathryn Richardson, and Larissa Glasser of the Arnold Arboretum. Acknowledgement is also made here to the Arnold Arboretum at Harvard University for providing access to the trees.

Thanks also to Virginia Small, Susan Bence, and Annemarie Sawkins in Milwaukee; Melissa Westbrook of the Office of the Architect of the Capitol; and Anthony Reed of the Frederick Law Olmsted National Historic Site. Georgia Silvera Seamans and Ken Chaya were very generous with their time in helping to identify some of the trees, and Dede Petrie of Olmsted 200 offered advice and assistance along the way.

My friends Riva Blumenfeld, Heather Cristol, Greg Conniff, Jon Gold, Mark Hellerman, Dennis Hrehowsik, John Shapiro, John Trotter, and Lisa Wilde all supported the book in their own separate ways. Lynn Yellen and Lena Greenberg were always up for talking about the trees and venturing out to look at them, too; this book is for them.

Thomas Zuhr at Hirmer enthusiastically responded to my book proposal after more rejections than I can count. Cordula Gielen and Sabine Frohmader, also at Hirmer, worked with me through the pandemic to make the book I wanted, under what I know were challenging circumstances. I'm grateful for their help.

— Stanley Greenberg

Impressum | Colophon

Autoren | Authors
Tom Avermaete, Kevin Baker, Mindy Thompson Fullilove

Projektmanagement | Project management
Cordula Gielen, Hirmer Verlag

Englisches Lektorat | English copyediting
James Copeland, Berlin

Deutsches Lektorat | German copyediting
Claudia Wagner, Starnberg

Übersetzung ins Deutsche | Translation from the English
Thomas Wollermann, Berlin

Gestaltung, Satz & Herstellung | Design, typesetting & production
Sabine Frohmader, Hirmer Verlag

Lithografie | Prepress
Reproline mediateam GmbH, München | Munich

Papier | Paper
Magno Volume 170 g/m^2

Vorsatzpapier | Endpaper
Apfelpapier Cartamela 135 g/m^2

Druck & Bindung | Printing & binding
Printer Trento s.r.l., Trient | Trento

Printed in Italy

Bibliografische Information der Deutschen Nationalbibliothek
Die Deutsche Nationalbibliothek verzeichnet diese Publikation in der Deutschen Nationalbibliografie; detaillierte bibliografische Daten sind im Internet über http://www.dnb.de abrufbar.

Bibliographic information published by the Deutsche Nationalbibliothek
The Deutsche Nationalbibliothek lists this publication in the Deutsche Nationalbibliografie; detailed bibliographic data are available online at http://www.dnb.de.

ISBN 978-3-7774-3857-3

www.hirmerverlag.de
www.hirmerpublishers.com

Umschlag | Cover image:
Ginkgo biloba, Ginkgo – Prospect Park, Brooklyn, New York, 2021
(S. | p. 37)

Umschlagrückseite | Back cover image:
Ulmus glabra "Camperdownii," Camperdown Elm, Lauben-Ulme – Prospect Park, Brooklyn, New York, 2019 (S. | p. 117);
Maclura pomifera, Osage-Orange, Milchorangenbaum – Central Park, New York, New York, 2020 (S. | p. 111)